ALTERNATIVE DISPUTE RESOLUTION

IN A NUTSHELL

THIRD EDITION

By

JACQUELINE M. NOLAN-HALEY
Professor of Law
Director of ADR & Conflict Resolution Program
Fordham University, School of Law

Mat #40582533

Thomson/West have created this publication to provide you with
accurate and authoritative information concerning the subject matter
covered. However, this publication was not necessarily prepared by
persons licensed to practice law in a particular jurisdiction.
Thomson/West are not engaged in rendering legal or other professional
advice, and this publication is not a substitute for the advice of an
attorney. If you require legal or other expert advice, you should seek the
services of a competent attorney or other professional.

Nutshell Series, In a Nutshell, the Nutshell Logo and West Group are
trademarks registered in the U.S. Patent and Trademark Office.

To Andrew and Martina

*

PREFACE

The first edition of this book was published sixteen years ago, and since that time the field of alternative dispute resolution (ADR) has undergone extraordinary growth. We have seen the passage of significant federal and state legislation, the Revised Uniform Arbitration Act, the Uniform Mediation Act, enactment of numerous court regulations, specific ethical rules to govern the conduct of lawyers engaged in ADR, and tremendous curricular development in law schools and universities. At the same time there has been a concerted effort to develop a culture of problem-solving in the legal profession and a growing recognition that understanding ADR processes can assist in creating that culture. My goal has been to present these developments and to help law students understand a wide variety of problem-solving approaches to resolving legal disputes. A selective bibliography can be found at the end of each chapter.

I am grateful to Fordham University School of Law for providing financial support. I also thank my research assistants Brian Wegrzyn, Marnie Cox and Brian Gulley for their excellent help and I am especially grateful to my ADR students who continue to stimulate my thinking in this field.

JACQUELINE M. NOLAN-HALEY

Fordham University School of Law
March 2008

*

V

ACKNOWLEDGEMENTS

The following authors and publishers gave me permission to reprint excerpts from copyright material. I gratefully acknowledge their assistance.

Chapter 2

American Bar Association (ABA), Model Rules of Professional Conduct and Model Code of Professional Responsibility. Copyright by the ABA. All rights reserved. Reprinted by permission of the American Bar Association.

Chapter 3

American Bar Association (ABA), Model Rules of Professional Conduct, and Resolution on Mediation and the Unauthorized Practice of Law. Copyright by the ABA. All rights reserved. Reprinted by permission of the American Bar Association.

Association of the Bar of the City of New York, Ethics Opinion, Committee on Professional and Judicial Ethics, Inquiry Reference No. 80-23.

Chapter 4

Restatement of the Law, Second, Judgments, Section 84, p. 286. Copyright 1982 by the American law Institute. Reprinted with the permission of the American Law Institute. All rights reserved.

ACKNOWLEDGEMENTS

Chapter 6

American Arbitration Association Mini-Trial Procedures. Printed with permission by the American Arbitration Association.

APPENDICES

Model Standards of Practice for Family and Divorce
Mediation (2000). Reprinted with permission of the
Association of Family and Conciliation Courts.

American Arbitration Association Materials

> AAA Commercial Arbitration Rules and
> Commercial Mediation Procedures
> (2007);
>
> Demand for Arbitration;
>
> Task Force on Alternative Dispute Resolu-
> tion in Employment, Due Process Protocol;
>
> Code of Ethics for Arbitrators in Commer
> cial Disputes (2004);

All of these materials are reprinted with permission
from the American Arbitration Association.

Uniform Arbitration Act. This Act has been reprinted with the permission of the National Conference
of Commissioners on Uniform State Laws.

Revised Uniform Arbitration Act. This Act has been
reprinted with the permission of the National Conference of Commissioners on Uniform State Laws.

ACKNOWLEDGEMENTS

Uniform Mediation Act. This Act has been reprinted with the permission of the National Conference of Commissioners on Uniform State laws.

ABA Model Rules of Professional Conduct, Rules 1.12, 3.3 and 5.5. Copyright by the ABA. All rights reserved. Reprinted by permission of the American Bar Association.

*

OUTLINE

Page

PREFACE --- V
ACKNOWLEDGEMENTS ------------------------------------ VII
TABLE OF CASES --------------------------------------- XIX

Chapter 1. Introduction ------------------------ 1
   I. Overview ------------------------------------- 1
  II. Why Study ADR? ----------------------------- 3
 III. Background of the Alternative Dispute
      Resolution Movement ----------------------- 5

Chapter 2. Negotiation ------------------------- 14
   I. Introduction --------------------------------- 14
  II. Definitions and Concepts --------------------- 16
     A. Dispute and Deal–Making Negotia-
        tion ----------------------------------- 17
     B. Distributive and Integrative Bar-
        gaining ------------------------------- 18
 III. Approaches to Negotiation ------------------- 23
     A. In General --------------------------------- 23
       1. Adversarial Approach ---------------- 23
       2. Problem–Solving Approach --------- 25
     B. Negotiation Approaches in Practice -- 29

		Page
IV.	Stages of the Negotiation Process	31
	A. Planning and Analysis	33
	B. Exchanging Information	37
	C. Concessions and Compromise	40
	D. Reaching Agreement	41
	E. Barriers to Settlement	42
	F. The Role of Emotions in Negotiation	43
	G. The Role of Culture in Negotiations	44
V.	Ethical Issues in Negotiation	45
	A. Relationship With Clients	47
	B. Truthfulness	48
	C. Misrepresentation	49
	D. Threats	54
VI.	Legal Aspects of Negotiation	56
	A. The Settlement Agreement	56
	1. Policy Favoring Settlement	56
	(i) The Agreement	56
	(ii) Consideration	57
	(iii) Legality	57
	2. Validity of Settlement Agreements	58
	(i) In General	58
	(ii) Guaranteed Verdict Agreements	58
	3. Court Approval of Settlement Agreements	59
	B. Protecting Confidentiality in Negotiation	60
	C. Incentives for Settlement	61
	1. Judicial Settlement Conferences	61
	2. Rule 68 FRCP	63

		Page
Chapter 3. Mediation		68
I.	Overview	68
	A. Definition	70
	B. Advantages and Disadvantages of Mediation	72
	1. Advantages	72
	2. Disadvantages	73
II.	The Mediation Process	74
	A. Specific Activities	74
	1. Mediator's Introduction	79
	2. Mediator Assists Parties With Information Exchange and Bargaining	82
	B. Drafting the Mediation Agreement	84
	C. Role of the Mediator	85
	D. Mediator Skills	90
	1. Listening	90
	2. Questioning	93
	3. Observation	95
	4. Reframing	96
	5. Cultural Awareness	96
	E. Mediator Requirements	96
III.	Ethical Concerns	99
	A. In General	99
	B. Good Faith Requirements	100
	C. Maintaining the Integrity of Mediation	101
	D. Mandatory Mediation Programs	103
	E. Ethical Concerns for the Lawyer–Mediator	104
	1. Conflict of Interest	105
	2. Advertising	109

	Page
IV. Mediation and the Law	110
A. The Role of Law	110
B. Informed Consent in Mediation	111
C. Lawyers and Mediation	112
1. Pre–Mediation Client Counseling	112
2. Representing Clients in Mediation	114
3. Lawyer as Mediator	116
D. Legal Issues	117
1. Confidentiality	117
(i) Evidentiary Exclusionary Rules	119
(ii) Privilege	120
(iii) Contract	123
(iv) Protective Orders	129
(v) Court Mediation Program Rules	129
2. Enforceability	130
(i) Agreements to Mediate Future Disputes	130
(ii) Agreements Reached in Mediation	131
3. Liability of Mediators	134
(i) Tort Liability Based in Negligence	135
(ii) Liability Issues in the Caucus	136
(iii) Contract Liability	138
(iv) Immunity	139
4. Unauthorized Practice of Law Restrictions	140

Page

  V. Mediation Approaches in a Litigated
      Case: One Example 144
      A. Some Indications for Mediation 147
      B. Possible Mediation Approaches 149

Chapter 4. Arbitration 153
  I. Introduction 153
  II. Historical Perspective 154
  III. The Traditional Model of Arbitration 159
  IV. Compulsory Arbitration 160
      1. Public Sector Arbitration 161
      2. Court–Annexed Arbitration 162
      3. Medical Malpractice Arbitration .. 162
      4. Employment Arbitration 163
  V. Arbitration Definitions 164
      1. Interest and Rights Arbitration ... 164
      2. Administered and Non-Adminis-
         tered Arbitration 165
      3. Final Offer Arbitration 165
      4. Tripartite Arbitration 166
  VI. Legal Issues 166
      1. Arbitrability 166
         (i) Substantive Arbitrability 167
         (ii) Procedural Arbitrability 175
      2. Separability 176
      3. Federalism Concerns 179
      4. Adhesion and Unconscionability .. 189
  VII. The Arbitration Proceeding 192
      1. Provisional Relief 192
      2. Initiating Arbitration 194
      3. Selection of Arbitrators 195
         (i) Qualifications of the Arbi-
           trator 195

Page

VII. The Arbitration Proceeding—Continued
        (ii) Arbitral Immunity 196
        (iii) Testimonial Immunity 197
    4. The Arbitration Hearing............ 197
    5. Law Applied by the Arbitrator..... 198
    6. Arbitration Ethics 199
VIII. The Arbitration Award 201
    1. Judicial Review of the Arbitration
       Award under the FAA 202
    2. Venue 206
    3. Punitive Damages 206
    4. Res Judicata, Collateral Estoppel
       and Arbitration 208
IX. International Arbitration 214

**Chapter 5. Dispute Resolution in the
Court System**.......................... 219
  I. Court–Annexed Arbitration 220
 II. Court–Annexed Mediation 222
III. The Summary Jury Trial.................. 223
    1. Overview........................... 223
    2. Governing Principles 224
    3. The Summary Jury Trial Process 226
    4. Major Advantages of the Sum-
       mary Jury Trial.................... 227
    5. Criticisms of the Summary Jury
       Trial............................... 229
    6. Case Law Development 230
       (i) Power to Compel Parties to
           Participate 230
       (ii) Right of Access.................. 231

Page

III. The Summary Jury Trial—Continued
    (iii) Authority of the Court to Empanel the Advisory Jury 231
IV. Early Neutral Evaluation 232
    1. Overview 232
    2. How ENE Operates 233
    3. On the Merits 234
V. Magistrates, Special Masters, and Neutral Experts 235
    1. Magistrates 236
    2. Special Masters 237
    3. Neutral Experts 241
VI. Restorative Justice: ADR in the Criminal Law Contexts 242

Chapter 6. Hybrid Dispute Resolution Procedures 246
I. The Mini–Trial 246
    1. Definition 246
    2. The Structure of a Mini–Trial 247
    3. The Settlement Discussions 249
    4. Appropriate Use of the Mini–Trial 250
II. Reference Procedures 254
III. MED–ARB 255
IV. Negotiated Rulemaking 257
V. Ombudsperson 259
VI. Conciliation 261
VII. Online Dispute Resolution 261
VIII. Consensus Building 262
IX. Dispute Review Boards 263

OUTLINE

Appendices

App.

A. Federal Rules of Evidence— Rule 408 268
B. Federal Rules of Civil Procedure—Rule 16 270
C. Federal Rules of Civil Procedure—Rule 68 276
D. Model Standards of Practice for Family and Divorce Mediation (August 2000) 278
E. The Model Standards of Conduct for Mediators 297
F. American Arbitration Association Commercial Arbitration Rules and Commercial Mediation Procedures 311
G. Mandated Participation and Settlement Coercion: Dispute Resolution as it Relates to the Courts 367
H. Ethical Standards of Professional Responsibility for the Society of Professionals in Dispute Resolution 371
I. The Uniform Arbitration Act...................... 378
J. Federal Arbitration Act 390
K. Revised Uniform Arbitration Act (2000) ... 406
L. Demand for Arbitration 431
M. Task Force on Alternative Dispute Resolution in Employment, Due Process Protocol 433
N. The Code of Ethics for Arbitrators in Commercial Disputes 438
O. Model Rules of Professional Conduct, Client-Lawyer Relationship, Rule 1.12 464
P. Model Rules of Professional Conduct, Advocate, Rule 3.3 466
Q. Model Rules of Professional Conduct, Law Firms and Associations, Rule 5.5 468
R. Uniform Mediation Act.............................. 471

INDEX 483

TABLE OF CASES

References are to Pages

Alexander v. Gardner–Denver Co., 415 U.S. 36, 94 S.Ct. 1011, 39 L.Ed.2d 147 (1974), *173, 210*

Allied–Bruce Terminix Companies, Inc. v. Dobson, 513 U.S. 265, 115 S.Ct. 834, 130 L.Ed.2d 753 (1995), *186*

AMF Inc. v. Brunswick Corp., 621 F.Supp. 456 (S.D.N.Y.1985), *130*

Application of (see name of party)

AT & T Technologies, Inc. v. Communications Workers of America, 475 U.S. 643, 106 S.Ct. 1415, 89 L.Ed.2d 648 (1986), *168*

Barrentine v. Arkansas–Best Freight System, Inc., 450 U.S. 728, 101 S.Ct. 1437, 67 L.Ed.2d 641 (1981), *173, 213*

Bernard v. Galen Group, Inc., 901 F.Supp. 778 (S.D.N.Y.1995), *130*

Bernhardt v. Polygraphic Co. of America, 350 U.S. 198, 76 S.Ct. 273, 100 L.Ed. 199 (1956), *179*

Boys Markets, Inc. v. Retail Clerks Union, Local 770, 398 U.S. 235, 90 S.Ct. 1583, 26 L.Ed.2d 199 (1970), *192*

Buckeye Check Cashing, Inc. v. Cardegna, 546 U.S. 440, 126 S.Ct. 1204, 163 L.Ed.2d 1038 (2006), *178, 183, 188*

Carman v. McDonnell Douglas Corp., 114 F.3d 790 (8th Cir. 1997), *260*

Charles, In re, 290 Or. 127, 618 P.2d 1281 (Or.1980), *55*

Cho v. Superior Court, 45 Cal.Rptr.2d 863 (Cal.App. 2 Dist.1995), *109*

Cincinnati Gas and Elec. Co. v. General Elec. Co., 854 F.2d 900 (6th Cir.1988), *231*

Circuit City Stores, Inc. v. Adams, 532 U.S. 105, 121 S.Ct. 1302, 149 L.Ed.2d 234 (2001), *163*

TABLE OF CASES

Cole v. Burns Intern. Sec. Services, 105 F.3d 1465, 323 U.S.App. D.C. 133 (D.C.Cir.1997), *174*

Commonwealth Coatings Corp. v. Continental Cas. Co., 393 U.S. 145, 89 S.Ct. 337, 21 L.Ed.2d 301 (1968), *199*

Cortez Byrd Chips, Inc. v. Bill Harbert Const. Co., 529 U.S. 193, 120 S.Ct. 1331, 146 L.Ed.2d 171 (2000), *206*

Dean Witter Reynolds, Inc. v. Byrd, 470 U.S. 213, 105 S.Ct. 1238, 84 L.Ed.2d 158 (1985), *183*

DeValk Lincoln Mercury, Inc. v. Ford Motor Co., 811 F.2d 326 (7th Cir.1987), *131*

Doctor's Associates, Inc. v. Casarotto, 517 U.S. 681, 116 S.Ct. 1652, 134 L.Ed.2d 902 (1996), *187*

Eastern Associated Coal Corp. v. United Mine Workers of America, Dist. 17, 531 U.S. 57, 121 S.Ct. 462, 148 L.Ed.2d 354 (2000), *205*

E.E.O.C. v. Waffle House, Inc., 534 U.S. 279, 122 S.Ct. 754, 151 L.Ed.2d 755 (2002), *164*

First Options of Chicago, Inc. v. Kaplan, 514 U.S. 938, 115 S.Ct. 1920, 131 L.Ed.2d 985 (1995), *174*

Foster v. Preston Mill Co., 44 Wash.2d 440, 268 P.2d 645 (Wash.1954), *144*

Garrity v. Lyle Stuart, Inc., 386 N.Y.S.2d 831, 353 N.E.2d 793 (N.Y.1976), *207*

Gateway Technologies, Inc. v. MCI Telecommunications Corp., 64 F.3d 993 (5th Cir.1995), *202*

G. Heileman Brewing Co., Inc. v. Joseph Oat Corp., 871 F.2d 648 (7th Cir.1989), *62*

Gilmer v. Interstate/Johnson Lane Corp., 500 U.S. 20, 111 S.Ct. 1647, 114 L.Ed.2d 26 (1991), *163, 171, 212*

Graham v. Scissor–Tail, Inc., 171 Cal.Rptr. 604, 623 P.2d 165 (Cal.1981), *190*

Green Tree Financial Corp. v. Bazzle, 539 U.S. 444, 123 S.Ct. 2402, 156 L.Ed.2d 414 (2003), *176*

Green Tree Financial Corp.–Alabama v. Randolph, 531 U.S. 79, 121 S.Ct. 513, 148 L.Ed.2d 373 (2000), *191*

TABLE OF CASES

Haghighi v. Russian–American Broadcasting Co., 577 N.W.2d 927 (Minn.1998), *133*

Halligan v. Piper Jaffray, Inc., 148 F.3d 197 (2nd Cir.1998), *203*

Hall Street Associates, L.L.C. v. Mattel Inc., 196 Fed. Appx. 476 (9th Cir.2006), *202*

Hoffman v. Red Owl Stores, Inc., 26 Wis.2d 683, 133 N.W.2d 267 (Wis.1965), *18*

Hoosac Tunnel Dock & Elevator Co. v. O'Brien, 137 Mass. 424 (Mass.1884), *196*

Howard v. Drapkin, 222 Cal.App.3d 843, 271 Cal.Rptr. 893 (Cal.App. 2 Dist.1990), *140*

Howsam v. Dean Witter Reynolds, Inc., 537 U.S. 79, 123 S.Ct. 588, 154 L.Ed.2d 491 (2002), *176*

Hume v. M & C Management, 129 F.R.D. 506 (N.D.Ohio 1990), *231*

In re (see name of party)

J.D. Booth v. Mary Carter Paint Co., 202 So.2d 8 (Fla.App. 2 Dist.1967), *58*

Jeld–Wen, Inc. v. Superior Court, 53 Cal.Rptr.3d 115 (Cal.App. 4 Dist.2007), *104*

John Wiley & Sons, Inc. v. Livingston, 376 U.S. 543, 84 S.Ct. 909, 11 L.Ed.2d 898 (1964), *175*

Kulukundis Shipping Co., S/A, v. Amtorg Trading Corporation, 126 F.2d 978 (2nd Cir.1942), *154*

Lange v. Marshall, 622 S.W.2d 237 (Mo.App. E.D.1981), *136*

Marek v. Chesny, 473 U.S. 1, 105 S.Ct. 3012, 87 L.Ed.2d 1 (1985), *63*

Mastrobuono v. Shearson Lehman Hutton, Inc., 514 U.S. 52, 115 S.Ct. 1212, 131 L.Ed.2d 76 (1995), *186, 207*

Mathews v. Weber, 423 U.S. 261, 96 S.Ct. 549, 46 L.Ed.2d 483 (1976), *236*

McDonald v. City of West Branch, Michigan, 466 U.S. 284, 104 S.Ct. 1799, 80 L.Ed.2d 302 (1984), *173, 213*

McKay v. Ashland Oil, Inc., 120 F.R.D. 43 (E.D.Ky.1988), *228, 230*

McKenzie Const. v. St. Croix Storage Corp., 961 F.Supp. 857 (D.Virgin Islands 1997), *109*

Merrill Lynch, Pierce, Fenner & Smith, Inc. v. Bobker, 808 F.2d 930 (2nd Cir.1986), *203*

Merrill Lynch, Pierce, Fenner & Smith, Inc. v. Bradley, 756 F.2d 1048 (4th Cir.1985), *194*

Merrill Lynch, Pierce, Fenner & Smith, Inc. v. Salvano, 999 F.2d 211 (7th Cir.1993), *193*

Michigan, State of, United States v., 471 F.Supp. 192 (W.D.Mich. 1979), *239*

Mitsubishi Motors Corp. v. Soler Chrysler–Plymouth, Inc., 473 U.S. 614, 105 S.Ct. 3346, 87 L.Ed.2d 444 (1985), *169*

Mitsubishi Motors Corp. v. Soler Chrysler–Plymouth, Inc., 723 F.2d 155 (1st Cir.1983), *168*

Moses H. Cone Memorial Hosp. v. Mercury Const. Corp., 460 U.S. 1, 103 S.Ct. 927, 74 L.Ed.2d 765 (1983), *181*

Mulder v. Donaldson, Lufkin & Jenrette, 224 A.D.2d 125, 648 N.Y.S.2d 535 (N.Y.A.D. 1 Dept.1996), *208*

NLO, Inc., In re, 5 F.3d 154 (6th Cir.1993), *231*

N.L.R.B. v. General Electric Co., 418 F.2d 736 (2nd Cir.1969), *40*

N.L.R.B. v. Joseph Macaluso, Inc., 618 F.2d 51 (9th Cir.1980), *120*

Olam v. Congress Mortgage Co., 68 F.Supp.2d 1110 (N.D.Cal. 1999), *121*

PacifiCare Health Systems, Inc. v. Book, 538 U.S. 401, 123 S.Ct. 1531, 155 L.Ed.2d 578 (2003), *175*

Pell City Wood, Inc. v. Forke Bros. Auctioneers, Inc., 474 So.2d 694 (Ala.1985), *50*

Perry v. Thomas, 482 U.S. 483, 107 S.Ct. 2520, 96 L.Ed.2d 426 (1987), *184*

Positive Software Solutions, Inc. v. New Century Mortg. Corp., 436 F.3d 495 (5th Cir.2006), *199*

Preston v. Ferrer, ___ U.S. ___, 128 S.Ct. 978 (2008), *189*

Prima Paint Corp. v. Flood & Conklin Mfg. Co., 388 U.S. 395, 87 S.Ct. 1801, 18 L.Ed.2d 1270 (1967), *177, 180*

RGI, Inc. v. Tucker & Associates, Inc., 858 F.2d 227 (5th Cir. 1988), *194*

Rodriguez de Quijas v. Shearson/American Exp., Inc., 490 U.S. 477, 109 S.Ct. 1917, 104 L.Ed.2d 526 (1989), *171*

Salvucci v. Sheehan, 349 Mass. 659, 212 N.E.2d 243 (Mass.1965), *193*

Shearson/American Exp., Inc. v. McMahon, 482 U.S. 220, 107 S.Ct. 2332, 96 L.Ed.2d 185 (1987), *170*

Simrin v. Simrin, 233 Cal.App.2d 90, 43 Cal.Rptr. 376 (Cal.App. 5 Dist.1965), *128*

Smith, Application of, 381 Pa. 223, 112 A.2d 625 (Pa.1955), *221*

Southland Corp. v. Keating, 465 U.S. 1, 104 S.Ct. 852, 79 L.Ed.2d 1 (1984), *182*

State of (see name of state)

Strandell v. Jackson County, Illinois, 838 F.2d 884 (7th Cir. 1987), *230*

Suquamish Indian Tribe, United States v., 901 F.2d 772 (9th Cir.1990), *237*

Tarasoff v. Regents of University of California, 131 Cal.Rptr. 14, 551 P.2d 334 (Cal.1976), *138*

Teradyne, Inc. v. Mostek Corp., 797 F.2d 43 (1st Cir.1986), *194*

Textile Workers Union of America v. Lincoln Mills of Alabama, 353 U.S. 448, 77 S.Ct. 912, 1 L.Ed.2d 972 (1957), *156*

United Paperworkers Intern. Union, AFL–CIO v. Misco, Inc., 484 U.S. 29, 108 S.Ct. 364, 98 L.Ed.2d 286 (1987), *204*

United States v. _____ (see opposing party)

United Steelworkers of America v. American Mfg. Co., 363 U.S. 564, 80 S.Ct. 1343, 4 L.Ed.2d 1403 (1960), *157*

United Steelworkers of America v. Enterprise Wheel & Car Corp., 363 U.S. 593, 80 S.Ct. 1358, 4 L.Ed.2d 1424 (1960), *158*

United Steelworkers of America v. Warrior & Gulf Navigation Co., 363 U.S. 574, 80 S.Ct. 1347, 4 L.Ed.2d 1409 (1960), *157*

Volt Information Sciences, Inc. v. Board of Trustees of Leland Stanford Junior University, 489 U.S. 468, 109 S.Ct. 1248, 103 L.Ed.2d 488 (1989), *159, 185*

Wagshal v. Foster, 28 F.3d 1249, 307 U.S.App.D.C. 382 (D.C.Cir. 1994), *140*

TABLE OF CASES

Werle v. Rhode Island Bar Ass'n, 755 F.2d 195 (1st Cir.1985), *141*

Wilko v. Swan, 346 U.S. 427, 74 S.Ct. 182, 98 L.Ed. 168 (1953), *170, 203*

Wright v. Universal Maritime Service Corp., 525 U.S. 70, 119 S.Ct. 391, 142 L.Ed.2d 361 (1998), *168, 212*

ALTERNATIVE DISPUTE RESOLUTION

IN A NUTSHELL

THIRD EDITION

*

CHAPTER 1

INTRODUCTION

I. OVERVIEW

The traditional legal response to disputes between parties has been for lawyers to initiate the litigation process by filing a complaint or motion. Most lawyers who graduated from law school before the mid-seventies would probably choose this option instinctively. Many law students would also probably choose this approach simply because in the majority of law school classrooms the litigation process is assumed to be the appropriate means of resolving a client's legal problems. Indeed, most law school courses on civil procedure are taught primarily through the study of adjudication. Law is studied chiefly through the analysis of appellate cases, all of which began with the filing of a complaint, motion or petition. When we add to this the television mystique of People's Court and Judge Judy, it is not surprising that much of the public and many lawyers think that the way to solve problems is by bringing a legal action.

The chief purpose of this book is to disabuse you of the "one size fits all" litigation mentality and to help you understand and appreciate more creative problem-solving processes that are available through *alternative* dispute resolution (ADR). ADR is an umbrella term that refers generally to alternatives to the court adjudication of disputes such as negotiation, mediation, arbitration, mini-trial and summary jury trial. It is also known as "appropriate dispute resolution" and in some international contexts such as the International Chamber of Commerce, it is called "amicable dispute resolution." ADR can be further distinguished between private contractual processes and public processes. Even though some of the "alternatives" such as negotiation, mediation and arbitration, have been practiced for hundreds of years, they have achieved a new familiarity today as part of the ADR movement.

This book does not blindly promote the use of alternatives to the traditional litigation process. Good lawyering demands more thoughtful legal and non-legal problem-solving to help clients achieve their goals. Rather, the purpose of this book is to help law students understand a wide variety of dispute resolution mechanisms, including litigation, so that they can help clients choose an appropriate process that fits their needs. The client's choice of process may not necessarily correspond to the ego needs of the attorney.

It is certainly not possible in this book to catalogue, let alone describe, every ADR procedure. Instead, the focus is on presenting the major processes of alternative dispute resolution—negotiation, mediation and arbitration as well as some well-known hybrids of these processes such as the summary jury trial, early neutral evaluation, the mini-trial, consensus-building, and negotiated rule-making. For purposes of analysis and client counseling, ADR processes should not be lumped together. Each one may offer different advantages to a client.

II. WHY STUDY ADR?

Studying ADR will help you to be a better lawyer. Most Americans who can afford to, consult a lawyer first when they believe they have been wronged. A lawyer's counseling, therefore, plays an important role in whether a party asserts a claim or brings a dispute into the public arena. Today, the professional responsibility codes of many states require that lawyers advise their clients of ADR options. If a lawyer decides that there is a legitimate claim and advises the client to proceed, the question becomes—what process or combination of processes should the client use to resolve the particular dispute?

For law students to focus exclusively on the litigation process is like medical students studying only surgery as a means of curing illness. Of course, that is not what medical students do. They study an extensive range of subjects for the treatment and cure of illnesses. Law students too must extend their focus beyond the litigation arena to a greater understanding of problem-solving approaches. The legal community's failure to do this for so long may be part of the reason for so much congestion in the civil justice system.

Law students cannot afford to ignore developments in ADR as many of these processes become institutionalized within the judicial system in court-annexed programs. They must understand ADR processes and develop the skills that are necessary to use them both as an advocate and as a neutral. It is important to learn to identify the factors that make a particular method the process of choice. If for example, there is a need to preserve an on-going relationship between the parties, litigation might not be appropriate because many relationships are terminated in the litigation process. Instead, the mediation process should be considered because it is known to work well where parties have an on-going or prior relationship. On the other hand, if a legal precedent is desirable, litigation may be a more appropriate dispute resolution process.

A useful way to enhance your ADR process skills is to keep a conflict journal. Make entries on a regular basis about disputes or conflicts you experience and then critically reflect on how you responded. How do you typically resolve conflicts? Through confrontation? Avoidance? Problem-solving? Would other methods be more appropriate? This process of critical self-reflection is what good lawyering is all about. Learn from your experiences. The study and practice of ADR is an on-going, active process and will continue to develop as long as creative lawyering exists.

III. BACKGROUND OF THE ALTERNATIVE DISPUTE RESOLUTION MOVEMENT

The study of ADR may be located within the broader field of conflict resolution. ADR assumed the attributes of a law reform movement in the early nineteen seventies when many observers in the legal and academic communities began to have serious concerns about the negative effects of increased litigation. Legislation enacted in the nineteen sixties granted a broad range of individual protections from consumer to civil rights. The search for redress of those rights through the legal system, however, was becoming a complex exercise. People began to look for alternatives to the court adjudication of disputes as docket congestion, high legal costs and waiting for your day in court became a way of life for Americans who encountered the judicial system either voluntarily or involuntarily.

One well known effort in the search for alternatives occurred in 1976 when former Chief Justice Warren Burger convened the Roscoe E. Pound Conference on the Causes of Popular Dissatisfaction with the Administration of Justice (Pound Conference) in Saint Paul, Minnesota. Academics, members of the judiciary, and public interest lawyers joined together to find new ways of dealing with disputes. Some of the papers that emerged from this conference such as Professor Frank Sander's classic, "Varieties of Dispute Resolution," formed the basic understanding of dispute resolution today.

"Isn't there a better way?" asked former Chief Justice Burger and the alternatives movement was officially off and running. The organized bar officially recognized the ADR movement in 1976 when the American Bar Association (ABA) established a Special Committee on Minor Disputes that has now become the Dispute Resolution Section of the ABA.

In the academic community, the late law professor Lon Fuller invited the legal profession to consider ways of resolving "polycentric" problems which have interconnected issues and which, therefore, do not easily lend themselves to resolution through the "all or nothing" approach of adjudication. Fuller offered as an example of a "polycentric" problem, the story of a wealthy testator who bequeathed a collection of paintings in equal parts to two museums. The adjudication process would have been totally inappropriate to resolve the issue in this case because it would simply result in a winner and a loser and therefore, fail to address the interconnected issue of each museum's interest. Thus, for the first time, the legal community as a group began to look thoughtfully at the *processes* by which disputes are resolved.

Professor Frank Sander proposed the idea of a multidoor courthouse where individual disputes would be matched to appropriate processes such as mediation, arbitration, fact finding or malpractice screening panels. The American Bar Association adopted his idea and established three multidoor courthouses in Houston, Texas, Tulsa, Oklahoma and the District of Columbia. The success of these programs has led other courts to begin similar programs.

Today, most state and federal bar associations have ADR committees. Law schools have gradually been adding ADR to the curriculum and now the majority of law schools offer one or more ADR courses or specialized courses in areas such as mediation and negotiation. Some schools offer graduate and certificate programs in dispute resolution. Several law reviews are devoted solely to the study of alternative dispute resolution. Similar ADR curricular developments have occurred in graduate and business schools.

ADR has also generated an enormous amount of study by cultural anthropologists, sociologists and lawyers on questions raised by the actual process of disputing. What kinds of disputes are resolved? How are they resolved? What are the effects of repeat players? How does culture affect dispute resolution processing? As the study and practice of ADR becomes more sophisticated, there has been a greater interest in problem-solving and consensus-building. ADR has generated interest in new forms of cooperative lawyering such as holistic lawyering and the Collaborative Law Movement. The latter operates in the family law context where lawyers and clients agree to focus on resolving their differences through a collaborative negotiation process. Parties agree not to resort to court unless all parties are in agreement.

As ADR became institutionalized in corporations, government agencies and other institutions, policy makers began to realize the importance of adopting a broader perspective and trying to understand how ADR procedures could be utilized at an early stage of disputing. From this realization came the development of "systems design", a scientific approach to establishing procedures for deciding what ADR processes should be used at particular phases of a dispute.

Over the last two decades, we have seen the beginning of a systematic implementation of ADR in the legal system as a result of the combination of statutes and court rules. Judges may order parties to participate in summary jury trials. Court rules require parties to arbitrate in specified categories of cases such as medical malpractice. In many courts, parties are required to try the mediation process before being permitted to have a trial. The increase in court ADR programs has been accompanied by a substantial decrease in the number of cases that go to trial. It is not clear however, to what extent the growth of ADR is responsible for what is known as the "vanishing trial" phenomena.

The growth of mandatory ADR raises a host of public policy issues. Some critics have charged that in our eagerness to adopt alternatives to litigation we risk losing the protection of the rule of law. Other critics have cautioned that some forms of ADR result in less justice for the poor. Professor Owen Fiss suggests that enthusiastic adoption of ADR minimizes the importance of lawsuits in responding to public policy issues. Professor Deborah Hensler worries that the privacy of ADR diminishes the individual's power to achieve social change through the justice system.

Federal ADR legislation has expanded significantly. The Civil Justice Reform Act of 1990, 28 U.S.C.A. § 1 required every federal district court to develop a "civil justice expense and delay reduction plan" (EDRP) to help streamline dockets. This statute was amended by the Alternative Dispute Resolution Act of 1998, 28 U.S.C.A. § 651 et seq., which required that all federal courts establish at least one ADR program. The Negotiated Rulemaking Act of 1990, 5 U.S.C.A. § 561, authorized the use of negotiated rulemaking as an alternative to adversarial rulemaking in federal agencies. Under the scheme established by the Act, parties who will be significantly affected by an agency rule, participate in the development of the rule. This Act was reauthorized in the Administrative Dispute Resolution Act of 1996, 5 U.S.C.A. §§ 571–584, Pub. L. No. 104–320, 110 Stat. 3870.

The Administrative Dispute Resolution Act of 1990, 5 U.S.C.A. § 581, extended in scope by the Administrative Dispute Resolution Act of 1996, requires all federal agencies to develop policies on the voluntary use of alternative dispute resolution. The purpose of the Act is "to offer a prompt, expert, and inexpensive means of resolving disputes as an alternative to litigation in Federal courts." In its findings, Congress stated that "the availability of a wide range of dispute resolution procedures, and an increased understanding of the most effective use of such procedures, will enhance the operation of the Government and better serve the public."

At the state level, in addition to legislation authorizing court-sponsored ADR programs, many states have offices of dispute resolution that coordinate state ADR activity and provide technical assistance to neutrals, conduct training, develop standards etc. for public dispute resolution. Finally, as noted above, several states have adopted ethical rules that require lawyers to advise clients of ADR options.

In the private sector, the ADR market is flourishing. Private ADR businesses offer a wide range of services ranging from private judging to mediation. Retired judges often act as neutrals to assist in resolving disputes. Many law firms have developed ADR departments and offer services that are similar to those offered by private ADR providers. The most recent marketing development of ADR is on the Internet with a growing number of dispute resolution services available to parties in cyberspace. Online dispute resolution (ODR) services are particularly helpful for parties who are separated geographically, although the lack of face-to-face communication may prove to be an impediment to a full understanding between disputing parties. Finally, with increasing globalization, ADR has had a significant impact on international commerce.

One thing that we have realized is that there are limits to the judicial process. High legal costs and long delays put a damper on the exercise of an individual's right to go to court. Once a case is in court, it is the judges and lawyers who are the major participants while the affected party often sits on the sidelines. A remedy will be fashioned by a neutral third party, applying the rule of law. Usually, it will be a money judgment. The judicial approach does not consider the affected party's feelings and allows little room for other values such as an apology to the malpractice victim or substitute employment for the injured worker.

Social scientists have begun to test the claims of ADR proponents. While the limited empirical research has not supported efficiency claims that ADR reduces cost or delay, it does suggest that ADR might increase the parties' personal satisfaction, particularly where procedural justice norms are honored. ADR remedies can be tailored to meet individual needs. The use of ADR personalizes what federal judge John Noonan calls the "faces and masks of the law." People's names and feelings are important in a process such as mediation. Private as well as public agendas are important in negotiation. The parties' notion of fairness is important in structuring an arbitration. Advising a client to apologize may be just as crucial as counseling her to file or defend a lawsuit.

Your study of ADR should be closely connected to developing your own theory of lawyering. What are the values that bring you to law school? What does it mean to be a lawyer at the beginning of the twenty-first century? Are you simply an advocate for clients? For a cause? What duties exist beyond those you owe your individual client? What do you hope to accomplish by being a lawyer? Beyond advocacy roles, lawyers are increasingly assuming the role of neutral in ADR proceedings and it is critical that they be aware of the developing ethical rules that govern neutral lawyering practice.

An ADR lawyering perspective goes beyond the bounds of advocacy to help clients help themselves. Implementing a problem-solving approach through processes such as negotiation and mediation advances that goal. Lawyers can educate their clients about the range of choices to accomplish their goals. The choice of process may depend upon who is doing the disputing—institutional disputants such as corporations, unions and government agencies, special interest groups, or individuals, and what is being disputed—individual rights, property rights, constitutional rights, etc.

Lawyers should also consider the standards by which they help their clients arrive at solutions. This requires them to reflect on some critical questions. How do lawyers insure the accuracy of information in ADR processes where parties take no oath to tell the truth? How do lawyers know that the outcome of an ADR method is a just and fair result? In many respects, these questions are more important than the answers.

Bibliography

M. Deutsch and P. Coleman, *The Handbook of Conflict Resolution: Theory and Practice* (2000);

O. Fiss, *Against Settlement,* 93 Yale L.J. 1073 (1984);

L. Fuller, *The Forms and Limits of Adjudication,* 92 Harv. L. Rev. 353 (1978);

M. Galanter, *A World Without Trials?* 2006 Journal of Dispute Resolution 7;

S. Goldberg, F. Sander and N. Rogers, S. Cole, Chapter 1 in *Dispute Resolution: Negotiation, Mediation and Other Processes,* 5th ed. (2007);

D. Hensler, *Our Courts, Ourselves: How The Alternative Dispute Resolution Movement is Reshaping Our Legal System,* 108 Penn. St. L. Rev. 165 (2003);

E. Katsh & J. Rifkin, *Online Dispute Resolution* (2001);

J. McArthur, *Inter-Branch Politics and the Judicial Resistance to Federal Civil Justice Reform,* 33 U.S.F.L. Rev. 551 (1999);

H. Perritt, Jr., *Dispute Resolution in Cyberspace: Demand for New Forms of ADR,* 15 Ohio St. J. on Disp. Resol. 675 (2000);

J. Robbennolt, *Apologies and Legal Settlement: An Empirical Examination,* 102 Mich. L. Rev. 460 (2003);

F. Sander, *Varieties of Dispute Resolution,* 70 F.R.D. 111 (1976);

R. Wissler, *Court-Connected Mediation in General Civil Cases: What We Know from Empirical Research,* 17 Ohio St. J. Disp. Resol. 641 (2002).

CHAPTER 2

NEGOTIATION

I. INTRODUCTION

Negotiation is a fundamental skill that all lawyers need. Corporate lawyers negotiate business deals. Government lawyers negotiate with administrative agencies. Even trial lawyers must negotiate because more often than not, the transaction costs of going to trial outweigh the benefits of a courthouse "victory." Thus, the vast majority of all civil and criminal cases are settled through negotiation.

The study of negotiation involves an analysis of process skills, procedural requirements, and professional responsibility standards as well as substantive law. If an agreement is reached in negotiation, the lawyer is concerned with its validity as well as whether it serves the client's needs and interests. Understanding how that result was reached involves the study of process, procedure, ethical norms and behavioral strategies as well as an appreciation of cultural differences.

The notion that somehow negotiators are born and not made is false. Negotiation is not simply an intuitive process. You can learn about bargaining theories and psychological obstacles to rational decisionmaking, develop strategic approaches and then practice and perfect your negotiation skills.

Legal negotiation differs from other types of negotiation because it involves lawyers acting as agents representing clients. The agency relationship adds a collaborative dynamic to the negotiation process. Prior to the actual negotiation, the lawyer works with the client to help determine the client's particular goals and objectives. Lawyers must develop an in-depth understanding of the underlying needs and interests that support the client's positions. During the negotiation, the lawyer-negotiator must keep the client informed of what is going on and also has the responsibility of protecting the client's interests. A lawyer is involved in the negotiation process not to accomplish personal goals but to serve the client. Lawyers, therefore, must assist clients in defining their goals for a particular negotiation. At the completion of the negotiation, the client, not the lawyer, decides ultimately whether to accept a particular settlement offer. The American Bar Association's Model Rules of Professional Conduct make this clear: "A lawyer shall abide by a client's decision whether to settle a matter." Rule 1.2(a) (1983).

The importance of negotiation skills in the dispute resolution universe cannot be overemphasized. Negotiation is the foundational skill for successful implementation of many ADR processes, such as mediation, the mini-trial and summary jury trial. A theoretical and practical understanding of negotiation enhances the lawyer's effectiveness in these procedures. Mediation, an extension of negotiation, is a process in which a neutral third party, the mediator, helps negotiating parties to reach a mutually acceptable agreement. Mediators who do not understand the dynamics of negotiation are of dubious assistance to the parties in the mediation process. The same is true for lawyers who represent clients in a mini-trial or summary jury trial. The post-hearing settlement talks may be more informed following these ADR proceedings, but they will not be effective if lawyers do not know how to make the negotiation process work effectively for clients.

II. DEFINITIONS AND CONCEPTS

Negotiation may be generally defined as a consensual bargaining process in which parties attempt to reach agreement on a disputed or potentially disputed matter. The whole point of parties negotiating is to achieve an advantage that is not possible by unilateral action. The focus of this chapter is on two-party negotiations. Multiparty or multilateral negotiations where three or more parties are involved, present additional challenges. In dealing with groups in multiparty negotiations, lawyers must be skilled in developing and maintaining coalitions, agreements with other individuals or groups to engage in joint action on particular issues.

Negotiation differs from other methods of dispute resolution in the degree of autonomy experienced by the disputing parties. In negotiation, parties attempt to reach agreement without the intervention of third parties such as judges, arbitrators or mediators. Parties also have the power to decide process norms in negotiation.

A. DISPUTE AND DEAL–MAKING NEGOTIATION

Negotiations may be classified in two categories: dispute and deal-making or transactional negotiations. In planning for a negotiation, lawyers must initially determine which type is involved. *Dealmaking* negotiation involves parties planning for a future event such as licensing a copyright agreement, drafting an employment contract or a long-term lease or other similar long-term goals. In a *dispute* negotiation the parties are in conflict over an event that has occurred—the contract that was breached, the patent that was infringed, the personal injury that was sustained. The issues in dispute negotiation are often susceptible to resolution by a third party such as a judge or arbitrator, while in deal-making negotiation, the issues are resolved by the parties themselves. It is not surprising then that dispute negotiation is often a prelude to litigation between the parties.

Strategic planning will obviously differ depending upon how a negotiation is classified. If preserving a relationship is important to the client in a dealmaking negotiation, for example, then any tactics which harm that relationship would be inappropriate. The lawyer-negotiator would attempt to avoid an unfavorable outcome in a deal-making negotiation in order to preserve the underlying transaction. In some cases, however, failed deal-making not only results in a loss of the bargain, but can even lead to litigation.

This is what occurred in *Hoffman v. Red Owl Stores, Inc.*, 26 Wis.2d 683, 133 N.W.2d 267 (1965), a case familiar to many first year law students because of its importance in common law developments in the law of promissory estoppel. In a series of detailed transactions, Joseph Hoffman and his wife negotiated with agents of the Red Owl stores to establish Hoffman as a franchise operator of a Red Owl store in Chilton, Wisconsin. Red Owl agents made representations to Hoffman that, if he fulfilled several conditions, he would become a franchise operator. The negotiations terminated between the parties when Hoffman informed Red Owl that he objected to some terms in their proposal. What result? Not only did the transaction negotiation fail, i.e. Hoffman never received the franchise, but extensive litigation ensued over alleged promises made during the negotiation.

B.　DISTRIBUTIVE AND INTEGRATIVE BARGAINING

Negotiation may be further classified into *distributive* or *integrative* bargaining situations. *Distributive* bargaining exists where the parties believe that there are limited resources to divide. Individual, rather than joint gain, is sought. Typically, the negotiator engages in *positional* bargaining, claiming a particular position and arguing for it throughout the negotiation process. To insure that the position is realized, the negotiator would usually take an extreme position, make few concessions and ultimately arrive at the desired position. Research shows that distributive bargaining is greatly influenced by information asymmetries and by manipulation of information to influence the opponents' perceptions.

There is a *zero-sum* dimension to distributive bargaining—more for me automatically means less for you. Consider a simple example where S, a second year law student, wants to sell her first year law books for the highest possible price. B, a first year law student, wants to pay the lowest possible price for the books. The negotiations between S and B over the price of the books can be described as a *zero-sum* situation where gain by S comes at the expense of B.

In an *integrative bargaining* situation, the parties' goals are not necessarily at odds with each other so that mutual gain is possible and oftentimes, desirable. Integrative bargaining usually involves multiple issues so that it is possible to develop several alternative and mutually beneficial solutions. The negotiator would engage in *interest* bargaining and focus on the underlying needs and concerns that support a particular position. The negotiator explores those interests and seeks opportunities to develop responsive solutions. Some scholars suggest that wherever possible, negoti-

ators should try to transform the bargaining context into integrative situations. Consider the following integrative approaches to negotiation.

Example 1

A Deal–Making or Transaction Negotiation

Eastern University wishes to recruit Professor X,
a national expert in governmental affairs to develop
its political science department. Professor X and her
husband, a chemist, currently teach at Western
University. The recruitment has the potential for
deadlock because of Professor X's salary demands.
Eastern has offered her a salary of $99,000.00 but
Professor X claims she would only leave Western
University for a salary of $120,000.00. Eastern is
not in a position to pay this salary. Hefty budget
cuts have affected all departments of the university
and it is unclear whether the political science department will receive outside funding this year.
Additionally, the highest paid professor in the political science department receives a salary of
$110,000.00 so that even if funds were available, it
might not be appropriate to bring in a newcomer at
a higher salary.

At first glance this looks like a *distributive* bargaining situation because the sole disputed issue is
the amount of money that Professor X will receive.
It is possible, however, to consider the opportunities
for joint gain and transform this into an *integrative
bargaining* situation. If Eastern University and
Professor X examine their goals, they would proba-

bly learn that Eastern wants to establish a first class political science department while Professor X is interested in establishing a national reputation in political science. Working collaboratively, they are better able to achieve those goals. If Professor X's salary demands are based on financial concerns, then additional items could be included with the Eastern's offer: assistance with locating a consulting or teaching position for her husband, health care benefits, housing assistance, travel grants, child care, an endowed chair etc. If scholarship is a concern, then items such as early sabbatical leave, lighter teaching load and additional research assistants could be discussed. While these are all separate issues, it may possible to resolve them interdependently, so that the result would then be a non *zero-sum* situation where both parties can gain by negotiating a settlement on all items together.

Example 2

A Dispute Negotiation

The tenants in an urban apartment complex suffered serious interruptions of services during a strike by maintenance workers. After conditions became close to intolerable as rats, roaches, and other vermin ran rampant, the tenants started a rent strike. The landlord demanded that the tenants pay their rent and threatened legal action. The tenants hired an attorney and agreed that if a case were brought to court by the landlord that they would all testify to the above-stated facts.

Consider the type of negotiation process that could take place in this case. The landlord and tenant's lawyers could view this as a *distributive* bargaining problem and posture the bargaining so that it becomes an adversarial, win-lose proposition. More money for the landlord means less money for the tenants or vice-versa.

If the negotiation failed, however, the parties would end up in court. Both sides would then risk a total loss. Litigation would only prolong the bad conditions in the building (assuming the maintenance strike continued) and the landlord's need for the rent money. The publicity from the litigation could be harmful to both the landlord and the tenants.

Alternatively, the lawyers could help their clients focus on the opportunities that exist for joint gain, thereby transforming this negotiation into an *integrative* bargaining context. Both the landlord and tenants could explore ways to furnish the services until the maintenance strike ended. The tenants could agree to pay the rent with an abatement until the repairs were made. Both sides have much to gain from a speedy resolution of the issue. The tenants hopefully would have the necessary repairs made to their building and the landlord would receive rent money with which he could arrange to have the repairs made and make the mortgage payments.

III. **APPROACHES TO NEGOTIATION**

A. IN GENERAL

The literature on legal negotiation identifies two major orientations that describe how lawyers generally negotiate: adversarial and problem-solving. Other dichotomies that describe these approaches include competitive and collaborative, value-claiming and value-creating, and interest-based and position-based. Scholars have described a number of variations within each model. Lawyers will adopt specific strategies, tactics and styles depending upon the model that is used. The early writings on legal negotiation focused primarily on the adversarial approach to negotiation. As the study of the legal negotiation process becomes more advanced, however, there is a growing recognition that a problem-solving approach may be more efficient and that it may result in more mutually satisfactory outcomes. As a practical matter, however, there is no "pure" adversarial or problem-solving approach and elements of value-claiming (adversarial) and value creating (problem-solving) may be present in most negotiations.

1. Adversarial Approach

The primary goal of the lawyer who engages in adversarial negotiation is to maximize individual gain. To achieve that goal, the negotiator engages primarily in positional bargaining, a strategy that has been described by Fisher, Ury and Patton in

Getting to Yes as one in which the negotiator adopts a particular position, advances arguments to support that position, makes some concessions and finally reaches a compromise solution. The adversarial negotiator stays close to the client's positions and maneuvers and structures the negotiation process so that it moves through those positions. The journey of the adversarial negotiator is, therefore, closely mapped out between the client's bottom line and stated position.

In *The Manager as Negotiator,* Lax and Sebenius characterize adversarial, competitive negotiators as the "value claimers" for whom "[T]he object of negotiation is to convince the other guy that he wants what you have to offer much more than you want what he has; moreover, you have all the time in the world while he is up against pressing deadlines." The adversarial negotiator usually perceives the issues in negotiation as distributive; the negotiator assumes that there is only one prize in the official jackpot and firmly believes that the negotiator's job is to get that prize for the client. The negotiation process is viewed as a zero-sum game, at the end of which there will be a winner and a loser.

The adversarial negotiator may use competitive or cooperative tactics to win this game. Professor Gerald Williams' empirical study of lawyers' negotiating behavior shows that the goals of the effective competitive negotiator include: maximizing settlement for their clients; obtaining profitable fees for themselves; and, outmaneuvering their opponents.

They are perceived as dominating, forceful, aggressive, tough, arrogant, and uncooperative. Hard bargaining tactics are common. Their strategy is to make high opening demands and offer few concessions. They use threats, are willing to stretch the facts in favor of their clients' positions, stick to their positions and are parsimonious with information about the case. The whole purpose of this behavior is to create substantial doubt in the mind of opposing negotiators about the validity of their positions. The opposing negotiators may lose confidence and arrive at a less than satisfactory solution for their clients.

Subsequent empirical research by other scholars shows that adversarial bargainers have become even more extreme in their behavior. Professor Andrea Schneider's study, conducted twenty-five years after Professor Williams' study, showed that adversarial lawyers are perceived as more extreme and less effective than those described in the Williams study. In her study, the top five adjectives describing effective adversarial negotiators are: egotistical, demanding, ambitious, experienced and confident.

2. Problem–Solving Approach

A problem-solving orientation in negotiation focuses on the opportunities for joint, rather than individual, gain. The negotiator views the dispute or transaction as a mutual problem that has the potential of being resolved to the parties' mutual satisfaction and then searches for ways to create value so that both sides may benefit. Negotiation is not just a "game" to be won. The problem-solving approach usually functions in an integrative (multiple issue), rather than a distributive (single issue) context. It is the predominant model advanced in negotiation theory today.

Lax and Sebenius characterize problem-solving negotiators as "value creators" who "advocate exploring and cultivating shared interests in substance, in maintaining a working relationship, in having a pleasant nonstrident negotiation process, in mutually held norms or principles, and even in reaching agreement at all." These negotiators use radically different tactics to achieve the same end as competitive negotiators.

There is a great deal of similarity between the cooperative negotiator described in Professor Williams' study of lawyers' negotiating behavior and the problem-solver. According to Professor Williams, the effective cooperative negotiator had the following characteristics: conducting self ethically; maximizing settlement for client; getting a fair settlement; meeting client's needs; avoiding litigation; and maintaining or establishing a good personal relationship with the opponent. These motivational objectives were observed in attorneys who were perceived as fair, objective, reasonable, logical, and willing to move from their established positions. Professor Schneider's study showed similar behavioral traits. Many of these characteristics apply to the problem-solving negotiator who tries to develop a relationship in which both parties can explore opportunities to create value. If there are distributive issues to be resolved, the problem-solving negotiator treats them as a shared problem that must be resolved fairly.

Professor Carrie Menkel–Meadow describes the methodology used in the problem-solving negotiation model in her seminal article, "Toward Another View of Legal Negotiation: The Structure of Problem Solving"—first, through extensive negotiation planning and brainstorming, the parties' underlying needs and objectives are identified; second, solutions which respond to those needs are formulated. In *Getting to Yes*, Fisher, Ury and Patton propose a bargaining model for using the problem-solving approach to negotiation. The authors suggest that as an alternative to the competitiveness of positional bargaining, negotiators engage in interest-based bargaining. This model requires that the negotiator distinguish the issues or problems from the parties involved in the dispute, and then concentrate on responding to the parties' underlying needs and interests rather than their stated positions.

Despite the growth and popularity of the problem-solving negotiation model, it has inspired several critiques. Some scholars have argued that it fails to address the problems raised by distributive bargaining situations where interests are clearly opposed. A second critique is that problem-solving requires good faith by both parties to the negotiation, an element that may be missing.

What approach should the negotiating attorney adopt? In every negotiation, lawyers must consciously consider what approach best serves their clients' interests. Thus, working collaboratively with their clients, lawyers must first determine the goals they hope to achieve in a negotiation. Whether the goal is to sever a relationship or to cement one, to open a deal or to close one, a conscious choice must be made about the appropriate negotiating approach.

In planning an approach to negotiation, lawyers should be mindful of some basic problems that must be managed if the negotiations are to be successful. The following tensions are among the more common problems identified by negotiation scholars. First, there is the tension between empathy and assertiveness, i.e., demonstrating to your opponent that you understand her point of view and asserting your own view. A second common tension arises with agency problems in conflicts between principal and agent. Such conflicts occur in legal negotiation when the interests of the client differ from those of the lawyer. A final example of the tensions that must be managed in negotiation are those that exist when competitive moves to claim value collide with cooperative moves to create value. As Lax and Sebenius have argued, the processes of value creating and value claiming are both present in every negotiation. At some point in the negotiation process, the resources that are available to the parties become fixed and must be divided among competing interests. One of the inherent tensions in every negotiation lies in making choices about the approach to use in determining how those resources will be divided. Behavior that makes the negotiator a successful value creator causes the same negotiator to become vulnerable when dealing with the value claimer. By the same token, the behavior necessary to claim value is counterproductive in creating value.

NEGOTIATION APPROACHES		
	ADVERSARIAL	PROBLEM–SOLVING
Goal:	maximize self gain	seeks joint gain
Behavior:	competitive positional bargaining	facilitative interest bargaining
Perception of issues:	distributive zero-sum win-lose	integrative non-zero sum win-win

B. NEGOTIATION APPROACHES IN PRACTICE

Problem

A owns a patent on a product (x), that could cure tuberculosis and for which there is a very large world market. A does not plan to develop or market (x). Instead, A is conducting clinical tests and awaiting government approval to sell a different, unpatented product (y), that also cures tuberculosis. This may take one to two more years. B already has government approval and has begun selling product (x) as a cure for tuberculosis without A's consent. B's sales of product (x) infringe A's patent. A tells B that his sale of product (x) infringes A's patent and warns B not to continue making, using or selling the product. B refuses.

Under an adversarial, competitive model, A might say—get off the market and stop selling my product (x) or I sue. This of course is classic, positional bargaining. To avoid a very costly lawsuit that could result in an injunction against B's future sales, damages for B's sales to date and punitive damages for B's willful infringement of A's patent, B might agree to stop selling product (x) if A would agree not to seek damages for past infringement or punitive damages. A would have given up the potential recovery from B of past damages and punitive damages, to retain the tuberculosis market for himself. The result, however, is that no one is on the market until A's product (y) is approved by the government and a product (x), potentially helpful to C, a tuberculosis patient, is unavailable.

Alternatively, under a problem-solving approach, using interest bargaining, a more beneficial and efficient outcome may be possible. A might say "I will agree to license B to use my patent to sell product (x)." A would benefit by receiving money from B and when A's product (y) reached the market, A would have an overall financial advantage over B. A would have no royalty obligation against the sales of product (y). B on the other hand would pay royalty to A, on all sales of B's product (x). A and B, however, would be permitted to sell their products and C, the potential tuberculosis patient, would be well served by a likely lower price (because of price competition between A and B for market share) and by a choice of two products from which to choose.

IV. STAGES OF THE NEGOTIATION PROCESS

Negotiation approaches will differ depending upon a number of variables including the client's goals, the subject matter, the personalities of the parties involved, the negotiator's individual preferences, and cultural considerations. Negotiating with your children is obviously quite different from negotiating with your clients. For an American lawyer, negotiating in New York may be quite different from negotiating in China. Before adopting an approach to negotiation, it is important to understand how a legal negotiation operates. The following elements constitute the generic negotiation process:

1. Planning and analysis

2. Exchanging information

3. Exchanging concessions and compromise

4. Reaching agreement

Negotiation is a fluid process and these stages do not necessarily occur in linear fashion. It is quite possible, for example, that a lawyer-negotiator may exchange substantial information about the value of a case before deciding on a planning approach to a particular negotiation. Or, after exchanging information with opposing counsel, the attorney may modify her initial approach. Consider the hypotheti-

cal case of a lawyer who represents a former mara-
thon runner in an orthopedic malpractice case. The
client's big toe was so severely damaged by the
orthopedic surgeon in a bunionectomy that the
client will not be able to run competitively in any
future marathons. During the initial planning
stages, the client tells the lawyer that he is very
angry, that he is nervous and tense all the time
because his sense of self-esteem was wrapped up in
his running. Now, money is the bottom line for him
and he wants no less than half a million dollars
from the orthopedic surgeon. The client asks the
lawyer to engage in aggressive advocacy. After de-
posing the orthopedic surgeon, the lawyer learns
that there are numerous ways to perform a bunionectomy and that the method used by the orthopedic surgeon on her client might even be considered
appropriate. The lawyer also learns from her client
that instead of running competitively, the client is
now race-walking and has already entered two regional competitions.

Given this information, the lawyer-negotiator
might well decide that an adversarial approach
would be totally inappropriate and probably counterproductive. Competitive strategies might result
in deadlock and the case would have to go to trial.
Because there are many methods of performing a
bunionectomy, there is a more than strong chance
that a jury would find no negligence. Even if the
jury found the surgeon to be negligent, the fact that
the client is still engaged in competitive sports
would significantly diminish the amount of dam-

ages. The lawyer would then explain all of these considerations to the client and suggest that it would be preferable to adopt a problem-solving approach or at the very least, a cooperative strategy, in the hope of inducing cooperation from the other side.

A. PLANNING AND ANALYSIS

Strategic planning is the key to successful negotiation and maximum time should be invested at this stage of the negotiation process. Just as a good trial lawyer would not dream of beginning a trial without a thorough knowledge of the facts and relevant substantive law and a well-designed strategic plan, neither should the negotiating lawyer.

At the initial planning and analysis stage the lawyer must work collaboratively with the client to identify and prioritize the client's goals. In order to accomplish this task, the lawyer needs to understand her client's underlying needs and interests, capabilities and resources. The skills used by lawyers in client interviewing and counseling, such as fact investigation and active listening, will be most helpful in the planning stages.

After learning the facts and the client's needs, interests and goals, the lawyer-negotiator must consider the appropriate method to satisfy those interests and achieve those goals. Just what does your client want out of this situation? Is money the bottom line or does your client wants to establish or maintain a business or other relationship?

In helping the client to identify goals and objectives, the lawyer-negotiator should consider how many parties are involved in or affected by the negotiation. This is a critical part of the planning analysis because the negotiation dynamic operates differently in a multi-party than in a two-party situation. For example, the negotiation of a class action where coalitions may develop will usually be a more complicated process than negotiating in a two party transaction. In *3–D Negotiation: Powerful Tools to Change the Game in Your Most Important Deal*, Lax and Sebenius focus on planning and analysis and emphasize the importance of paying attention to what they call "setup" actions away from the bargaining table that shape what happens at the table. These would include actions such as making sure that the correct parties have been contacted, and being aware of the consequences of walking away from the table if there is no deal.

In the planning and analysis stage, lawyer-negotiators must also examine whether there are any related transactions that may impact on the instant negotiation. A simple example of this would be representing the seller of a residential home where the buyer's ability to close the transaction depends upon his sale of his home within a six month period.

Throughout the planning and analysis stage, the lawyer should continuously explain all of the pa-

rameters of the case as openly as possible so that
there can be meaningful involvement by the client
who should also have some input on negotiation
strategy. This is consistent with the dictates of the
Model Rules of Professional Conduct which provide
in Rule 1.4(b) that "[a] lawyer shall explain a
matter to the extent reasonably necessary to permit
the client to make informed decisions regarding the
representation." Working collaboratively with the
client, the lawyer then maps out specific objectives,
a strategic plan and tactical approaches that will
achieve the client's desired goals. Ultimately, it will
be the client who decides whether or not to accept a
settlement proposal.

Clients who are actively involved in the planning
and analysis stage of a negotiation are much more
likely to be satisfied with the end result and with
their lawyer than are clients who are kept in the
dark by their lawyers. Consider the case of two
clients X and Y who had similar personal injury
cases against Z arising out of the same automobile
accident. Both X and Y claimed $100,000.00 in
damages. However, they each received only
$20,000.00 in settlement. X had several meetings
with her lawyer where X helped him understand
the interests and goals that were important to her
in the case and the lawyer explained what was
likely to happen. X and her lawyer talked about how
best to pursue those goals. Y's lawyer, on the other
hand, had one meeting with her and wrote her one
letter in three years which told her to come to a
deposition. At the end of three years both X and Y

receive a letter from their respective attorneys which said "Congratulations, I have just settled your case for $20,000.00." Who will be the more satisfied client?

Planning checklist

1. learn underlying facts of dispute

2. determine whether additional information is needed

3. determine weakest aspects of client's case—vulnerability points and the strongest aspects of client's case

4. analyze issues (distributive or integrative), identify positions and distinguish them from the clients' interests

5. assist client in determining goals and objectives

6. determine whether the client will participate in the negotiation and what parties should be at the table

7. research and review relevant law

8. determine alternatives to reaching a negotiated agreement—e.g., the deal will be lost; a lawsuit will be filed; Fisher, Ury & Patton refer here to one's BATNA or best alternative to a negotiated agreement

9. decide upon initial strategy and tactics (subject to change depending upon opposing counsel's behavior)

10. determine what information to give the opposing party

B. EXCHANGING INFORMATION

The information exchange begins the "getting to know you" part of the negotiation. Lawyers meet each other through phone calls, letters or personal contact. Each party offers an initial assessment of the case. How lawyers react to each other may determine the future of the negotiation in terms of the strategy and tactics which each side will use. Will I cooperate? Do I trust this negotiator? Will she be open with me? What is her reputation for fairness? Do I want to show that I am tough? Lawyers should be aware of the importance of framing at this initial stage of the negotiation. Framing refers to the way a negotiation story is told. It reveals a negotiator's understanding of the issues that are at stake. The manner in which issues are framed at the beginning of a negotiation may well determine whether the negotiation proceeds in a problem-solving or adversarial approach.

Control over the information acquisition process is crucial to the success of negotiation. How we acquire and disclose information will often determine the outcome and efficiency of the negotiation. Here, it is likely that ethical issues related to truthfulness and fairness in negotiation may be raised.

Listening is an important skill to develop in the information exchange. By listening carefully, we try to learn what our opponents are really seeking.

Listening skills, however, are often not easily acquired by many lawyers who find it difficult to resist the urge to interrupt conversation with another question.

Effective listening can be a passive experience simply involving moments of concentrated silence or it can require active participation in summarizing what you have heard from the other party. Active participatory listening tells the other party not only that you hear her story but that you understand the feelings and emotions which are connected with that story. Listening is discussed in more detail in Chapter 3 on mediation.

Generating Options

As information is exchanged, parties further explore ways to enlarge the pie both in terms of possible solutions and available resources. What besides money damages would satisfy the client's or opponent's needs? If money damages alone are the priority, should they be paid in a lump sum or as part of a structured settlement? This exploration is an on-going process throughout the negotiation.

First Offer

A crucial part of the information exchange is the first offer. Who makes it? What are its contents? When should it be made? The negotiation literature is replete with advice about the merits and demerits of making the first offer. There is an important anchoring effect in making the first offer and this may affect the final outcome. Some negotiation scholars suggest that when negotiators have good information about their opponents' reservation value [the point below which they will not go] then making the first offer may be beneficial in order to anchor expectations. However, without knowledge of an opponent's reservation value, it may be preferable to allow your opponent to begin. As a practical matter, the only general rule with respect to who makes the first offer, is that it depends upon the circumstances. In some competitive bargaining situations, it may not matter who makes the first offer because opening offers are usually quite extreme and therefore less likely to establish a credible zone of bargaining. In other situations, however, a major advantage of making the first offer lies in the offeror's potential control of the outer limits of the bargaining zone.

Negotiators should exercise caution and obtain as much reliable information about the case and the parties as possible before making the first offer. Without a thorough knowledge of the case and parties, an initial offer may be below the range within which the case could be settled. For example, in the tuberculosis patent licensing case, discussed earlier, A, looking only to the present market, could offer to settle the patent infringement dispute by giving a license to B for ten thousand dollars a year. A has obviously limited the settlement by her initial offer. If the market is likely to grow rapidly, however, A's opening "present-day" bid will have cost it dearly over the life of the patent.

In thinking about the content and range of the first offer the negotiator should leave room for maneuvering by the other party. Making the first offer on a "take it or leave it basis" leaves no opportunity for the other side to engage in any semblance of bargaining. This tactic, known as "Boulwarism," derives from Lemuel R. Boulware who used the "take it or leave it" technique during his tenure as vice-president of General Electric Company during the 1950's. General Electric avoided working with the union representatives in the collective bargaining process by going directly to the workers with what it considered to be fair and reasonable proposals. Generally, the company's first offer was its final offer. The practice of bypassing union representatives and going to the workers with firm first offers was finally held to be an unfair labor practice by the National Labor Relations Board because it represented a failure to bargain in good faith. *N.L.R.B. v. General Electric Co.*, 418 F.2d 736 (2nd Cir.1969).

C. CONCESSIONS AND COMPROMISE

By the time that the legal and factual issues have been distilled, the dispute is sufficiently refined to begin the "give and take" aspect of the negotiation process. Usually there are external factors such as impending deadlines that initiate this movement by the parties. By exchanging concessions, the parties begin to narrow the zone of the dispute. If compromise is reached on at least some of the issues involved, the parties create a good climate which is conducive to a final agreement.

Concessions are a crucial component of the negotiation process, a part of the reciprocity norm. Lawyers who fail to reciprocate risk bringing negotiations to an impasse. The lawyer who decides to be "up front" and reveal a client's bottom line at the beginning of the negotiation has foreclosed the opportunity to make concessions and thus, cannot really participate in the bargaining process in any meaningful fashion. Professor Gerald Williams' empirical study of lawyers' negotiating behavior shows that making few concessions is one of the characteristics of the competitive negotiator. If opposing counsel does not reciprocate with concessions, caution should be exercised.

Negotiators adopting a cooperative or problem-solving strategy may use the "logrolling" tactic of offering concessions on some issues in exchange for concessions by the other party. Joint gain results because the parties have traded concessions based on their priorities.

D.   REACHING AGREEMENT

When the parties finally reach a settlement, then the actual mechanics of the agreement must be worked out. This process demands prudent exercise of the same process skills that produced the agreement because packaging all the details of the final agreement may involve a separate negotiation. The lawyer who drafts the final settlement agreement should always be mindful of contract law principles regarding the validity and effect of settlement agreements and consider whether some type of penalty provisions should be included in the case of noncompliance.

E. BARRIERS TO SETTLEMENT

Of course, not all negotiations will result in settlement and it is important to be aware of the impediments to successful negotiation. Over the last twenty-five years, scholars have devoted considerable attention to the study of barriers to negotiation in order to understand why some negotiations are unsuccessful when they could have resulted in settlement. It is important for negotiators to understand these impediments to successful negotiation and consider techniques and processes that may help to overcome them. The following list is illustrative of some major barriers that impede successful negotiations.

1. *Strategic barriers*

    Example 1: The negotiator conceals real interests.

    Example 2: The negotiator engages in hardball tactics.

2. *Psychological barriers*

    Example 1: *Loss aversion.* The negotiator risks a large loss that is uncertain rather than accept smaller loss that is certain.

Example 2: *Reactive devaluation.* The negotiator may discredit a proposal that is received from an opponent even if the same proposal would have been acceptable if offered by a neutral party.

3. *Structural barriers*

Example 1: *Agency problems.* The interests of the lawyer-negotiator (agent) differ from those of the client (principal) who is represented in the negotiation.

Example 2: *Representation of multiple groups*: All parties affected by the outcome are not represented at the bargaining table.

F.   THE ROLE OF EMOTIONS IN NEGOTIATION

People do not negotiate in an emotional vacuum—human emotions are an inherent aspect of negotiation. Lawyers need to appreciate this reality, particularly when they are engaged in complex legal negotiations. One suggestion from Stone, Patton and Heen in their book, *Difficult Conversations: How to Discuss What Matters Most,* is to think about difficult conversations as if there were really three conversations going on, involving the facts, the emotions and the identities of the parties.

Responding to the complexity of human emotions is challenging and the legal profession is just beginning to appreciate the research of social psychologists on dealing with psychological biases and emotions such as fear, anxiety, anger, and stress that can arise during negotiations. Most lawyers, of course, are not therapists, and will never be experts in managing the parties' emotional concerns. Rather than attempt to deal with the range of human emotions that can surface in any bargaining situation, Fisher and Shapiro suggest in *Beyond Reason: Using Emotions As You Negotiate* that negotiators focus on five core concerns: appreciation, affiliation, autonomy, status and role.

Appreciation: Parties are more likely to reach a wise agreement if they each appreciate each other;

Affiliation: When parties work together (affiliation), there is a sense of connectedness;

Autonomy: When autonomy is honored, there is respect for the other party as well as one's self;

Status: It is important to acknowledge both social status and status based on expertise; appreciate the status of others and be proud of your own;

Role: In addition to your conventional role, you have the power to reshape your role and choose temporary roles that empower you and encourage joint work.

G. THE ROLE OF CULTURE IN NEGOTIATIONS

The relationship between culture and conflict is receiving increased attention from negotiation scholars, and there is now a substantial literature on how cultural differences may affect negotiations. According to Professor Kevin Avruch "culture refers to the socially transmitted values, beliefs and symbols that are more or less shared by members of a social group." Culture also includes boundaries such as gender, race, religion, and ethnicity.

Negotiating in cross-cultural situations requires an awareness of one's own cultural values and an alertness to the cultural interests of others. Professor Jeanne Brett's research suggests that cultures differ in negotiation styles in a number of ways including the manner in which information is communicated; the extent to which direct confrontation is preferred to indirect approaches; the extent to which parties are drawn by self-interest or collective interests; and the value of fairness. Other cultural differences include the parties' attitude towards time, and gender stereotypes. While the extent to which culture affects negotiation is unclear, failure to be aware of cultural differences may doom a negotiation.

V. ETHICAL ISSUES IN NEGOTIATION

Legal negotiations should be distinguished from market place dealings by the integrity and professionalism of the lawyers who negotiate. This ideal is reflected in the Preamble to the Model Rules of Professional Conduct (Model Rules) adopted by the American Bar Association in 1983: "(a)s negotiator a lawyer seeks a result advantageous to the client but consistent with requirements of honest dealings with others." The practice of "honest dealings with others" is most difficult to define with dispute negotiations in on-going litigation. Federal Magistrate Wayne Brazil has written of the negative aspects of settlement negotiations:

Some of the most exaggerated and obvious abuses of the litigator's manipulative and deceptive tools take place during settlement negotiations. Occasional melodramatic performances only highlight the somewhat more subtle acts of subterfuge, concealment, and emotional posturing that seem to be the perennial attendants of settlement negotiations. The goal is to manipulate your opponent, through whatever emotional pressures or rational arguments will have the desired effect, into giving your client the best "deal" possible. If that deal happens to coincide with what is fair, fine; but the goal all too frequently is that best "deal," not fairness. Short of bald lying, many attorneys will resort to almost any device that "works" in the settlement process, *e.g.*, appealing to feelings of guilt, pandering to vanities, exploiting fears, generating confusions, and, above all, hiding as many of the damaging balls of evidence as possible.

The Attorney as Victim: Toward More Candor About the Psychological Price Tag of Litigation Practice, 3 J. Legal Prof. 107 (1978).

Negotiating behavior is constrained generally by the substantive law of crimes, torts and contract.

For lawyers, there are additional constraints imposed by professional codes, either the Model Code of Professional Responsibility promulgated by the American Bar Association in 1969 or the Model Rules of Professional Conduct, adopted by almost two-thirds of the states. Additional guidance is provided by the American Law Institute's Restatement (Third) of the Law Governing Lawyers, and Lawyers Ethical Guidelines for Settlement Negotiations (2002), developed by a Task Force of the ABA Section on litigation and available at http://www.abanet.org/litigation/ethics/settlementnegotiations.pdf.

A.   RELATIONSHIP WITH CLIENTS

Before beginning a negotiation, lawyers and client should be clear about the extent to which the lawyer has authority to enter into a binding agreement on behalf of a client. It is good practice to have this agreement in writing. During negotiations, lawyer's have an on-going responsibility under Model Rule 1.4 to keep their clients informed about the status of their negotiations. When a lawyer receives an offer of settlement from opposing counsel, the client must be informed unless the client has previously indicated that a proposal would be unacceptable or has authorized the lawyer to accept or reject offers. Clients have the right to make the final determination about whether or not to accept a settlement offer. Rule 1.2 of the Model Rules states that "a lawyer shall abide by a client's decisions concerning the objectives of representation...[and] shall abide by a client's decision whether to settle a matter."

B. TRUTHFULNESS

One of the recurring ethical issues in legal negotiation concerns truthfulness. How much are we required to reveal? How honest must we be in our statements? Truthfulness may seem antithetical to the competitive negotiator who is trying to create doubt in the mind of an opponent about the validity of a position.

The fundamental tension in this area derives from two obligations imposed on the negotiating lawyer: the legal and ethical disclosure requirements of negotiation and the lawyer's duty to protect her client's interests. The reality is that negotiation is essentially a private activity and there are few, if any, mechanisms to enforce a requirement of truthfulness. Professor James White has cogently characterized the dilemma:

If one negotiator lies to another, only by happenstance will the other discover the lie. If the settlement is concluded by negotiation, there will be no trial, no public testimony by conflicting witnesses, and thus no opportunity to examine the truthfulness of assertions made during the negotiation. Consequently, in negotiation, more than in other contexts, ethical norms can probably be violated with greater confidence that there will be no discovery and punishment.

Machiavelli and the Bar: Ethical Limitations on Lying in Negotiation, 1980 Am. B. Found. Res. J. 926 (1980).

C. MISREPRESENTATION

Where lack of truthfulness in negotiation rises to the level of deliberate misrepresentation, a lawyer may be subject to liability under tort and contract law depending upon the level of deception involved.

The negotiator who deliberately misrepresents a fact, opinion, intention or law so that the opposing negotiator will rely on it, may be liable for fraudulent misrepresentation (*Restatement (Second) of Torts* § 525). For example, a lawyer who deliberately tells her opposing negotiator that her client has only $25,000.00 of liability insurance, when in fact her client has $100,000.00 policy, may be exposed to tort liability if the opposing counsel settles the case for $25,000.00 based on that representation.

What about disclosure requirements? When does a negotiator's silence subject her to liability? There are two situations where a negotiator may incur civil liability for silence. The first is where a negotiator intentionally conceals a material fact or does something that prevents the other party from acquiring the information. The second situation involves failure to disclose where there is a duty to disclose, where for example, there is a fiduciary relationship between the parties.

Contract law also provides redress if there has been a misrepresentation that is either fraudulent or material. (*Restatement (Second) of Contracts*, § 164). In the same example above with the lawyer who misrepresented the amount of her client's liability insurance, the settlement agreement that resulted from that misrepresentation could be set aside.

Both contract and tort law recognize a puffing exception for statements upon which a person would not reasonably rely. For example, in one case, the statements of an auctioneer that "the trucks are in good condition," and "the trucks are ready to work tomorrow" were considered permissible "puffing" even when the same truck broke down shortly after purchase because of a crack in the engine block. *Pell City Wood, Inc. v. Forke Bros. Auctioneers, Inc.*, 474 So.2d 694 (Ala.1985).

The lawyer-negotiator is a member of a profession and quite apart from substantive law, lawyers' professional codes govern bluffing, puffing and lying in the negotiation context. Model Rule 4.1, Truthfulness in Statements to Others, describes the extent to which a lawyer must speak the truth in negotiation:

> In the course of representing a client a lawyer shall not knowingly: (a) make a false statement of material fact or law to a third person; or (b) fail to disclose a material fact to a third person when disclosure is necessary to avoid assisting a criminal or fraudulent act by a client, unless disclosure is prohibited by Rule 1.6.

Model Rule 4.1 corresponds to EC 7–102(A)(5) under the Code of Professional Responsibility.

The official explanatory comment to Model Rule 4.1 states that:

> A lawyer is required to be truthful when dealing with others on a client's behalf, but generally has no affirmative duty to inform an opposing party of relevant facts. A misrepresentation can occur if the lawyer incorporates or affirms a statement of another person that the lawyer knows is false. Misrepresentation can also occur by partially true but misleading statements or omissions that are the equivalent of affirmative false statements. [check]

The Comment then delineates three categories where certain statements are not considered material fact—

> Estimates of price or value placed on the subject of a transaction and a party's intentions as to an acceptable settlement of a claim are in this category, and so is the existence of an undisclosed principal except where nondisclosure of the principal would constitute fraud.

It is important to balance the truthfulness requirements of Rule 4.1 with the attorney's overarching duty to honor client confidences. Model Rule 1.6(a) provides that "[a] lawyer shall not reveal information relating to the representation of a client unless the client gives informed consent, the disclosure is impliedly authorized in order to carry out the representation." The mandate of Rule 1.6(a) is qualified somewhat in Rule 1.6(b) by allowing a lawyer to reveal information to the extent that the lawyer reasonably believes necessary in the following circumstances:

(1) to prevent reasonably certain death or substantial bodily harm;

(2) to prevent the client from committing a crime or fraud that is reasonably certain to result in substantial injury to the financial interests or property of another and in furtherance of which the client has used or is using the lawyer's services;

(3) to prevent, mitigate or rectify substantial injury to the financial interests or property of another that is reasonably certain to result or has resulted from the client's commission of a crime or fraud in furtherance of which the client has use the lawyer's services;

(4) to secure legal advice about the lawyer's compliance with the Rules;

(5) to establish a claim or defense on behalf of the lawyer in a controversy between the lawyer and the client, to establish a defense to a criminal charge or civil claim against the lawyer based upon conduct in which the client was involved, or to respond to allegations in any proceeding concerning the lawyer's representation of the client; or

(6) to comply with other law or a court order.

Thus, lawyers' ability to share information in negotiation is constrained by the rules on client confidentiality. Lawyers may not reveal information in negotiations without their clients' informed consent. It is important therefore, that lawyers understand from their clients what information may be revealed to their opponents.

A lawyer's professional credibility is at stake in every negotiation situation. If I negotiate with you and you deliberately mislead me, I will have a low level of trust the next time that we negotiate. Even though negotiation is essentially a private activity, lawyer-negotiators should always conform their conduct to the highest standards of professionalism. In addition to the constraints of substantive law and the ethical codes, the individual lawyer's own sense of professionalism should require the highest aspirations of integrity in the bargaining process. The important thing to remember is that once lost, a lawyer's reputation for honesty and fair dealing is not easily retrieved.

D. THREATS

Making threats is characteristic of a competitive, adversarial bargaining style. Empirical evidence suggests that threats often result in concessions from the other negotiator, which is precisely the result desired by the competitive negotiator. Of course, to have this effect, the threats must be credible. Threats also have an informational function. Depending on the nature of the threat, the opposing negotiator learns the depth of your commitment to your position.

Is making threats consistent with the Model Code's requirement of honest dealings with others? The Model Rules do not address threats in the negotiation context specifically but simply prohibit lawyers from engaging in conduct that adversely reflects on fitness to practice law. Model Rule 8.4(b) and (c) provide:

It is professional misconduct for a lawyer to:

. . .

(b) commit a criminal act that reflects adversely on the lawyer's honesty, trustworthiness or fitness as a lawyer in other respects;

(c) engage in conduct involving dishonesty, fraud, deceit or misrepresentation;

Clearly some threats are part of a lawyer's permissible negotiating baggage. "If we can't settle this matter today, we'll go to trial and hear what the judge thinks." "These are my client's settlement figures and either you accept them or we go to the jury." On the other hand, a lawyer who threatens to harm one of the parties in negotiation may be liable under the criminal laws of extortion. A lawyer who threatens to bring criminal charges against a party in the context of settlement negotiations may be in violation of the Model Code, DR 7–105(a) which provides: "A lawyer shall not present, participate in presenting, or threaten to present criminal charges solely to obtain an advantage in a civil matter." In the case of *In re Charles*, 29 Or. 127, 618 P.2d 1281 (1980), for example, a lawyer who participated in threatening to bring criminal charges during the course of settlement negotiations was held to have violated DR 7–105(a) even though the charges were never brought and the settlement was never consummated.

VI. LEGAL ASPECTS OF NEGOTIATION

A. THE SETTLEMENT AGREEMENT

1. Policy Favoring Settlement

The general policy of the law favors compromise and settlement for the obvious benefits that settlement brings—less litigation and thus less cost in terms of time and money for the parties and the courts. When there is a legal challenge to the validity of a settlement agreement, the courts will usually articulate a general legal policy favoring compromise and enforce the disputed agreement. Encouraging settlement however, is a legal policy, not an absolute goal, and the courts will overturn settlement agreements that fail to meet the basic requirements of contract law. In negotiating a settlement agreement therefore, it is important to keep in mind general contract law principles regarding the validity and enforcement of contracts.

(i) The Agreement

Settlement agreements are created, like other contracts, with a valid offer and acceptance. General contract principles apply here with respect to the requirements of an offer and the time within which it may be accepted. While as a general rule, settlement agreements need not be in writing, local court rules or the statute of frauds may require a writing.

(ii) Consideration

The general rules of contract apply to consideration in settlement agreements. By compromising a disputed claim, an aggrieved party gives up the right to litigate and at the same time avoids the transaction costs of going to court, i.e., expense, delay and uncertainty of court outcome. If the disputed claim turns out to be invalid, the settlement agreement will still be upheld as long as the party giving up the claim reasonably believes in its validity.

(iii) Legality

Despite the policy of the law favoring settlement agreements, disputing parties do not forfeit their contract rights when they enter into settlement agreements. Like all other contracts, settlement agreements may be challenged on the grounds of fraud, duress, illegality, misrepresentation, lack of capacity, mistake, undue influence, and as violative of public policy.

It is important to pay attention to the relevant statute of limitations during settlement discussions. If negotiations continue until the statute of limitations runs out, the other disputing party has a potential defense to an action. For, unless a potential defendant has engaged in wrongful conduct, courts hold that continuing settlement negotiations do not prevent the statute of limitations from running.

2.   Validity of Settlement Agreements

(i) In General

General contract principles apply to the validity of settlement agreements. Even though courts usually adopt a policy of favoring settlement agreements, if traditional contract defenses such as fraud, duress, undue influence, illegality and lack of capacity are established, the agreement may be set aside.

(ii) Guaranteed Verdict Agreements

Courts also set aside settlement agreements where public policy interests are implicated. One such area concerns contribution issues with joint tortfeasors and "Mary Carter" or "guaranteed verdict" agreements which guarantee that the plaintiff will obtain a minimum recovery and establish a ceiling on the settling defendant's liability. Mary Carter agreements, the name of which derives from the case of *J.D. Booth v. Mary Carter Paint Company*, 202 So.2d 8 (Fla.App. 2 Dist.1967), operate generally as follows: one or more defendants agrees to settle with the plaintiff for a specific amount of money. If the plaintiff recovers more than this amount from the non-settling defendants in a subsequent court action, the liability of the defendants who settled is reduced by that amount.

Mary Carter agreements have received mixed reviews from the legal community. Despite their popularity with defendants in complex tort litigation, legal scholars have criticized them because of the potential prejudice to non-settling defendants. Several states have held them void on public policy grounds, as constituting maintenance and champerty (supporting or promoting another person's litigation) as well as being violative of the cannons of ethics.

3. Court Approval of Settlement Agreements

Even though negotiation is essentially a private activity, there are some situations that require court approval before a settlement agreement becomes binding on the parties. Settlement agreements in class action litigation or involving minors are classic examples. In determining whether to approve such a proposed agreement, a trial court must analyze the facts and law relevant to the proposed compromise. The court must focus its inquiry on the actual terms of the settlement and compare them with the likely rewards the class or minor would have received following a successful trial of the case. Approval will be granted if the court finds that the settlement is fair, reasonable and is not the result of collusion. The court must document this conclusion in the record so that an appellate court will have a basis for review.

Other examples of agreements requiring judicial approval include divorce settlements, agreements by fiduciaries for the benefit of their wards, agreements where the public interest may be implicated such as antitrust, patent or trademark cases and, of course, criminal plea bargains.

B. PROTECTING CONFIDENTIALITY IN NEGOTIATION

Good lawyering demands careful consideration of what to disclose in a settlement negotiation. No lawyer wants to expose a client to the possibility of having admissions of liability introduced at a future trial if the negotiation breaks down. Confidentiality is, therefore, an essential ingredient in the negotiation process and the rules of evidence play an important role in protecting it.

Under the common law, an offer to compromise a disputed claim is inadmissible in a later trial to prove the validity or amount of the claim on the theory that the offer has little probative value. Rather than being construed as an admission of liability, the offer is viewed as an effort to avoid the transaction costs associated with litigation. It is therefore excluded from a later trial because of the public policy favoring the compromise of claims. Factual statements made during compromise negotiations may be admissible in a later trial, however, unless such statements are made in hypothetical terms or are prefaced with such phrases as "without prejudice," or "for purposes of discussion only."

Federal Rule of Evidence 408 (Appendix) expands the common law evidentiary exclusionary rule to include not only offers of compromise but also "evidence of conduct or statements made in compromise negotiations," thereby avoiding the distinctions between hypothetical and factual statements. Like the common law rule, Federal Rule 408 is limited to situations where evidence is introduced at trial to prove the validity or amount of the claim. Rule 408 does not allow exclusion if the evidence is offered for other purposes such as proving bias or prejudice, undue delay or obstruction of justice. A majority of states have adopted some version of Federal Rule 408.

While Rule 408 and its state counterparts give broad protection when the issue is admissibility, it does not necessarily protect information from discovery. The Federal Rules of Civil Procedure provide for a very liberal range of discovery. Rule 26(b) provides generally that "Parties may obtain discovery regarding any matter, not privileged, that is relevant to the claim or defense of any party." Relevance in the context of discovery is broader than that required for admissibility at trial.

C. INCENTIVES FOR SETTLEMENT

1. Judicial Settlement Conferences

Judicial activism in settling lawsuits has received increasing attention in recent years. Rule 16 of the Federal Rules of Civil Procedure (Appendix) and its state counterparts, is a powerful tool for judges to hold pre-trial conferences and gain early control over litigation. In complex cases, judges may assign magistrates to conduct pre-trial conferences.

Many lawyers believe that judicial involvement enhances the settlement process. Instead of having to decide whether to be the first to initiate settlement discussions and risk appearing to have a weak case, the lawyer can rely on the judge to call the parties together for initial settlement talks. The judge offers a neutral perspective and gives the litigating parties a sense of where the case might be going. The negotiating lawyers bring this perspective back to their clients who may then be more inclined to accept a settlement offer.

Some commentators have expressed concern where judges go beyond managerial settlement techniques and take on the role of the mediator. They warn that judges should not mediate cases assigned to them for trial because the risk of judicial coercion is too great. Additional concerns about the dangers of judicial coercion have been expressed where parties have been compelled to attend settlement conferences. In *G. Heileman Brewing Company, Inc. v. Joseph Oat Corporation*, 871 F.2d 648 (7th Cir.1989) the Seventh Circuit Court of Appeals upheld the right of a federal magistrate to compel the Joseph Oat Corporation to send a "corporate representative with authority to settle" to a pretrial conference. The court relied on the Rules of Civil Procedure, particularly Rule 16, and the inherent power of a court to manage its docket. In a dissenting opinion Judge Posner expressed concerns about judicial coercion and wrote that "there are obvious dangers in too broad an interpretation of the federal courts' inherent power to regulate their procedure.

One danger is that it encourages judicial high-handedness...."

2. Rule 68 FRCP

Rule 68 of the Federal Rules of Civil Procedure (Appendix) and its state counterparts, give the party who is defending a claim the opportunity to settle by making a formal offer of judgment. The party who rejects the settlement offer does so at her economic peril for she is liable for sanctions if she obtains a final judgment that is not "more favorable" than the settlement offer. In order to determine whether the final judgment is more or less favorable than the Rule 68 settlement offer, courts usually do a simply money calculation and compare the money amounts of the offer with the amount of the judgment. If the amount of final judgment is less than the settlement offer, the prevailing plaintiff is required to pay all "costs incurred after the making of the offer."

The purpose of Rule 68 is to encourage pretrial settlement of civil suits by imposing court costs on a plaintiff who rejects an offer of settlement and subsequently receives a less favorable judgment. It has been used infrequently, however, since its enactment in 1938 largely because of its complexity. Despite numerous criticisms and proposals to amend the Rule, it remains unchanged.

The Supreme Court's decision in *Marek v. Chesny*, 473 U.S. 1, 105 S.Ct. 3012, 87 L.Ed.2d 1 (1985) is perhaps the most significant case interpreting

Rule 68. *Marek* arose under 42 U.S.C.A. § 1983 and involved a civil rights action against three police officers. In responding to a domestic violence call, the officers shot and killed plaintiff Chesny's son. Prior to trial, the officers made a timely Rule 68 settlement offer of $100,000 that specifically included costs and attorneys fees. The plaintiff rejected the offer and the case was tried before a jury that awarded him less than the Rule 68 offer. Subsequently, the plaintiff filed a request for costs and attorney's fees pursuant to the Civil Rights Attorney's Fees Awards Act of 1976, 42 U.S.C.A. § 1988, under which a prevailing party in a § 1983 action may be awarded attorney's fees as part of the costs. The police officers opposed the granting of any post-offer attorney's fees on the ground that these fees were part of the costs that plaintiff was required to pay as sanctions under Rule 68. The district court agreed with the police officers and refused to award the plaintiff costs, including attorney's fees, incurred after the offer of judgment. This decision was reversed by the Court of Appeals for the Seventh Circuit.

The Supreme Court held that the officers had made a valid offer of judgment under Rule 68 and that the term "costs" as used in Rule 68 included attorneys fees awarded under 42 U.S.C.A. § 1988. The Court rejected the assertion that subjecting civil rights plaintiffs to Rule 68 curtails their access to the courts or deters them from bringing lawsuits. Rather, Rule 68 would serve as a disincentive for the plaintiff's attorney to continue litigation after the defendant makes a settlement offer.

———

Negotiation Bibliography

J. Alfini, *Risk of Coercion Too Great: Judges Should Not Mediate Cases Assigned to Them for Trial*, 6 No. 1 Disp. Resol. Mag. 11 (ABA Section of Dispute Resolution) (Fall 1999);

K. Arrow, R. Mnookin, L. Ross, A. Tversky & R. Wilson, Editors, *Barriers to Conflict Resolution* (1995);

K. Avruch, *Culture as Context, Culture as Communication: Considerations for Humanitarian Negotiators*, 9 Harv. Negot. L. Rev. 391 (2004);

L. Bonney, R. Tribeck & J. Wrona, *Rule 68: Awakening A Sleeping Giant*, 65 Geo. Wash. L. Rev. 379 (1997);

R. Bastress and J. Harbaugh, *Interviewing, Counseling and Negotiating: Skills For Effective Representation* (1990);

D. Binder, P. Bergman, S. Price, P. Tremblay, *Lawyers as Counselors: A Client–Centered Approach*, 2nd edition (2004);

R. Birke & C. Fox, *Psychological Principles in Negotiating Civil Settlements*, 4 Harv. Neg. L. Rev. 1 (1999);

J. Brett, *Negotiating Globally: How to Negotiate Deals, Resolve Disputes, and Make Decisions Across Cultures* (2001);

W. Brazil, *Effective Approaches to Settlement: A Handbook for Lawyers and Judges* (1988);

W. Brazil, *The Attorney as Victim: Towards More Candor About the Psychological Price Tag of Litigation Practice,* 3 J. of the Legal Profession 107, 112 (1978);

P. Chew, *The Conflict and Culture Reader* (2001);

R. Fisher, W. Ury & B. Patton, *Getting to Yes: Negotiating Agreement Without Giving In* (2nd ed. 1991);

R. Fisher and D. Shapiro, *Beyond Reason: Using Emotions as You Negotiate* (2005);

D. Gifford, *Legal Negotiation: Theory and Applications*, 2nd edition (2007);

D. Lax and J. Sebenius, *The Manager as Negotiator: Bargaining for Cooperation and Competitive Gain* (1986);

D. Lax and J. Sebenius, *3–D Negotiation: Powerful Tools to Change the Game in Your Most Important Deals* (2006);

R. Lewicki and J. Litterer, *Negotiation*, 4th edition (2003);

C. Menkel–Meadow, *Toward Another View of Legal Negotiation: The Structure of Problem–Solving,* 31 UCLA L. Rev. 754 (1984);

C. Menkel–Meadow and M. Wheeler, *What's Fair: Ethics for Negotiators* (2004);

B. Merenstein, *More Proposals To Amend Rule 68: Time To Sink The Ship Once and For All*, 184 F.R.D. 145 (1999);

R. Mnookin, *Why Negotiations Fail: An Exploration of Barriers to the Resolution of Conflict*, 8 Ohio St. J. on Disp. Resol. 235 (1993);

R. Mnookin, S. Peppet & A. Tulumello, *Beyond Winning: Negotiating to Create Value in Deals and Disputes* (2000);

M. Moffitt and R. Bordone, Editors, *The Handbook of Dispute Resolution* (2005);

M. L. Nelken, *Negotiation: Theory and Practice,* 2nd ed. (2007);

H. Raiffa, *The Art and Science of Negotiation* (1982);

T. Schelling, *The Strategy of Conflict* (1980);

A. Schneider, *Shattering Negotiation Myths: Empirical Evidence on the Effectiveness of Negotiation Style,* 7 Harv. Negotiation L. Rev. 143 (2002);

Stone, Patton and Heen, *Difficult Conversations: How to Discuss What Matters Most* (1999);

L. Teply, *Legal Negotiation in a Nutshell*, 2nd edition (2005);

G. Williams, *Legal Negotiation and Settlement* (1983);

G. Williams and C. Craver, *Legal Negotiating* (2007).

CHAPTER 3

MEDIATION

I. OVERVIEW

Mediation is an extension of the negotiation process. Parties who have been unable to resolve a dispute or conflict use an impartial third party to assist them in reaching a resolution. Unlike the adjudication process where a third party applies law to the facts to reach a result, in mediation a third party assists the disputants in applying their values to the facts and reaching a result. These values may include: the law; cultural interests; a sense of fairness; religious preferences; morals; and ethical concerns. The distinguishing feature of mediation is that the disputing parties, rather than the mediator, choose the norms that will influence the outcome of their dispute.

The use of mediation to resolve disputes is not a new phenomenon in the United States. Early immigrant groups resorted to their own mediation models rather than embrace the American system of justice. For some of these groups, including the Quaker, Chinese and Jewish communities, their own mediation mechanisms operated to insulate them from a foreign legal culture.

Organized labor has used mediation since the passage of the Arbitration Act of 1888 which provided for mediation as well as arbitration of railway labor disputes. The Erdman Act of 1898 also provided for mediation of railway disputes and the Newlands Act of 1913 established an official dispute resolution mechanism to manage railway disputes— the Board of Mediation and Conciliation. Mediation continued to be used in labor disputes with the passage of the Railway Labor Act of 1926, which created the National Mediation Board and the Taft–Hartley Act (1947), which established the Federal Mediation and Conciliation Service. Title II of the Taft–Hartley Act reflects a strong Congressional policy favoring mediation:

> It is the policy of the United States that ... the settlement of issues between employers and employees through collective bargaining may be advanced by making available full and adequate governmental facilities for conciliation, mediation, and voluntary arbitration to aid and encourage employers and the representatives of their employees to reach and maintain agreements ...

Section 201(b) of Title II of the Taft Hartley Act.

Since the early 1970's, mediation has transcended religious, ethnic, and labor interests to become a method of processing disputes in a wide variety of contexts including corporate, commercial, community, family and environmental settings. The rapid growth of mediation in the private sector has been accompanied by its institutionalization in the judicial system. Mediation programs are no longer limited to the informal courts, i.e., small claims, family and housing courts, but they are now a common feature in state and federal courts. In a growing number of jurisdictions, mediation has become a mandatory prerequisite to trial.

A. DEFINITION

Mediation is generally understood to be a short-term, structured, task-oriented, participatory intervention process. Disputing parties work with an impartial third party, the mediator, to negotiate towards a resolution of their conflict. The core value of mediation is the principle of self-determination. This means that the parties who are affected by a dispute decide the outcome of the dispute. Unlike the adjudication process, where a third party intervenor *imposes* a decision, no such compulsion exists in mediation. The mediator aids the parties in reaching a consensus by facilitating their communications and negotiations but it is the parties themselves who shape their agreement. Thus, mediation is at all times a consensual process.

The traditional ideal of mediation contemplates a voluntary, private setting with individual members of ethnic or religious groups. The disputants share common values and have relatively equal bargaining strength. This assumption is being challenged today with the growth of mandatory and court-annexed mediation programs. Empirical studies of some court-annexed mediation programs suggest that even where parties have no prior or continuing relationship or shared values, the mediation process may still be successful. More empirical study is needed, however, to identify the principles that underlie successful mediation in mandatory and court-annexed programs.

The growth of non-traditional mediation programs today has led to further classification of mediation as either *rights-based* or *interest-based*. In a rights-based mediation process, the parties' decision-making is tempered by what they think would be available to them in court if the case were litigated. In this type of process, there is more focus on the immediate dispute rather than the underlying conflict. An exclusive emphasis on rights, however, encourages positional bargaining and undercuts the inherent value of the mediation process. Interest-based mediation, on the other hand, is a somewhat more therapeutic process. It more closely resembles the traditional ideal of mediation that emphasizes the value of relationships and attempts to help disputing parties understand the underlying needs and interests of the other party. In short, interest-based mediation calls for much more focus on the underlying conflict that gave rise to the dispute.

B. ADVANTAGES AND DISADVANTAGES OF MEDIATION

1. Advantages

The mediation process is viewed as more expeditious, inexpensive, and procedurally simple than adversarial problem solving. It enables the parties to define what is satisfactory to them by transcending the narrow issues in the dispute to focus on the underlying circumstances that contributed to the conflict. What looks like an isolated harassment case may well be a long story about years of hostilities between the parties. In the mediation process, the disputing parties are able to deal with these long-standing hostilities and vent their anger in ways that would not be possible in the adversarial process that is confined by the rules of evidence and procedure.

Moreover, mediation helps the parties re-adjust their conflicting perspectives and view their concerns in a much broader framework than simply "legal" issues in a legal system. Disputing parties begin to see themselves and their opponents in a different light. As Professor Lon Fuller observed in his classic essay on the central quality of mediation: mediation has the "capacity to reorient the parties toward each other, not by imposing rules on them, but by helping them to achieve a new and shared perception of their relationship, a perception that will redirect their attitudes and disposition toward one another."

Finally, mediation has great potential as an empowering process. Disputing parties have considerably more autonomy in mediation than they would in an adjudication process where a judge or arbitrator would impose a decision. In mediation, the disputants control the outcome of the process and this usually results in a high degree of compliance with mediated agreements. Empirical studies of some court-annexed mediation programs show that parties have a greater commitment to abide by a mediated agreement than with a court judgment.

2. Disadvantages

Mediation as a process is independent of the judicial system and therefore lacks the procedural and constitutional protections of adversarial justice, such as the right to a jury trial and the right to counsel. The expected tradeoff is that mediation will result in an agreement that is more responsive to individual needs than a court judgment. The underlying assumption here is that the agreement reached will be a fair one.

Fairness, however, is not an easily identifiable outcome, particularly where third parties not present at the mediation sessions may be affected. For example, what may be an acceptable agreement to parents in a divorce mediation, may seem quite unfair to the children who will be affected by the agreement. Furthermore, if parties reach an agreement in mediation without a general awareness of what is available to them from the legal system, there is a risk of unfairness in the agreement. Additionally, in those instances where one of the parties has greater bargaining power whether from sheer force of personality, knowledge of law, better grasp of the facts or emotional or economic power, the resulting agreement may be unfair to the weaker party.

Looking beyond the issue of fairness to participants, it is important to understand that mediation is neither a "truth" nor a "fault" inquiry. The question of who is right and who is wrong is less important than the question of how the problem can be resolved or the future defined. Disputing parties who need a vindication of their rights or a determination of fault will probably be unsatisfied with the mediation process.

Finally, successful mediation depends upon the parties' willingness to come to the bargaining table in good faith. Good faith is a difficult requirement to enforce in any dispute resolution process including litigation. Some parties may be using the process as a fishing expedition or simply to stall the litigation process. The mediator must guard against these abuses and be prepared to suspend or terminate the process if necessary.

II. THE MEDIATION PROCESS

A. SPECIFIC ACTIVITIES

In the mediation process, an impartial third party assists disputing parties in negotiating towards the resolution of their conflict. The disputing parties are responsible for deciding the outcome of the resolution. The core activities in this process are the information exchange and bargaining between the parties. These activities may be carried out in joint sessions, in private meetings known as caucuses or in a combination of both.

The mediation process usually begins in a joint session with opening remarks by the mediator followed by opening statements from the disputing parties. After the initial discussion of each parties' view of the situation, and depending upon the issues involved, the mediator may meet separately with the parties in private caucus sessions. If however, there is a high level of hostility between the parties, the mediator may begin the process by meeting separately with each party before the joint session.

Mediation works best when it is a private, confidential proceeding. Confidentiality helps the mediator to build trust and develop a constructive rapport with the parties. It creates a safe space where parties can share information about their interests and needs without fear of reprisals. It is critical, therefore, that the mediator be aware of and honor the parties' expectations for confidentiality.

Preliminary Matters

Pre-mediation Discussions: The mediator may conduct preliminary discussions to address certain procedural issues such as scheduling, document exchanges or other pre-mediation written submissions.

Disclosure of Conflict of Interest: In order to insure the mediator's impartiality, before accepting a case, the mediator should undertake reasonable inquiries to determine whether there are any facts that would reasonably affect her impartiality and then disclose such facts as soon as practical. Conflict-of-interest facts would include any financial or personal interest in the outcome of the mediation as well as existing or past relationships with a disputing party or any known or foreseeable participant in the mediation.

The Uniform Mediation Act (UMA) (Appendix), approved by the National Conference of Commissioners on Uniform State Laws and the American Bar Association Section on Dispute Resolution in 2002, has a specific requirement that directs mediators to make disclosures about conflicts of interest. Section 9(a) of the UMA provides that before accepting a case for mediation, a mediator must:

(1) make an inquiry that is reasonable under the circumstances to determine whether there are any known facts that a reasonable individual would consider likely to affect the impartiality of the mediator, including a financial or personal interest in the outcome of the mediation and an existing or past relationship with a mediation party or foreseeable participant in the mediation; and

(2) disclose any such known fact to the mediation parties as soon as is practical before accepting a mediation.

Screening: Mediation is not a panacea for the ills of the adversary system and not every case is appropriate for this process. In order to conduct a meaningful screening assessment, the mediator should gather information regarding the parties' relationship, the cause of the dispute, the legal and factual issues in dispute, the interests and needs of the parties and the parties' expectations for the mediation process. Then, before beginning the mediation, the mediator should conduct two preliminary inquiries: (a) Is this an issue that is properly the subject of mediation? (b) Are these parties ready for this process?

Depending upon the setting, the initial screening assessment may or may not be conducted by the mediator. Some types of disputes, such as those related to the custody of children, are subjected to mediation by virtue of statutes or local court rules. Thus, the mediator may be encountering resistant parties for the first time at the mediation session itself. Screening is also affected by public policy questions related to the appropriateness of mediating certain cases such as those involving domestic violence, antitrust violations and criminal matters. Additionally, in any situation where a precedent is desirable, mediation may not be appropriate.

The second screening inquiry focuses on the parties' disposition and the stage of the conflict. Are there power imbalances between the parties? Are these parties ready for the process of mediation or are they too hostile to negotiate? Are they too polarized or entrenched in their positions to negotiate in good faith? Mediation is less likely to be effective if a good faith desire for resolution is missing.

Stages of the Process

The number of actual stages in the mediation process has been variously identified. In developing a protocol for mediation, it is useful to consider the variety of approaches suggested by different scholars. It is important to keep in mind, however, that there may be differences across cultures with respect to any of these models. Professor Kimberlee Kovach describes the following thirteen stages, four of which, in parentheses, are optional: (1) preliminary arrangements; (2) mediator's introduction; (3) opening statements by the parties; (4) (ventilation); (5) information gathering; (6) issue and interest identification; (7) (agenda setting); (8) (caucus); (9) option generation; (10) (reality testing); (11) bargaining and negotiation; (12) agreement; and (13) closure.

Christopher Moore describes twelve stages: (1)establishing a relationship with disputing parties; (2) selecting a strategy for mediation; (3) collecting and analyzing background information; (4) designing a detailed plan; (5) building trust and cooperation; (6) beginning the session; (7) defining issues and setting an agenda; (8) uncovering hidden interests of the disputing parties; (9) generating options for settlement; (10) assessing options for settlement; (11) final bargaining; (12) achieving formal settlement.

Jay Folberg and Alison Taylor describe seven stages: (1) introduction; (2) fact-finding and isolation of issues; (3) creation of options and alternatives; (4) negotiation and decisionmaking; (5) clarification and writing a plan; (6) legal review and processing; (7) implementation, review and revision. As a practical matter, mediators may incorporate these stages into their own approach.

Mediation is a highly contextual process. How it is conducted depends upon a host of variables ranging from subject matter and mediator style to whether legal or judicial review is required. But, there are specific activities associated with the mediation process that are constant. Although mediation is usually depicted as a linear process, there is often a high degree of interaction between the various activities. The mediator's work may be described generally as follows:

1.   Mediator's Introduction

Even though one or both of the parties may understand how mediation works, it is useful for the mediator to explain the process in the presence of both parties at the initial joint session so that all parties share the same information. This is typically accomplished in an opening statement by the mediator. The mediator's introduction will vary in scope and complexity depending upon (a) whether or not the parties are represented by attorneys at the mediation and (b) whether attorneys appear at the mediation without the parties. The following sample opening is directed toward parties who are not represented by attorneys at the mediation session.

[Sample]   Contents for an opening statement:

- (a) *Introduction of Mediator.* e.g., "Good morning. My name is Mary Smith. I am an attorney and have practiced family law for five years. I have mediated several custody disputes over the last three years."

- (b) *Impartiality.* This is the time to tell the parties of any prior relationship you may have had with either of them or any bias you may have in connection with the dispute. e.g., "I have not met either one of you before this meeting today and I have no opinion on the merits of this dispute."

- (c) *Explanation of the process and role of the mediator.* e.g., "Mediation is a process where both of you have the opportunity and the power to decide how to resolve this dispute. I am here to help you do this. I am not here to tell you what to do or to impose an agreement upon you."

- (d) *Mechanics.* e.g., "Each of you will have the opportunity to discuss how you view the situation and you should not interrupt each other. I may meet with each of you privately. These meetings are called caucuses and sometimes they are quite helpful in giving people a chance to express fully how they feel about a particular problem. You can decide how much of our discussion remains private. Whatever information you tell me not to repeat, I will keep confidential." At this point if there have not been any preliminary discussions, the mediator may discuss other matters such as fees, number of helpful persons who may sit in on the sessions, number of sessions and scheduling, etc.

(e) *Confidentiality.* The parties may decide to agree about the extent to which their communications will be kept confidential. Otherwise, the mediator should discuss the limits of confidentiality within a particular jurisdiction, including relevant evidentiary exclusion rules and privilege statutes.

(f) *Mediation outcomes.* This will depend upon the law in individual jurisdictions. If an agreement is reached in mediation, it may be enforceable as a contract. In some court-annexed programs, the mediation agreement becomes a court judgment. If an agreement is not reached, however, the parties have the option of deciding whether or not to pursue their claim in another forum.

2. Mediator Assists Parties With Information Exchange and Bargaining

Before beginning to assist parties with the information exchange and bargaining, the mediator must be conscious of the parties' behavior towards each other. If there is a high level of hostility between the parties, it may be necessary for the mediator to be particularly assertive about the groundrules at the beginning of the session so that the parties do not recreate the same behavior that led to the dispute. Mutual respect is the cornerstone rule. It is important to remember that throughout the process, the mediator models behavior for the disputing parties.

The information exchange begins when the mediator makes the initial contact with the parties and they begin to educate each other about the dynamics of the controversy. For instance, are there entrenched positions, long-standing hostilities, misperceptions, poor communications? Information is not just limited to the substantive and factual aspects of the dispute but it also includes the parties' feelings, attitudes and mindsets.

Disputing parties bring much factual and psychological baggage to mediation. There is, at one level, the dispute that brought them there, e.g., the custody battle, the breached contract, the unpaid rent. At another level, there is an emotional component. Often, parties may be confused, angry, or hurt when they believe that they have been wronged. Other parties may have the need for an apology or revenge. This emotional baggage may present the real stumbling blocks to a mediated settlement. Therefore, the mediator must be skilled at understanding and acknowledging these feelings and drawing out hidden agendas if the final agreement is to satisfy the parties' real needs and interests.

The initial information acquisition process is a necessary prelude to helping parties distinguish the issues from their underlying interests. The mediator assists parties in framing issues, isolating points of agreement and generating options for settlement. It is important to remember however, that mediation is not a linear, but, an on-going interactive process. Information is constantly being acquired and re-interpreted. Issues are framed and re-framed as information is offered and refined.

Use of the Caucus

If it appears that a resolution may be difficult to achieve during joint sessions, the mediator may decide to meet separately with the parties in a caucus. This individual meeting provides each party with the opportunity to share concerns privately with the mediator. Often, parties may be uncomfortable revealing certain types of information in the joint session. In a caucus, parties may sketch their ideas for settlement and offer suggestions that they may be reluctant to offer in the joint session for fear of being considered too weak. In general, a caucus is a confidential session and the mediator shares only the information that the parties wish to reveal.

B. DRAFTING THE MEDIATION
AGREEMENT

Mediation agreements may be oral or written and they will vary considerably depending upon the context. In some cases, the parties' lawyers or the mediator may draft a memorandum of understanding at the completion of a mediation session before the official mediation agreement is drafted. In court-annexed or mandatory mediation programs, the agreement may be written on a one page stipulation form, whereas in custody, divorce or commercial cases, the agreement may be quite lengthy and detailed. Disputing parties should consider including a clause that they will return to mediation if there is a breach of the agreement.

As a general rule, the parties' lawyers prepare the mediation settlement agreement. If the parties are not represented by counsel, then depending upon the nature of the dispute, the mediator should advise the parties to have independent legal review of the agreement before signing it. In all cases, the mediator should make diligent efforts to insure that the parties fully understand the content of their agreement and the consequences of failing to comply with it. Informed decisionmaking is crucial to a durable agreement.

Some mediators have been reluctant to draft settlement agreements because they fear liability under unauthorized practice of law (UPL) restrictions, a topic that is discussed later in this chapter. In response to UPL concerns, the American Bar Association Section of Dispute Resolution adopted a resolution in 2002 that addressed the relationship between drafting mediation agreements and the UPL doctrine. It is available at http://www.abanet. org/dispute/webpolicy.html.

Single Negotiating Text

Fisher and Ury describe a technique, the "single negotiating text," which helps disputing parties produce an agreement that focuses primarily on their interests, rather than their positions. It operates in the following manner. The parties share their interests and needs with a mediator who then identifies them in a document. The parties review the document and make further suggestions based on their real interests. Then mediator then drafts a proposed agreement that both sides review. The process of mutual review and input continues until a final agreement is accepted or rejected by the parties.

C. ROLE OF THE MEDIATOR

Throughout the mediation session, the mediator is in control of the process, interpreting concerns, relaying information between the parties, framing issues and re-focusing the problems. How these functions are accomplished depends upon the mediator's personal style and the level of hostilities between the parties. In some cases, the mediator facilitates the session by giving the parties control of the agenda and walking them through a problem-solving process. Other conflict situations may require more intense intervention efforts by the mediator such as making specific suggestions, deliberately controlling the agenda and limiting conversation.

Mediation Styles and Approaches

As discussed earlier, mediation is a contextual process and there is a great deal of variety in mediator styles and approaches. Based on empirical studies of mediator behavior, scholars have described several approaches ranging from problem-solving to "hashing, bashing and trashing." Two sets of the more generic mediator approaches are described below.

(1) ***Bargaining and Therapeutic:*** Silbey and Merry have described two types of mediation styles based on their study of mediation: the bargaining and the therapeutic style. The *bargaining* mode is a pragmatic approach to reaching a settlement with more emphasis on the parties' bottom line than on hidden feelings. The mediator assumes a directive style and leads the parties towards agreement. Silbey and Merry report some comments of mediators who adopt a bargaining mode:

(a) I get people talking, then focus on some issues to get to agreement points. You can't just keep talking.

(b) I take a ball of broad issues and expand it by breaking it down into concrete ones. I see what issues really matter to them and I work on those.

(c) As a mediator, your job is to convince one or the other party to give up something; to negotiate together. The essence of the process is negotiation. You don't accept blame from others of each other, and you also don't accept their version of the facts. I am firm with a loudmouth. In small claims cases, I say that when a person won't settle, I will give it back to the judge and the judge will give him only 30 days to pay.

A *therapeutic* strategy emphasizes the emotional content of disputes and focuses on the communicative aspects of the mediation process. Disputing parties are taught the value of resolving conflict through peaceful discourse and are encouraged to express their feelings fully. The following comments illustrate the strategy of mediators who adopt a therapeutic strategy:

(a) My strategy is to try to get the recalcitrant person to see the other's view. If the other person doesn't do it, I do it in caucus myself. It usually works to point out how the other person sees things—that usually produces an agreement.

(b) I look for people's concerns, the reasons why this is important to each of them, and try to create an environment where they feel safe enough to articulate that concern. I do this by being open and non-judgmental and by listening to their feelings.

(c) I try just to get people talking, to get them to explain their side fully so that the other side really understands them. The problem is that people don't understand each other's thinking. I try to help them look for solutions.

(2) *Facilitative and Evaluative:* A *facilitative* mediator assists parties with their communications and negotiations. The mediator's strategies are designed to help parties identify the issues in dispute, understand their real needs and interests and formulate options for settlement. Several models have emerged within the facilitative mediation framework:

• *Narrative Mediation:* focuses on culture and shared stories as the forces which shape parties' interests and positions. It encourages parties to resolve problems through a deep understanding of their shared narratives and culture.

• *Transformative Mediation:* seeks party empowerment and recognition. Rather than focus on settlement, the mediator seeks to assist parties in creating a new relationship.

• *Understanding-Based Mediation:* aims to resolve conflict through deeper understanding by the parties of their own and each other's perspectives. It emphasizes the parties' responsibility for their own decisions.

Evaluative mediation goes beyond facilitation and usually involves some type of professional assessment. This may consist of an opinion or prediction as to a specific court outcome or legal advice on a specific issue. The subject of mediator evaluation is a topic of considerable debate. In general, the argument in favor of evaluation argues for flexibility in the mediator's role while the opposing argument holds that evaluation compromises the mediator's neutrality. Quite apart from the ongoing debate, mediators should be aware of the relevant statutes and court rules in their jurisdiction that may limit their ability to engage in evaluative techniques.

In sum, mediation is a malleable and highly contextual process. The above-described approaches and models are just some examples of how mediators operate. There is no one "correct" way to mediate. Whether a mediator adopts a bargaining or therapeutic style, a facilitative or evaluative orientation or a variation of these behaviors, depends upon the mediator's own comfort level with each approach, the nature of the issues involved and the needs of the disputing parties. Mediating a commercial dispute between two business persons with an ongoing relationship may well call for a different approach than mediating a disputed child custody case with hostile parents. The important point is that the parties are able to engage in informed decisionmaking. Thus, the mediator should inform the parties of his or her approach to mediation so that parties may make informed judgments in selecting a mediator.

D. MEDIATOR SKILLS

There is no magic formula that guarantees a successful mediation. Certainly, a mediator must be tolerant, patient, resourceful and articulate. She should have a clear understanding of her own fundamental beliefs about human beings' ability to resolve their own disputes. In connecting mediation practice to a theory of lawyering, other skills of a good mediator are quite similar to those of the lawyer in listening, questioning, observing, interviewing, counseling and negotiating.

1. Listening

Listening skills are essential. The mediator listens to acquire information and to model behavior for the disputing parties. Many lawyers have a difficult time practicing the art of listening. They may be thinking of the next question while their client is talking or wondering whether their client is telling the truth or trying to make the facts fit a specific cause of action. The lawyer who acts as a mediator must overcome this occupational handicap and temporarily suspend the "lawyering" mindset.

The importance of acknowledging the role of emotions in the negotiation process was discussed in Chapter Two. The same is true in mediation. In developing the skill of listening, it is important to distinguish between the factual and substantive aspects of a dispute and the emotional feelings that react to those facts. The mediator who is really listening will hear the facts as well as understand the emotions attached to them. Mediators must also listen in order to understand and distinguish between a party's interests and positions.

It is important that all parties perceive that they are being heard throughout the mediation process. It may well be that ultimately, the outcome of a particular dispute is not resolved according to a party's original expectations. Parties who believe that someone has really listened to them, however, are more likely to be satisfied with the process. This is particularly true in some forms of court-annexed mediation where parties may simply want their day in court. In these instances, they do not necessarily need or desire black-robed justice but simply an impartial third party to listen with understanding to their grievances.

Developing good listening skills is not just an intuitive process. Mediators must be attentive for clues about what is really going on between the parties. They must concentrate on understanding what has been said and relay this understanding back to the parties using active listening techniques such as rephrasing or reflecting. Good listening is not simply repeating what has been said.

Example 1

The husband in a custody dispute tells the mediator: "My wife is such a selfish person. She cares only about her patients and nothing else. If her own kids were sick, she would still be off to the hospital to care for her patients. That's just the type of driven nut that she is. I can't imagine her giving any time to the kids if they were really in trouble and any judge that would grant her custody would have to be deranged."

Mediator Response

"You seem to have real concerns about how your children would be cared for if your wife were given custody considering how much time she spends with her work. It seems that your wife is very committed to her responsibilities at the hospital."

Comment: The mediator's response in this case focuses on the husband's real concern, the children, and deflects attention away from the husband's image of the wife as an evil person. Instead of labeling the wife as a workaholic or repeating the husband's comment that she is a "driven nut," the mediator in more positive language says that she is "very committed to her responsibilities at the hospital." This response may help the husband to see his wife in a new light and re-focus his energy and concerns on the children.

Example 2

The landlord in a housing dispute tells the mediator: "I want this bum out right away. He was late with his rent this month and I don't want this kind of trouble. The apartment looks like a cyclone hit it. It's a royal mess. Everything is broken. You know, these people are all the same. They have no sense of cleanliness or respect for property."

Mediator Response

"It sounds to me like you are worried about future non-payment of rent. You think that since your tenant was late this month, that he will probably continue to pay his rent late. You also seem to be concerned with how the apartment is being kept up and whether you will have to make expensive repairs."

Comment: The mediator acknowledges the landlord's anxious feelings instead of reminding him that the tenant is a "bum." The mediator's response also focuses the issue on the landlord's concern that this tenant's non-payment of rent may set a precedent with the other tenants. By re-phrasing the landlord's comments in non-judgmental language that acknowledges the real fear, i.e., future non-payment of rent, the mediator establishes a good setting for a trust relationship with the landlord.

2.   Questioning

Information is also acquired by questioning, a process that should always reinforce the mediator's impartiality. A good way to begin is to use open-ended questions. "Ms. Jones, can you tell us how you see the situation that brings you to mediation?" When Ms. Jones finishes her story, the mediator will turn to Ms. Smith and ask an equally open-ended question. "Ms. Smith, can you tell us how you view the situation?" As the mediation session progresses and additional information is acquired, questioning should remain non-judgmental.

Lawyer-mediators should shift gears away from any overly technical or cross-examination style questioning that may have been acquired as part of their adversarial skills training. For example, consider the following question based on the hypothetical disputed custody case in the first listening example: "Dr. Smith, isn't it a fact that you work very long hours at the hospital?" This confrontational approach limits the mediator's potential for developing a constructive rapport with the wife. A better question might be: "Dr. Smith, could you describe a typical work day at the hospital beginning with the time you arrive until the time you leave for home?" The latter non-threatening, non-judgmental question will probably elicit more information than the adversarial one.

Folberg and Taylor have identified two specific questioning skills, reflection and clarification, that are also useful to mediators in acquiring information throughout the process.

The mediator *reflects* when trying to understand or interpret unacknowledged feelings or when suggesting to a person the missing meaning behind his or her words. For example, the mediator might say to a parent in a custody dispute: "It is not uncommon for the parent who agrees to give up custody to feel depressed and a little guilty. Do you feel this way now?" This type of reflecting statement can reduce tension and increase rapport with that parent. When people know that you understand what they are trying to say, they are more comfortable in opening up.

Clarification confirms what has been said and eliminates conflicting information. The mediator gives the parties a more definite sense of where they are going. For example, in a landlord-tenant dispute, a mediator might say to the landlord: "A while ago you said that you would be willing to accept a payment schedule for prior rent due and work out an agreement regarding repairs. Can we move forward with that understanding?"

3.   Observation

The mediator also acquires information by observing what the parties do and how they act in the presence of each other as well as in a private caucus. When do they become silent? When do they appear nervous, uneasy, restless? The mediator must interpret non-verbal communications such as body language and eye contact. Is one party's refusal to look at the other party a sign of nervousness or is it hostility? In observing the parties, it is important to be aware of possible cultural differences. For example, the fact that a person never makes eye contact with the mediator or the other party may be a sign of respect in one culture and a sign of guilt in another.

4. Reframing

The manner in which a problem is framed can have a significant influence on the outcome of mediation, particularly in cases where emotions run high. When angry or hostile language is used by a party, the mediator can try to change the tone of the conversation by reframing the statement and restating it in more neutral terms. This can help to diffuse volatile situations and help parties view the problem in a more positive way. It may also help others who are present in the mediation to have a different perception of the problem. The mediator should always make sure to confirm that her reframe is accurate.

5. Cultural Awareness

The important role that culture plays in negotiation was discussed in Chapter Two. Likewise, mediating in cross-cultural situations also requires an awareness of one's own culture and alertness to cultural differences in others. Mediators must keep in mind that cultures differ in their approach to conflict resolution. Race, ethnicity, religion, and gender and are just some examples of factors that suggest distinct cultural profiles for which mediators should be sensitive.

E. MEDIATOR REQUIREMENTS

Mediators are drawn from numerous backgrounds and disciplines including law, education, psychology and social work. As an interdisciplinary field, mediation is at a crossroads and it is not clear what skills and knowledge base are essential. Although efforts are underway to identify the requirements, mediators are not currently compelled to comply with any uniform standards for education, training or practice. States have addressed the issue of mediator requirements in a variety of ways. Some take a certification approach in specific contexts such as court-annexed or marital mediation. Other states regulate mediators by statute, specifying so many hours of training or the subjects that must be studied in such training. For example, a Massachusetts statute provides:

... For the purposes of this section a "mediator" shall mean a person not a party to a dispute who enters into a written agreement with the parties to assist them in resolving their disputes and has completed at least thirty hours of training in mediation and who either has four years of professional experience as a mediator or is accountable to a dispute resolution organization which has been in existence for at least three years or one who has been appointed to mediate by a judicial or governmental body. M.G.L.A. ch. 233, § 23C.

The Society of Professionals in Dispute Resolution (SPIDR), a national interdisciplinary organization of dispute resolvers, created a commission in 1987 to study the qualifications of mediators and arbitrators. [SPIDR merged with the Academy of Family Mediators and the Conflict Resolution Education Network in 2001 to become the Association for Conflict Resolution (ACR)]. One of the main principles recognized by the commission is that performance rather than paper credentials should be the central qualification criteria. The SPIDR commission identified the following skills as necessary for competent performance as a mediator:

(a) ability to understand the negotiating process and the role of advocacy;

(b) ability to earn trust and maintain acceptability;

(c) ability to convert parties' positions into needs and interests;

(d) ability to screen out non-mediable issues;

(e) ability to help parties to invent creative options;

(f) ability to help the parties identify principles and criteria that will guide their decision making;

(g) ability to help parties assess their nonsettlement alternatives;

(h) ability to help the parties make their own informed choices;

(i) ability to help parties assess whether their agreement can be implemented.

National Institute of Dispute Resolution (NIDR) *Dispute Resolution Forum* 9 May 1989. See also *Ensuring Competence and Quality in Dispute Resolution Practice*, Report No. 2 of the SPIDR Commission on Qualifications 7 (April 1995); *Qualifying*

Dispute Resolution Practitioners: Guidelines for Court–Connected Programs (SPIDR 1997).

III. ETHICAL CONCERNS

A. IN GENERAL

Concern with ethical behavior should permeate all areas of mediation practice to insure the highest quality process. Mediation is an interdisciplinary field and uniform control of the practice is difficult because there are several sources of regulation including federal and state law, court rules and numerous ethics codes and professional standards. Most standards address the more common ethical issues in practice including confidentiality, conflicts of interest, competency, impartiality, neutrality, informed consent, providing professional advice, party self-determination, advertising and fees.

Some of the most notable and comprehensive efforts to date in the development of uniform ethical standards are the Model Standards of Conduct for Mediators (2005) developed by the American Arbitration Association, the American Bar Association and the Society of Professionals in Dispute Resolution, and the Model Standards of Practice for Family and Divorce Mediation (2000), developed as a collaborative effort of the Association of Family and Conciliation Courts, the Family Law Section of the American Bar Association, the National Council of Dispute Resolution Organizations as well as prominent individuals in the mediation field. Both standards are reprinted in the Appendix.

The standards advanced in the Model Standards are aspirational in nature and are intended to provide guidance in the development of national ethical guidelines for mediation practice. They address nine topics: self-determination; impartiality; conflicts of interest; competence; confidentiality; quality of the process; advertisements and solicitation, fees, and advancement of mediation practice. The Family and Divorce Standards are more specific in orientation and seek to provide guidance to family mediators, to inform participants in mediation about the process and to promote public confidence in mediation as a process for resolving family disputes. Like the Model Standards, the Family and Divorce Standards are aspirational in nature and are not intended to establish legal rules.

B.　GOOD FAITH REQUIREMENTS

As noted earlier in this chapter, successful mediation depends, in part, upon the parties' willingness to come to the bargaining table in good faith and good faith is a difficult requirement to enforce in any dispute resolution process. In the context of court-related mediation programs, there has been considerable debate about whether courts should have the power to sanction parties for bad faith participation in mediation Some scholars believe that this is necessary in order to honor the integrity of the process. Others have argued that such an approach threatens self-determination and other core values of the mediation process. An alternative approach advanced by Professor John Lande, argues for the use of system design principles to promote good faith participation in mediation.

In response to the debate over good faith participation requirements, the ABA Section of Dispute Resolution issued a Resolution on Good Faith Requirements for Mediators and Mediation Advocates in Court–Mandated Mediation Programs (2004). The Resolution calls for a re-examination and revision of statutes and rules requiring good faith participation in light of three core values of mediation: self-determination, confidentiality, and mediator impartiality. It identifies three policy areas that should be considered by court-mandated mediation programs:

(1) what conduct should be sanctionable;

(2) what conduct or other information mediators may be required to report to court administrators or judges; and

(3) what actions court-mandated mediation programs should take to promote productive behavior in mediation.

The complete text of the ABA resolution is available at www.abanet.org/dispute/webpolicy.html.

C. MAINTAINING THE INTEGRITY OF MEDIATION

Process integrity is critical in mediation. If the integrity of the mediation process is to be maintained consistently, mediators must be alert to the possibility of physical or mental impairment, coercion, unfairness and bargaining imbalance between the parties. This awareness is consistent with the directives given to mediators in several professional standards including the Model Standards of Conduct for Mediators (2005) and the Family and Divorce Standards (2000).

The Comments to the Model Standards of Conduct for Mediators are instructive. They authorize the mediator to "...take appropriate steps including, if necessary, postponing, withdrawing from or terminating the mediation," if the mediator believes that participant conduct, including that of the mediator, jeopardizes conducting a mediation consistent with the Standards. Likewise, in the context of family and divorce mediation, the Family and Divorce Standards direct the mediator to "suspend or terminate the mediation process when the mediator reasonably believes that a participant is unable to effectively participate or for other compelling reasons." These Standards identify the following seven circumstances under which a mediator may consider suspending or terminating the mediation process:

(1) the safety of a participant or well-being of a child is threatened;

(2) a participant has or is threatening to abduct a child;

(3) a participant is unable to participate due to the influence of drugs, alcohol, or physical or mental condition;

(4) the participants are about to enter into an agreement that the mediator reasonably believes to be unconscionable;

(5) a participant is using the mediation to further illegal conduct;

(6) a participant is using the mediation process to gain an unfair advantage;

(7) the mediator believes the mediator's impartiality has been compromised ...; (Family and Divorce Standards, *Standard XI*).

These examples are helpful for all mediators to consider because they offer guidance in a wider context than family or divorce mediation.

D. MANDATORY MEDIATION PROGRAMS

Beyond the ethical concerns that affect all mediation programs, mandatory mediation programs raise particular ethical considerations related to funding, coercion and quality control. The Committee on Law and Public Policy of the Society of Professionals in Dispute Resolution (SPIDR) addressed these issues in an excellent report on mandatory participation in ADR programs. A summary of the SPIDR report is reprinted in the Appendix.

Mandatory mediation is generally associated with court-connected programs and it raises important issues related to consent and party self-determination. Ideally, mediation is a voluntary process that takes place in private and requires the good faith and meaningful participation of the parties. These characteristics may be diluted, however, as mediation becomes institutionalized within the judicial system. When disputing parties are told by a court that they *must* submit to mediation before they are entitled to a trial, coercion issues arise. While parties may be required to attend court mediation sessions, they may never be required to reach an agreement. Compulsion should never be a part of the mediation process. If an agreement is reached in mediation, parties should always leave the process with a sense of ownership of the agreement that resulted from it. Finally, while mandatory court mediation programs are considered permissible as long as there is no coercion in the process, at least one court has held that parties cannot be compelled to attend and pay for private mediation. *Jeld-Wen, Inc. v. Superior Court,* 146 Cal.App.4th 536, 53 Cal.Rptr.3d 115 (4th Dist.2007).

E. ETHICAL CONCERNS FOR THE LAWYER–MEDIATOR

In addition to the general ethical issues that confront all mediators, there are more specific concerns for lawyers who serve as mediators. When lawyers have dual roles as partisan representatives and as third party neutrals within their law firms, courts or private mediation programs, they are confronted with different obligations than lawyers who act solely as partisan representatives for clients. Whether or not sufficient guidance exists for these lawyers is debatable.

1. Conflict of Interest

A) Lawyers Serving as Third Party Neutrals

Conflict of interest is an increasingly complex problem in lawyers' mediation practice. In the early years of lawyer involvement in mediation practice, conflict of interest issues were primarily concerned with the permissible limits of divorce mediation. Several bar associations issued formal and informal ethics opinions on the propriety of lawyer-mediation practice. Most of the opinions related to the conflict of interest problems that arise with divorce mediation.

One of the most enlightened early opinions regarding the permissible extent of a lawyer's involvement in the mediation process was issued by the Association of the Bar of the City of New York. While the opinion responds specifically to an inquiry about a non-profit divorce mediation program, it provides helpful parameters for lawyers who wish to become involved in mediation. The factual background of the opinion involved an organization with a staff of licensed mental health professionals which provided marital and family therapy. The organization proposed to offer "structured mediation" in marital cases, a process which involves a trained therapist working with separating or divorcing couples to help them resolve issues such as property division, child custody, visitation and support. Part of the inquiry concerned whether a lawyer could (a) become part of the mediating team, (b) give impartial legal advice to the parties, such as advice on the tax consequences of a separation or divorce agreement, or (c) draft a divorce or settlement agreement after the terms of such agreement have been approved by the parties. After a thorough and thoughtful examination of a lawyer's involvement in mediation the opinion provides the following guidelines:

... we have concluded that lawyers may participate in the divorce mediation procedure proposed in the inquiry here, only on the following conditions.

To begin with, the lawyer may not participate in the divorce mediation process where it appears that the issues between the parties are of such complexity or difficulty that the parties cannot prudently reach a resolution without the advice of separate and independent legal counsel.

If the lawyer is satisfied that the situation is one in which the parties can intelligently and prudently consent to mediation and the use of an impartial legal adviser, then the lawyer may undertake these roles provided the lawyer observes the following rules:

First, the lawyer must clearly and fully advise the parties of the limitations on his or her role and specifically, of the fact that the lawyer represents neither party and that accordingly, they should not look to the lawyer to protect their individual interests or to keep confidences from the other.

Second, the lawyer must fully and clearly explain the risks of proceeding without separate legal counsel and thereafter proceed only with the consent of the parties and only if the lawyer is satisfied that the parties understand the risks and understand the significance of the fact that the lawyer represents neither party.

Third, a lawyer may participate with mental health professionals in those aspects of mediation which do not require the exercise of professional legal judgment and involve the same kind of mediation activities permissible to lay mediators.

Fourth, lawyers may provide impartial legal advice and assist in reducing the parties' agreement to writing only where the lawyer fully explains all pertinent considerations and alternatives and the consequences to each party of choosing the resolution agreed upon.

Fifth, the lawyer may give legal advice only to both parties in the presence of each other.

Sixth, the lawyer must advise the parties of the advantages of seeking independent legal counsel before executing any agreement drafted by the lawyer.

Seventh, the lawyer may not represent either of the parties in any subsequent legal proceedings related to the divorce.

Ethics Opinion, Committee on Professional and Judicial Ethics, Association of the Bar of the City of New York, Inquiry Reference No. 80–23.

In 2002, after much scholarly discussion and debate, the American Bar Association amended ABA

Rule of Professional Conduct 2.4 to specifically acknowledge the role of a lawyer acting as a third-party neutral. That rule now reads as follows:

Rule 2.4 Lawyer Serving as Third–Party Neutral
ABA Model Rules of Professional Conduct

(a) A lawyer serves as a third-party neutral when the lawyer assists two or more persons who are not clients of the lawyer to reach a resolution of a dispute or other matter that has arisen between them. Service as a third-party neutral may include service as an arbitrator, a mediator or in such other capacity as will enable the lawyer to assist the parties to resolve the matter.

(b) A lawyer serving as a third-party neutral shall inform unrepresented parties that the lawyer is not representing them. When the lawyer knows or reasonably should know that a party does not understand the lawyer's role in the matter, the lawyer shall explain the difference between the lawyer's role as a third-party neutral and a lawyer's role as one who represents a client.

ABA Model Rules of Professional Conduct, 2007 Edition, published by the American Bar Association Center for Professional Responsibility.

B) Law Firm Screening Issues

Today, conflict of interest problems encompass a wide range of issues beyond those associated with divorce mediation. With the growth of court mediation programs, an increasing number of attorneys in law firms are involved as neutrals in mediation practice. It is difficult for them to know with certainty how mediation work will affect future business for their law firm. One of the critical questions in this area concerns the imputation of disqualifying conflicts to the neutral lawyer's law firm in future representational relationships. A recurring question in the courts has been whether appropriate screening can avoid disqualification of a law firm. In several cases, courts have found that screening has been insufficient to defeat a law firm's disqualification. E.g., *McKenzie Const. v. St. Croix Storage Corp.,* 961 F.Supp. 857 (D.Virgin Islands 1997); *Cho v. Superior Court of Los Angeles County,* 39 Cal.App.4th 113, 45 Cal.Rptr.2d 863 (1995).

The American Bar Association has taken a screening approach to conflict of interest problems. In 2002, it expanded Rule 1.12 which previously dealt with former judges and arbitrators to include mediators and other third-party neutrals. That rule is reprinted in the Appendix.

2. Advertising

Bar association ethics opinions have responded to lawyer-mediator concerns about the permissible limits of advertising. In general, written lawyer advertising is permissible unless it is deceptive or misleading. Standard VII, Comment two of the Model Standards provides: "A mediator should only claim to meet the mediator qualifications of a governmental entity or private organization if that entity or organization has a recognized procedure for qualifying mediators and it grants such status to the mediator." Although some bar associations have permitted lawyers to identify themselves as practicing lawyers when advertising mediation services, there is no uniformity in this area. A potential lawyer-mediator should check the status of advertising in the relevant jurisdiction and, if necessary, request an advisory opinion from the bar association.

IV. MEDIATION AND THE LAW

A. THE ROLE OF LAW

Mediation often occurs in the shadow of the legal system. Rules and laws may impact on the kind of outcome that the parties consider. The primary concern of mediation, however, is not legal rights but shared interests and values. Law is one among many choices of values that may influence the outcome of a dispute. Legal rules exist simply as a reference point in the mediation process and are not dispositive of the outcome. They do, however, provide some indication of how the parties' positions would balance should they go to court.

For example, law is relevant to two disputing business persons, A and B, who know that A has the legal right to sue B for B's breach of contract in failing to deliver computers on time when time was of the essence in the contract. A lawsuit, however, cannot achieve the same result as mediation in this case. A lawsuit will result in a determination that B was either right or wrong but the inherently adversarial nature of the litigation process may impair any future business relationship between A and B. On the other hand, it is not the function of mediation to determine who is right and who is wrong. In the mediation process, A and B will both decide what they think is a fair resolution of the problem. When they reach a mutually advantageous result, their business relationship has the possibility of continuing.

The role of law becomes increasingly more significant in court-annexed mediation programs where parties go to court in the first instance to seek a vindication of their legal rights. In jurisdictions where mediation is a mandatory prerequisite to trial, it is important that the parties have a basic understanding of the legal parameters of their case. While there is no guarantee of how a judge will rule in a particular case, there is usually a predictable range of possible outcomes. When disputing parties enter into mediation settlement agreements, they should have some awareness of what these outcomes might be. Otherwise, the danger is too great that legal rights might be relinquished without informed consent and that expediency rather than justice might become the goal of the mediation process. If this happens, the resulting agreement may well be unfair to one of the parties.

B.   INFORMED CONSENT IN MEDIATION

The principle of informed consent is a means of achieving the fundamental goal of fairness in mediation. Fairness is a difficult concept to define in mediation but at the very least, it contemplates a minimum level of knowledge by the parties engaged in the mediation process. Parties should understand the consequences of participating in mediation. They should also understand all aspects of the decisionmaking process in mediation including their right to withdraw consent to participation and to discontinue negotiations at any time. Finally, parties should understand the substantive outcomes reached in mediation. In this way, the principle of informed consent enhances the psychological and legal interests connected to the values of self-determination and efficiency, and protects the human dignity of the parties who participate in the mediation process.

C. LAWYERS AND MEDIATION

Lawyers may assume a wide variety of participatory roles in the mediation process. From the initial client counseling session, to representing clients in the mediation process, reviewing the mediation agreement, serving as a third party neutral in mediating or co-mediating, mediation is becoming a familiar area of practice for lawyers.

1. Pre–Mediation Client Counseling

Most Americans usually consult a lawyer before beginning a lawsuit. Thus, in the interviewing and counseling process that accompanies legal consultation, lawyers are able to assist clients in choosing between the available range of dispute resolution processes from negotiation to full scale litigation. A growing number of states have imposed upon attorneys an ethical obligation to inform clients of ADR options, including mediation. Lawyers, therefore, often help clients to decide whether they should try mediation before or during litigation.

In the counseling session, deliberations between lawyers and client should be governed by the principle of informed consent. Lawyers should understand both the factual and emotional background of the clients' disputes. They should not presume to know their clients' goals but seek consciously to understand them. Clients must be educated about the mediation process and understand how it differs from adjudication. They should also have a general understanding of the relevant laws involved in their case in order to engage in informed decisionmaking.

Some of the factors that should be considered in helping clients decide whether to choose the mediation process include: (a) the client's desire to settle, i.e., does the client really want to resolve the problem or just "get even;" (b) the nature of the relationship between the disputing parties, i.e., long-term, on-going or a one-shot deal; (c) the type of relief desired, i.e., whether a precedent is desirable; (d) the client's financial situation; (e) time considerations; (f) predictability of legal outcome; (g) the parties' positions; (h) desirability of a private settlement.

If a client decides to engage in the mediation process, then several practical decisions must be made. These include decisions about appropriate mediation style, whether the mediator's evaluation might be requested, the identity of the mediator, the client's role and the lawyer's role in the mediation process.

2. Representing Clients in Mediation

Lawyers should prepare their clients and themselves to work with the mediator and to negotiate on the merits in a creative, problem-solving process. They should refrain from traditional adversarial tactics when representing clients in mediation. It is important for a lawyer to begin establishing credibility with the mediator by providing him or her with sufficient background information so that the mediation process will be productive. This would include information about the barriers to settlement, prior negotiation efforts, an understanding of the clients' interests and a range of solutions that might be explored.

In some situations, clients may prefer that their attorney function in a traditional lawyering role and act as a negotiator for them during the mediation session. Some clients may feel more comfortable with this approach particularly in some court-annexed mediation programs where their attendance at mediation is mandated by court rule. There are considerable downsides however, in having the lawyer, rather than the client, dominate the mediation process. Typically, the client becomes a non-participatory fixture who defers to the attorney's sense of fairness. The client never directly experiences the benefits of mediation and the total experience is focused as a rights-based process. This is similar to what happens in the adjudication process where the client is also essentially a non-participant and the lawyer tells the client's story. The story is constructed as a "cause of action" with the total emphasis on the client's "rights" and little or no understanding of the client's underlying needs and interests. Thus, to the extent possible, disputing parties themselves should become involved in working through the mediation process to fully appreciate the sense of empowerment and satisfaction that mediation offers.

Whether or not lawyers are present at the mediation, they have an important role in reviewing a mediation agreement for a client. In performing the review function, assuming the agreement is otherwise fair, lawyers must be cautious about substituting their own judgment for their client's. What is unacceptable for lawyers who judge agreements through a legal prism may be more than satisfactory to clients who feel that their needs have been satisfied.

Ethical Concerns

A recent ethics opinion issued by the ABA discusses the extent of a lawyer's obligation to be truthful when making statements on behalf of the client in a caucused mediation. ABA Formal Opinion 06–439, makes clear that Model Rule 4.1, discussed in Chapter 2 in connection with truthfulness in negotiation, also applies to caucused mediation. Thus, a lawyer representing a client in a caucused mediation may not make a false statement of material fact to a third person. However, statements regarding a client's negotiating goals, willingness to compromise, or statements considered to be "puffing", are not considered false statements of material fact within the meaning of the Model Rules.

3. Lawyer as Mediator

As noted earlier in the section on ethical concerns for the lawyer-mediator, the ABA amended the Model Rules of Professional Conduct, Rule 2.4, to acknowledge the role of a lawyer serving as a third-party neutral. One of the chief benefits of choosing a lawyer as a mediator is the lawyer's ability to help the parties explore the legal as well as the non-legal consequences of conduct. Lawyers are better able to help the parties engage in reality testing about what is involved in the litigation process as well as to understand the likely range of legal outcomes.

There has been a great deal of discussion and debate about whether lawyer-mediators should be permitted to offer professional legal advice to the parties during a mediation session. Model Standard VI, Comment 5, addresses this issue directly: "The role of a mediator differs substantially from other professional roles. Mixing the role of a mediator and the role of another profession is problematic and thus, a mediator should distinguish between the two roles. A mediator may provide information that the mediator is qualified by training or experience to provide, only if the mediator can do so consistent with these Standards."

D. LEGAL ISSUES

1. Confidentiality

The mediation process works effectively when the disputing parties participate in good faith and are willing to share their real needs and interests with each other and the mediator. The parties may be reluctant to speak openly, however, for fear that their statements will come back to haunt them and the mediator in future litigation if the mediation session breaks down. Other parties may fear that their opponent is using the mediation process as a discovery-type fishing expedition. Some lawyers, therefore, are reluctant to encourage their clients to participate in the mediation process, particularly in the face of on-going litigation.

These concerns have resulted in a great deal of writing about the need for protecting confidentiality in the mediation process. Not all commentators agree, however, on the extent to which confidentiality should be honored. Is absolute confidentiality necessary to safeguard the integrity of the mediation process? Or, should confidentiality be honored on a more limited basis? In either case, what happens to the well-established principle of law which holds that the public is entitled to every person's evidence?

There is no uniform approach in this area. While almost every state has enacted confidentiality protections of some type, existing statutes vary by state and even within a given state. Statutes may also differ by type of program and subject matter of the dispute. Court decisions are inconsistent. Thus, it is difficult to predict with certainty how much protection will be afforded to communications made in mediation. In an effort to avoid the current patchwork protection of confidentiality in mediation and to achieve greater uniformity, the National Conference of Commissioners on Uniform State Laws and the American Bar Association Section on Dispute Resolution drafted a model Uniform Mediation Act (UMA) that addresses issues related to confidentiality and privilege. The UMA is reprinted in the Appendix and is discussed more fully below in the section on mediation privilege.

Given the current lack of uniformity regarding the parameters of mediation confidentiality, in counseling clients about protecting the confidentiality of the mediation process, lawyers should be aware of several means of protection: the evidentiary exclusionary rules, privilege, contract, protective orders and where relevant, the rules of specific court-connected mediation programs,

(i) Evidentiary Exclusionary Rules

Under the common law, an offer to compromise a disputed claim is inadmissible in a later trial to prove the validity or amount of the claim on the theory that the offer has little probative value. The underlying support for the rule is a strong public policy favoring settlement of disputes. Federal Rule of Evidence 408 (Appendix) expands the common law rule to include not only offers of compromise but also "evidence of conduct or statements made in compromise negotiations." These evidentiary exclusionary rules are discussed more fully in Chapter 2 on the negotiation process.

Mediation is an extension of the negotiation process. Thus, communications from a mediation session arguably fall within the evidentiary exclusionary rule. The scope of protection, however, is limited under this approach. For example, Rule 408 and its state counterparts, only apply to hearings in which the tribunal is required to apply the rules of evidence. This would exclude protection in a number of situations such as discovery hearings and arbitration proceedings. Additionally, the exclusions within Rule 408, particularly that permitting the use of settlement discussions to prove matters other than liability or amount, could pave the way for a wide use of mediation communications at trial. Finally, Rule 408 offers no protection from the discovery of information from mediation sessions.

(ii) Privilege

A mediation privilege allows a disputant to refuse to disclose and to prevent another from disclosing particular communications. Thus, it may provide a greater degree of protection to communications made in the mediation process than is available with the evidentiary exclusionary rules.

Courts have recognized a mediation privilege based on public policy considerations. For example, in *N.L.R.B. v. Joseph Macaluso, Inc.*, 618 F.2d 51 (9th Cir.1980), a case involving unfair labor practices, the testimony of a labor mediator was critical in resolving a factual dispute. The court, however, recognized a mediator privilege and held that the National Labor Relations Board could revoke the subpoena of a mediator even though the mediator could have provided information that was crucial to the resolution of the dispute in that case. The operative statutes and regulations in *Macaluso*, gave strong support to a public policy of complete exclusion of mediator testimony in labor cases. Thus, the court held "that the complete exclusion of mediator testimony is necessary to the preservation of an effective system of labor mediation, and that labor mediation is essential to continued industrial stability, a public interest sufficiently great to outweigh the interest in obtaining every person's evidence." Judicial decisions, however, are inconsistent in this area. In some cases, a mediator's privilege not to testify has been trumped by other policy considerations. See *Olam v. Congress Mortgage Co.*, 68 F.Supp.2d 1110 (N.D.Cal.1999).

The modern statutory trend favors a privilege structure. The majority of states that have enacted mediation confidentiality legislation use a privilege approach. Under many of these statutes, information from a mediation session is both inadmissible at trial and also protected from discovery. There is, however, little uniformity among the states and the statutes vary concerning the content of what is privileged and the conditions under which the privilege may be invoked. For example, in New York where mediation is conducted within a community dispute resolution program, there is a broad privilege that applies to all communications made in the mediation session. The Judiciary Law, section 849–b(6) provides in relevant part:

> ... all memoranda, work products, or case files of a mediator are confidential and not subject to disclosure in any judicial or administrative proceeding. Any communication relating to the subject matter of the resolution made during the resolution process by any participant, mediator, or any other person present at the dispute resolution shall be a confidential communication.

The UMA contains the following three mediation privileges:

Uniform Mediation Act

Section 4. Privilege Against Disclosure; Admissibility; Discovery

(a) Except as otherwise provided in Section 6, a mediation communication is privileged as provided in subsection (b) and is not subject to discovery or admissible in evidence in a proceeding unless waived or precluded as provided by Section 5.

(b) In a proceeding, the following privileges apply:

   (1) A mediation party may refuse to disclose, and may prevent any other person from disclosing, a mediation communication.

   (2) A mediator may refuse to disclose a mediation communication, and may prevent any other person from disclosing a mediation communication of the mediator.

   (3) A nonparty participant may refuse to disclose, and may prevent any other person from disclosing, a mediation communication of the nonparty participant.

(c) Evidence or information that is otherwise admissible or subject to discovery does not become inadmissible or protected from discovery solely by reason of its disclosure or use in a mediation.

It should be noted that the privileges recognized by the UMA are limited to disclosures of mediation communications in arbitrations, court proceedings, other adjudicative processes and legislative hearings. There is no general requirement of confidentiality that operates outside the context of legal proceedings. Rather, the UMA, Section 8 provides that "mediation communications are confidential to the extent agreed by the parties or provided by other law or rule of this State."

(iii) Contract

Whether or not a privilege exists, parties who participate in the mediation process may establish additional safeguards by entering into a written confidentiality agreement. Such a contract could be a simple release in which the parties agree not to subpoena the mediator or request production of any information related to the mediation. Alternatively, a more detailed contract could be executed between the parties and the mediator specifically providing what is and is not confidential, e.g. the fact that the agreement was reached, the terms of the agreement itself and any details relating to the actual mediation process.

The Model Standards adopt a contractual approach providing that "A mediator shall maintain the confidentiality of all information obtained by the mediator in mediation, unless otherwise agreed to by the parties or required by applicable law." (Model Standards, *Standard V*) Comment D. provides: "Depending on the circumstances of mediation, the parties may have varying expectations regarding confidentiality that a mediator should address. The parties may make their own rules with respect to confidentiality, or the accepted practice of an individual mediator or institution may dictate a particular set of expectations."

A contract approach is also adopted in the Mediation Procedures of the International Institute for Conflict Prevention & Resolution (formerly the CPR Institute for Dispute Resolution)(April 1998). The model procedures, which can be incorporated by reference into a business agreement as well as into a post-dispute submission agreement, provide in relevant part:

9. The entire mediation process is confidential. Unless agreed among all the parties or required to do so by law, the parties and the mediator shall not disclose to any person who is not associated with participants in the process, including any judicial officer, any information regarding the process (including pre-process exchanges and agreements), contents (including written and oral information), settlement terms or outcome of the proceeding. If litigation is pending, the participants may, however, advise the court of the schedule and overall status of the mediation for purposes of litigation management. Any written settlement agreement resulting from the mediation may be disclosed for purposes of enforcement.

Under this procedure, the entire process is a compromise negotiation subject to Federal Rule of Evidence 408 and all state counterparts, together with any applicable statute protecting the confidentiality of mediation. All offers, promises, conduct and statements, whether oral or written, made in the course of the proceeding by any of the parties, their agents, employees, experts and attorneys, and by the mediator are confidential. Such offers, promises, conduct and statements are privileged under any applicable mediation privilege and are inadmissible and not discoverable for any purpose, including impeachment, in litigation, between the parties. However, evidence that is otherwise admissible or discoverable shall not be rendered inadmissible or non-discoverable solely as a result of its presentation or use during the mediation.

The exchange of any tangible material shall be without prejudice to any claim that such material is privileged or protected as work-product within the meaning of Federal Rule of Civil Procedure 26 and all state and local counterparts.

The mediator and any documents and information in the mediator's possession will not be subpoenaed in any such investigation, action or proceeding, and all parties will oppose any effort to have the mediator or documents subpoenaed. The mediator will promptly advise the parties of any attempt to compel him/her to divulge information received in mediation.

The **CPR Institute** is a nonprofit initiative of 500 general counsel of major corporations, leading law firms and prominent legal academics whose mission is to install alternative dispute resolution (ADR) into the mainstream of legal practice.

Parties who seek the assistance of private ADR organizations to administer their mediation may be adopting a contract approach if they agree to abide by the rules of that organization. For example, the American Arbitration Association's Commercial Mediation Procedures (2007) have specific regulations governing the confidentiality of the mediation session. Rules 9 and 10 provide as follows:

M–9. *Privacy*. Mediation sessions and related mediation communications are private proceedings. The parties and their representatives may attend mediation sessions. Other persons may attend only with the permission of the parties and with the consent of the mediator.

M–10 *Confidentiality*. Subject to applicable law or the parties' agreement, confidential information disclosed to a mediator by the parties or by other participants (witnesses) in the course of the mediation shall not be divulged by the mediator. The mediator shall maintain the confidentiality of all information obtained in the mediation, and all records, reports, or other documents received by a mediator while serving in that capacity shall be confidential.

The mediator shall not be compelled to divulge such records or to testify in regard to the mediation in any adversary proceeding or judicial forum.

The parties shall maintain the confidentiality of the mediation and shall not rely on, or introduce as evidence in any arbitral, judicial or other proceeding the following, unless agreed to by the parties or required by applicable law:

   i.   By the execution of a settlement agreement by the parties; or

   ii.   Admissions made by a party or other participant in the course of the mediation proceedings;

   iii.   Proposals made or views expressed by the mediator; or

   iv.   The fact that a party had or had not indicated willingness to accept a proposal for settlement made by the mediator.

While the contract approach overcomes the gaps inherent in the evidentiary exclusionary rules, it has some downsides. First, confidentiality contracts would not be binding on non-parties to the agreement who might be able to obtain the desired information through discovery requests.

Second, it is unclear whether the courts will enforce a private confidentiality agreement arising out of the mediation process. If, for example, there is a claim that a mediation agreement resulted from fraud, duress or coercion, a court might examine evidence from the mediation session in order to determine whether the agreement should be enforced. Certainly, the existence of a confidentiality agreement in mediation should not shield illegal behavior.

Many commentators rely on a marriage counseling case, *Simrin v. Simrin*, 233 Cal.App.2d 90, 43 Cal.Rptr. 376 (Cal.App. 5 Dist.1965) for the proposition that courts will enforce a confidentiality agreement in mediation. In *Simrin,* a rabbi acting as a marriage counselor, agreed to counsel a husband and wife only after they had expressly agreed that their communications to him would be confidential and that neither would call him as a witness in the event of a divorce. After the parties were divorced, the wife sought the rabbi's testimony in a custody action and he refused to testify based on the prior confidentiality agreement. Responding to the wife's claims that suppression of evidence was against public policy, the court noted that public policy also favors procedures designed to preserve marriages. Thus, the court ruled that the rabbi need not reveal his conversations with the parties.

Equally strong public policy arguments can be made in the case of mediation. As an extension of the negotiation process, mediation helps parties to resolve disputed claims. It can be argued therefore, that because public policy favors the settlement of disputed claims, and assuming they are otherwise legal, that confidentiality agreements arising out of the mediation process should be honored.

(iv) Protective Orders

As noted earlier, mediation confidentiality agreements are not binding on those who are not parties to the agreement. If disputants are concerned that communications made during mediation may be disclosed to non-parties who might be involved in other litigation, they could jointly request a protective order. In situations where only one of the parties seeks a protective order against a discovery request regarding statements made during a mediation session, Rule 26 and comparable state discovery rules give courts authority to issue such an order. In general, the court would be required to engage in a balancing test, weighing the burdensome nature of the request against the need of the party seeking disclosure.

(v) Court Mediation Program Rules

Protection of confidential mediation communications is a serious concern in court mediation programs. The Federal Alternative Dispute Resolution Act of 1998, 28 U.S.C.A. §§ 651 et seq. provides that local court rules should address confidentiality and "prohibit disclosure of confidential dispute resolution communications" until such time as confidentiality rules are adopted under the Act. A growing number of state and federal court mediation programs have confidentiality rules that prohibit disclosures by court-appointed mediators or the parties. Lawyers have been sanctioned for failure to abide by these rules. See *Bernard v. Galen Group, Inc.*, 901 F.Supp. 778 (S.D.N.Y.1995).

2. Enforceability

There are two questions raised by the issue of enforceability in mediation: (1) whether an agreement to mediate a future dispute is enforceable and (2) whether an agreement reached in mediation is enforceable.

(i) Agreements to Mediate Future Disputes

One way to encourage the use of mediation is to insert a clause in a contract which provides that the parties will attempt to resolve all disputes arising out of the contract through mediation before resorting to arbitration or litigation. This agreement acts as a type of guarantee that the reluctant mediation user will cooperate. An example of a simple clause would be:

Mediation: If a dispute arises related to this contract, we agree to use our best efforts to resolve the dispute through the mediation process. We will both select the mediator. The costs of mediation shall be shared equally by us.

There is little case law concerning the enforceability of such clauses. Some courts have upheld written agreements for nonbinding ADR. For example, in *AMF Inc. v. Brunswick Corp.*, 621 F.Supp. 456 (S.D.N.Y.1985), the court considered the enforceability of a nonbinding ADR clause in a settlement agreement which required that disputes over advertising claims be submitted to an advisory third party for a non-binding opinion. The clause at issue read as follows:

Both parties agree to submit any controversy which they may have with respect to data based comparative superiority of any of their products over that of the other to such advisory third party for the rendition of an advisory opinion. Such opinion shall not be binding upon the parties, but shall be advisory only.

In holding that the agreement was enforceable, the court noted that "public policy favors support of alternatives to litigation when these alternatives serve the interests of the parties and of judicial administration." Similarly, in *DeValk Lincoln Mercury, Inc. v. Ford Motor Co.,* 811 F.2d 326 (7th Cir. 1987) compliance with a mediation clause in a commercial agreement was considered to be a condition precedent to seeking other remedies.

(ii) Agreements Reached in Mediation

Generally, under current practice, a mediation agreement is considered to be a contract and is enforced under the general principles of contract law. These rules requires an offer, acceptance, consideration, capacity, legality, compliance with the Statute of Frauds and with rules of construction. The same grounds for setting aside contracts, i.e., fraud, duress, unconscionability, exist with respect to mediation agreements. Many cases dealing with the enforceability of mediation agreements result from coercion, duress and lack of informed consent.

It is important to note, however, that enforcement issues may be complicated by confidentiality provisions. If, for example, parties have entered into a contractual agreement regarding communications made during mediation, it may be difficult to introduce evidence from the mediation session to prove a valid agreement. Conversely, it may be difficult to set aside an agreement on the grounds of fraud, duress or undue influence. Some states have addressed the latter issue by statute. A Virginia statute is a good example of one state's concern for upholding the integrity of the mediation process and encouraging informed decisionmaking.

Va. St. § 8.01–576.12 Vacating orders and agreements.

Upon the filing of an independent action by a party, the court shall vacate a mediated agreement reached in a dispute resolution proceeding pursuant to this chapter, or vacate an order incorporating or resulting from such agreement, where:

1. The agreement was procured by fraud or duress, or is unconscionable;

2. If property or financial matters in domestic relations cases involving divorce, property, support or the welfare of a child are in dispute, the parties failed to provide substantial disclosure of all relevant property and financial information; or

3.   There was evident partiality or misconduct by the neutral, prejudicing the rights of any party.

For purposes of this section, "misconduct" includes failure of the neutral to inform the parties in writing at the commencement of the mediation process that: (i) the neutral does not provide legal advice, (ii) any mediated agreement may affect the legal rights of the parties, (iii) each party to the mediation has the opportunity to consult with independent legal counsel at any time and is encouraged to do so, and (iv) each party to the mediation should have any draft agreement reviewed by independent counsel prior to signing the agreement.

In an effort to enhance the quality of mediation practice and also to protect parties in the process, some states have enacted statutes that modify existing contract law regarding the enforcement of mediation agreements. In Minnesota, for example, a mediation agreement is not binding unless the parties state specifically that it *is* binding. See *Haghighi v. Russian–American Broadcasting Co.*, 577 N.W.2d 927 (Minn.1998). Minn.Stat.Ann. § 572.35 provides:

Effect of mediated settlement agreement

Subdivision 1. General. The effect of a mediated settlement agreement shall be determined under principles of law applicable to contract. A mediated settlement agreement is not binding unless:

(1) it contains a provision stating that it is binding and a provision stating substantially that the parties were advised in writing that (a) the mediator has no duty to protect their interests or provide them with information about their legal rights; (b) signing a mediated settlement agreement may adversely affect their legal rights; and (c) they should consult an attorney before signing a mediated settlement agreement if they are uncertain of their rights; or

(2) the parties were otherwise advised of the conditions in clause (1).

3. Liability of Mediators

Outside the labor field, organized mediation practice is a relatively recent phenomena. It is not surprising, therefore, that there is very little case law on mediator liability. Beyond the general understanding that mediators must act impartially and avoid conflicts of interest, commentators have advanced a number of theories under which a mediator could be held liable by the parties. These include general negligence, breach of contract including confidentiality agreements, breach of fiduciary duty, invasion of privacy, defamation, false imprisonment, fraud, and tortious interference with contractual relationship. As a practical matter, tort and contract will be the most feasible theories of liability.

Professional liability insurance is generally available today for third party neutrals who practice as mediators. Lawyers who serve as mediators should determine whether their liability policy covers mediation practice or whether they may be required to obtain additional coverage.

(i) Tort Liability Based in Negligence

One of the obstacles to imposing tort liability on mediators is the difficulty of pinpointing the specific duties that mediators owe to participants or third parties. Traditional negligence theory is predicated on the existence of a duty, breach of that duty, causation and damages. Mediators work in many different contexts and therefore, their duties may vary. Some indication of the minimal expectations for mediator conduct are found in well known ethical codes and professional standards such as The Ethical Standards of Professional Responsibility of the Society of Professionals in Dispute Resolution (SPIDR)(Appendix), the Model Standards of Conduct for Mediators (Appendix) and the Family and Divorce Mediation Standards(Appendix). These codes however, are aspirational in nature and are not intended to establish standards of liability.

Even where the plaintiff is able to show that the mediator owed and breached a duty, there is the additional difficulty of satisfying the causation requirement. The case of *Lange v. Marshall*, 622 S.W.2d 237 (Mo.App.E.D.1981), is instructive. In *Lange,* an appellate court reversed a $74,000 jury verdict against a lawyer-mediator on the grounds that the plaintiff failed to prove that the mediator caused her injury. The plaintiff argued that in attempting to assist her and her husband terminate their marriage of twenty-five years, the lawyer-mediator breached several duties. Specifically, he failed to (1) inquire as to the financial state of her husband and advise her accordingly; (2) negotiate for a better settlement; (3) advise her that she would obtain a better settlement if she litigated the matter; and (4) fully and fairly disclose to her the extent of her rights as to marital property, custody and maintenance. The plaintiff's causation argument was that, but for the lawyer-mediator's actions, her husband would have agreed to a more favorable divorce settlement. The *Lange* court found this argument highly speculative, stating that the causal connection between the mediator's conduct and the harm asserted was merely conjectural. Such weak evidence of causation, the court concluded, provided insufficient grounds for recovery, even if the defendant mediator had acted negligently.

(ii) Liability Issues in the Caucus

Use of the caucus raises some complicated issues related to confidentiality and mediator liability. Mediators must honor the expectations of the parties regarding confidentiality. Thus, typically, in a caucus, the mediator will ask the parties to specify what information should be kept confidential. The mediator then assures the party that she will not disclose that information. Suppose the mediator learns in a caucus that child abuse has occurred in a family. Should that information remain confidential? In some states information related to child abuse is not considered confidential. Absent such a policy, however, the question arises as to what, if any, duty the mediator has to inform the proper authorities? Moreover, if the mediator learns information in a caucus that serious bodily harm will occur to the other party, the issue arises as to whether there is a duty to warn despite the prior assurances of confidentiality.

As outlined above, for a mediator to be found liable on a theory of negligence, she must owe a duty to the plaintiff. In the usual case the plaintiff will have been a party in the mediation process. But what about third parties who are not present at the mediation? Whether a mediator may also owe a duty to these individuals has been the subject of some debate.

As an example of a third-party scenario, suppose that two disputing parties in a commercial mediation case request that the mediator keep all information from the session confidential. The mediator agrees and then learns in a private caucus that one of the parties intends to inflict serious physical harm on her competitor, a third party. Does the mediator have a duty to inform the competitor of what she heard despite the earlier assurances of confidentiality?

Some commentators have looked to a California case, *Tarasoff v. Regents of the University of California*, 17 Cal.3d 425, 131 Cal.Rptr. 14, 551 P.2d 334 (1976), to support a theory of mediator liability in this type of case. In *Tarasoff,* a psychotherapist was found to be negligent for failing to warn a young woman of his patient's threats to murder her. According to the California Supreme Court, the doctor had a duty to disclose the threats because of the special relationship existing between doctor and patient. This special relationship, the *Tarasoff* court posited, required the psychotherapist to control his patient's conduct. In the aftermath of *Tarasoff*, many state statutes and court rules, as well as the UMA and the Model Standards of Practice for Family and Divorce Mediation require mediators to report threats of violence if the mediator believes that the threats will be acted upon.

(iii) Contract Liability

It is common for mediators to use written employment contracts in their practice. This is a wise approach because a contract clarifies the extent of the mediators' responsibilities and gives the parties a clear understanding of what is and is not promised. This is particularly important in the case of lawyer-mediators where parties' expectations for the mediator's performance may go beyond the bounds of appropriate mediator activity. For example, the lawyer-mediator may want to make sure that the parties understand that legal representation is not part of the mediation process or that specific legal advice will not be given to either party. This type of contract would have protected the attorney in a *Lange v. Marshall* situation where one of the parties later claims that the attorney mediator failed to represent her interests.

In addition to providing a measure of protection for the parties and the mediator, contracts can also serve as a basis of liability against the mediator. Thus, lawyers should be cautious in drafting mediation contracts and consider including such items as time limits for the mediation and specific demands on the mediator's performance. In some cases, it may even be appropriate to include an exculpatory clause in the contract or to negotiate a contractual waiver of civil liability claims.

(iv) Immunity

A majority of states have enacted statutes that grant some type of civil immunity to mediators. The nature and extent of the immunities vary depending upon subject matter, e.g. farm debt, medical malpractice, or what type of program is involved, e.g. court-annexed mediation. Immunity may also be limited to certain types of behavior, such as reckless or wanton misconduct.

Court-annexed mediation programs share many of the characteristics of judicial settlement conferences. The mediator is a neutral third party appointed by the court who tries to assist litigants in arriving at a settlement. Common law judicial immunity has been extended to persons who are appointed by the court to perform a wide range of tasks within the judicial system. Thus, absent a statute, mediators in a growing number of court-annexed programs may be protected under some species of judicial immunity. See *Wagshal v. Foster*, 28 F.3d 1249, 307 U.S.App.D.C. 382 (D.C.Cir.1994); *Howard v. Drapkin*, 222 Cal.App.3d 843, 271 Cal. Rptr. 893 (Cal.App. 2 Dist.1990).

4. Unauthorized Practice of Law Restrictions

The unauthorized practice of law (UPL) doctrine restricts the practice of law to licensed attorneys who have satisfied specific educational requirements and have demonstrated good moral character. Canon 3 of the Model Code states that "a lawyer should assist in preventing the unauthorized practice of law." The Model Rules contain a similar provision. Model Rule 5.5(a). While this doctrine has come under attack in recent years as an attempt by the legal profession to preserve its professional monopoly, every jurisdiction still has laws that, with a few exceptions, prohibit non-lawyers from the practice of law.

The relationship between UPL and mediation has generated much discussion about whether mediation is the practice of law, and if so what results flow from that determination. Some states, notably

Virginia and North Carolina, have issued extensive ethical guidelines in this area. Certainly, mediators should become familiar with the rulings in their own jurisdictions before engaging in the practice of mediation. Overall, however, despite concern with unauthorized practice regulations, there are few reported cases. *Werle v. Rhode Island Bar Ass'n*, 755 F.2d 195 (1st Cir.1985).

The UPL issue has arisen most frequently within the context of divorce mediation and several bar association ethics committees and supreme court committees have issued opinions on the permissible boundaries of divorce mediation for lawyers and non-lawyers. Typical inquiries in the opinions concern whether mediation constitutes the practice of law, the extent to which non-lawyers may participate in the mediation process, mediator's discussion of legal issues, drafting settlement agreements, and the extent to which lawyers may participate in mediation with non-lawyers or on their own.

In response to these concerns and the confusion about whether mediation constitutes the practice of law the ABA Section of Dispute Resolution adopted a Resolution on Mediation and the Unauthorized Practice of Law in February 2002. It provides in relevant part:

Mediation is not the practice of law. Mediation is a process in which an impartial individual assists the parties in reaching a voluntary settlement. Such assistance does not constitute the practice of law. The parties to the mediation are not represented by the mediator.

Mediators' discussion of legal issues. In disputes where the parties' legal rights or obligations are at issue, the mediator's discussions with the parties may involve legal issues. Such discussions do not create an attorney-client relationship, and do not constitute legal advice, whether or not the mediator is an attorney.

Drafting settlement agreements. When an agreement is reached in mediation, the parties often request assistance from the mediator in memorializing their agreement. The preparation of a memorandum of understanding or settlement agreement by a mediator, incorporating the terms of settlement specified by the parties, does not constitute the practice of law. If the mediator drafts an agreement that goes beyond the terms specified by the parties, he or she may be engaged in the practice of law. However, in such a case, a mediator shall not be engaged in the practice of law if (a) all parties are represented by counsel and (b) the mediator discloses that any proposal that he or she makes with respect to the terms of settlement is informational as opposed to the practice of law, and that the parties should not view or rely upon such proposals as advice of counsel, but merely consider them in consultation with their own attorneys.

The complete text of the resolution is available at http://www.abanet.org/dispute/webpolicy.html.

Resolution on Mediation and the Unauthorized
Practice of Law, 2002, published by the American
Bar Association Section of Dispute Resolution.
© 2002 by the American Bar Association.

Multijurisdictional Practice

UPL has also become an issue in some states in
connection with multijurisdictional law practice.
With the expansion and institutionalization of ADR,
lawyers frequently represent clients in out-of-state
mediations. Many states lack procedures for allowing out of state lawyers to enjoy pro hac vice status
so that they may represent their clients without
violating unauthorized practice of law statutes. Although this issue has arisen more frequently with
arbitration practice, it is an emerging problem in
mediation. In 2002, the ABA responded to this issue
in its Report on the Commission on Multijurisdictional Practice. The ABA drafted a rule, Model Rule
of Professional Conduct, Rule 5.5 (Appendix) that
permits lawyers to represent clients in ADR proceedings, including mediation. The rule provides in
relevant part:

Rule 5.5 Unauthorized Practice of Law;

Multijurisdictional Practice of Law

ABA Model Rules of Professional Conduct

. . .

5.5 (c) A lawyer admitted in another United
States jurisdiction, and not disbarred or suspended from practice in any jurisdiction, may provide

legal services on a temporary basis in this jurisdiction that:

(3) are in or reasonably related to a pending or potential arbitration, mediation, or other alternative dispute resolution proceeding in this or another jurisdiction if the services arise out of or are reasonably related to the lawyer's practice in a jurisdiction in which the lawyer is admitted to practice and are not services for which the forum requires pro hac vice admission.

. . .

V. MEDIATION APPROACHES IN A LITIGATED CASE: ONE EXAMPLE

Until recently, the adversarial mindset has prevailed in the practice of law. In counseling clients with disputes, most lawyers have assumed that litigation was the norm and have had little encouragement to advise a client to try the mediation process. Court reporters are filled with cases that might have been settled through mediation with better results than those produced by litigation.

An example of a case that might have been a possible candidate for mediation is *Foster v. Preston Mill Co.*, 44 Wash.2d 440, 268 P.2d 645 (Wash. 1954). It is unclear from the reported facts whether mediation was attempted in this case. The facts are relatively straightforward. Blasting operations conducted by Preston Mill Company (defendant), frightened mother mink owned by B.W. Foster, (plaintiff) and caused the mink to kill their kittens. Foster sued his neighbor, Preston Mill to recover damages. The case was tried on a theory of absolute liability and in the alternative, a nuisance theory. Following a non-jury trial, the court rendered a judgment for Foster in the amount of $1953.68 on the theory that after Preston received notice of the effect which its blasting operations were having upon the mink, it was absolutely liable for all damages of that nature thereafter sustained. Preston Mill Company appealed this decision.

On appeal, the Supreme Court of Washington reversed the judgment of the trial court and held that the doctrine of absolute liability was inapplicable under the facts of the case.

Resolving this case through the adjudication process required that the court apply ''law'' to the ''facts'' and arrive at a conclusion. Excerpted below are a few passages that illustrate this process.

The primary question presented by appellant's assignments of error is whether, on these facts, the judgment against appellant is sustainable on the theory of absolute liability.

The modern doctrine of strict liability for dangerous substances and activities stems from Justice Blackburn's decision in Rylands v. Fletcher ... As applied to blasting operations, the doctrine has quite uniformly been held to establish liability, irrespective of negligence, for property damage sustained as a result of casting rocks or other debris on adjoining or neighboring premises....

There is a division of judicial opinion as to whether the doctrine of absolute liability should apply where the damage from blasting is caused, not by the casting of rocks and debris, but by concussion, vibration, or jarring.... This court has adopted the view that the doctrine applies in such cases....

However the authorities may be divided on the point just discussed, they appear to be agreed that strict liability should be confined to consequences which lie within the extraordinary risk whose existence calls for such responsibility....

This restriction which has been placed upon the application of the doctrine of absolute liability is based upon considerations of policy....

Applying this principle to the case before us, the question comes down to this: Is the risk that any unusual vibration or noise may cause wild animals, which are being raised for commercial purposes, to kill their young, one of the things which make the activity of blasting ultrahazardous?

We have found nothing in the decisional law which would support an affirmative answer to this question. The decided cases, as well as common experience, indicate that the thing which makes blasting ultrahazardous is the risk that property or persons may be damaged or injured by coming into direct contact with flying debris, or by being directly affected by vibrations of the earth or concussions of the air . . . .

It is the exceedingly nervous disposition of mink, rather than the normal risks inherent in blasting operations, which therefore must, as a matter of sound policy, bear the responsibility for the loss here sustained.

Obviously, if the parties' goal was to obtain a precedent on the issue of absolute liability, then litigation was the proper choice of process. But consider the litigation "results" here. Three years passed before this dispute was resolved by the court. The case was tried, appealed, and decided again, with all the attendant financial, emotional, and temporal costs associated with litigation. The result was a "winner" and a "loser." Preston won a victory of sorts but at the cost of "saving" less than $2000.00. There were the transaction costs of legal fees, and time lost in testifying, etc. The mink farmer lost the income from thirty to forty kittens and remained uncompensated despite his foray into court.

A. SOME INDICATIONS FOR MEDIATION

(a) *Parties Desire to Settle:* The facts certainly show an initial willingness to compromise. When Preston told Foster about the damage to his minks from the blasting, he did not demand that the blasting stop. Foster, on the other hand, agreed to reduce the force of the blast.

(b) *Nature of Relationship:* The parties were neighbors and presumably intended to remain neighbors. Both businesses operated within a short distance from each other. The lumber company had been there for fifty years. The rancher operated an established business.

(c) *Nature of the Dispute:* This appears to be a short-term dispute. Blasting, the cause of the dispute, was done in order to build a road. Once it was built, the blasting would stop, but the acrimony attendant on a winner/loser resolution would perhaps poison the relationship forever.

(d) *Uncertainty of Legal Outcome:* Judicial decisions were divided as to whether the doctrine of absolute liability should apply where the damage from blasting was caused by concussion, vibration or jarring. The lack of decisive case law leaves both parties unsure of what might happen in court.

(e) *Desirability of a Private Settlement:* If this case arose today, Foster might be concerned with avoiding publicity and its possible attendant pressure from animal rights activist groups concerned with his treatment of the minks (i.e. keeping mink in steel cages in wood sheds). Foster could face boycotts and possibly demonstrations near his property which is located near a major highway. The company might also have an interest in a private settlement to avoid exposing its blasting operations.

B.   POSSIBLE MEDIATION APPROACHES

A.   By asking questions, the mediator could help the parties recognize the evidence which indicated that only during the whelping season is the mother mink disturbed by unaccustomed noises, and that regular and continuous noises such as the continuous noise from the highway do not disturb her. If the company were unwilling to put off the blasting for the six week whelping season, it might have agreed to blast more frequently using smaller shots of ammunition. Instead of twice a day using 50 pound charges, they could have blasted five times a day using 20 pound charges, or ten times using 10 pound charges. The noise would be continuous, but it would cause less vibration while the area would be cleared for road building. Both parties would be able to continue their business with minimal losses.

B.   Another possible solution might have been for the parties to try to insulate the mother minks from the noise and the vibrations. Perhaps Foster could have traded some mink pelts in exchange for wood to reinforce and insulate the cages. This would certainly have minimized the vibrations.

C.   It may also have been possible for Preston to warn Foster each time the blasting was to occur. According to the evidence, this was twice a day. In this way, the mothers could be isolated from the kittens during that time. Other solutions come to mind if the parties are aware of the potential problems before the whelping season begins, such as conditioning the minks, constructing special cages, etc.

Mediation Bibliography

H. Abramson, *Mediation Representation: Advocating in a Problem–Solving Process* (2004);

J. Alfini, S. Press, J. Sternlight and J. Stulberg, *Mediation Theory and Practice,* 2nd ed. (2006);

D. Binder, P. Bergman, S. Price, and P. Tremblay, *Lawyers as Counselors: A Client–Centered Approach*, 2nd ed. (2004);

D. Bowling and D. Hoffman, *Bringing Peace Into the Room: How the Personal Qualities of the Mediator Impact the Process of Conflict Resolution* (2003);

R. Bush and J. Folger, *The Promise of Mediation: The Transformative Approach to Conflict* (2004);

A. Chaykin, *The Liabilities and Immunities of Mediators: A Hostile Environment for Model Legislation,* 2 Ohio St. J. on Disp. Res. 47 (1986–87);

S. Cole, *Unauthorized Practice of Law Charges: A Risk for Lawyers Representing Clients in Mediation and Arbitration in a Multi–Jurisdictional Practice Environment,* 13 Disp. Resol. Mag. 26 (Fall 2006);

S. Cole, Rogers and C. McEwen, *Mediation: Law, Policy, Practice,* 2nd edition (2006 Supp.);

J. Feerick, *Toward Uniform Standards of Conduct for Mediators,* 38 S. Tex. L. Rev. 455 (1997);

J. Folberg and A. Taylor, *Mediation: A Comprehensive Guide to Resolving Conflicts Without Litigation* (1984);

L. Fuller, *Mediation—Its Forms and Functions,* 44 S. Cal. L. Rev. 305 (1971);

G. Friedman & Jack Himmelstein, *Resolving Conflict Together: The Understanding–Based Model of Mediation,* 4 J. Amer. Arb. 225 (2005);

D. Golann and J. Folberg, Mediation: *The Roles of Advocate and Neutral* (2006);

D. Kolb, *When Talk Works: Profiles of Mediators* (1994);

K. Kovach, *Mediation: Principles and Practice,* 3rd edition (2004);

J. Lande, *Using Dispute System Design Methods to Promote Good–Faith Participation in Court–Connected Mediation Programs,* 50 UCLA L. Rev. 69 (2002);

C. Menkel–Meadow, *Ethics and Professionalism in Non-Adversarial Lawyering,* 27 Fla. St. U. L. Rev. 153 (1999);

C. Menkel–Meadow, L. Love and A. Schneider, *Mediation: Practice, Policy and Ethics* (2006);

M. Moffitt, *Suing Mediators,* 83 B.U. L. Rev. 147 (2003);

C. Moore, *The Mediation Process: Practical Strategies for Resolving Conflict*, 3rd edition (2003);

A. Rau, E. Sherman, S. Peppet, *Processes of Dispute Resolution: The Role of Lawyers*, 4th edition (2006);

J. Nolan-Haley, *Court Mediation and the Search for Justice Through Law,* 74 Wash. U. L.Q. 47 (1996);

J. Nolan-Haley, *Informed Consent in Mediation: A Guiding Principle for Truly Educated Decisionmaking,* 74 Notre Dame L. Rev. 775 (1999);

J. Nolan–Haley, H. Abramson and P. Chew, I*nternational Conflict Resolution: Consensual ADR Processes,* Chapter 3, *The Role of Culture in Transborder Conflict Resolution* (2005);

L. Riskin, *Toward New Standards for the Neutral Lawyer in Mediation,* 26 Ariz. L. Rev. 329 (1984);

L. Riskin, *Decisionmaking in Mediation: The New Old Grid and the New New Grid System,* 79 Notre Dame L. Rev. 1 (2003);

K. Scanlon, *Mediator's Deskbook* (CPR Institute for Dispute Resolution 1999);

S. Sibley and S. Merry, *Mediator Settlement Strategies*, 8 L. & Pol'y Q. 7 (1986);

W. Simkin & N. Fidandis, *Mediation and the Dynamics of Collective Bargaining* (2nd ed. 1986);

J. Stulberg, *Taking Charge/Managing Conflict* (2002);

J. Winslade & G. Monk, *Narrative Mediation: A New Approach to Conflict Resolution* (2000).

CHAPTER 4

ARBITRATION

I. INTRODUCTION

Arbitration is the most formalized alternative to the court adjudication of disputes and enjoys a dominant position in the American legal system. In the arbitration process, disputing parties present their case to one or more impartial third persons who are empowered to render a decision. Pragmatic and policy considerations have led courts and legislatures to endorse arbitration as the preferred process in resolving a wide range of disputes. As a result, arbitration has been transformed today into a flexible adjudicatory process, operating both in the mandatory, public context, as well as in voluntary, private settings.

American arbitration practice is governed by the Federal Arbitration Act (FAA) and by individual state arbitration statutes patterned after the Uniform Arbitration Act (UAA) (Appendix) that was promulgated in 1955. In August 2000, the National Conference of Commissioners on Uniform State Laws voted to adopt the Revised Uniform Arbitration Act (RUAA) (Appendix), a comprehensive model statute that addresses many issues arising in modern arbitration cases that were not addressed in the UAA. Such issues include questions related to who decides arbitrability, whether arbitrators have discretion to order discovery, and when a court can award attorney's fees and costs to a prevailing party in an appeal of an arbitrator's award. The RUAA is intended to promote fairness and predictability in arbitral proceedings by enhancing the procedural protections in the process. Thus far, it has been adopted by twelve states and is under consideration in several others.

II. HISTORICAL PERSPECTIVE

There is nothing new about arbitration as a method of private adjudication in America. Commercial arbitration has flourished in this country since the 18th century even though the courts have not always looked kindly toward the arbitration process. No doubt the early American mistrust of arbitration was influenced by the English court's hostility as exemplified in Lord Coke's famous statement in *Vynior's Case* that arbitration agreements were against public policy because they "oust the jurisdiction" of the courts. The rationale for this judicial hostility is not entirely clear. Lord Campbell has suggested that it may have been based on economic interests since judges depended upon fees for their services. Or, it could simply be what the Second Circuit Court of Appeals has described as the "hypnotic power of the phrase, 'oust the jurisdiction.' " (*Kulukundis Shipping Co., S/A v. Amtorg Trading Corporation*, 126 F.2d 978 (2nd Cir.1942)).

For a long period in American legal history the courts adopted the English courts' antagonism towards executory arbitration agreements and routinely refused to enforce contract clauses which required the arbitration of future disputes. If the parties did submit a dispute to the arbitration process, they were often permitted to withdraw before the arbitration decision was rendered.

Judicial attitudes toward arbitration began to change in the early twentieth century with the passage of state and federal statutes promoting arbitration. In 1920, New York became the first state to enact an arbitration statute giving parties the right to control future disputes as well as settle existing disputes through the arbitration process. The New York statute provided a model for the Uniform Arbitration Act of 1955 (UAA) (Appendix). Today, the majority of states have adopted arbitration statutes modeled on the UAA.

In 1925, Congress enacted the United States Arbitration Act, known today as the Federal Arbitration Act (FAA) (Appendix), 9 U.S.C.A. §§ 1 et seq., to place arbitration agreements on the same footing as other contracts and to encourage the use of commercial arbitration as an alternative to court. The FAA was intended to reverse centuries of judicial hostility towards the arbitration process. Section 2, the primary substantive provision of the Act, provides that a written agreement to arbitrate "in any maritime transaction or a contract evidencing a transaction involving commerce ... shall be valid, irrevocable, and enforceable, save upon such grounds as exist at law or in equity for the revocation of any contract." In effect, Section 2 created a body of federal substantive law of arbitrability, applicable to any arbitration agreement within the coverage of the Act.

The Act provides in Section 3 for a stay of proceedings in a case where a court is satisfied that the issue before it is arbitrable under the agreement. Section 4 of the Act directs a federal court to order parties to proceed to arbitration if there has been a "failure, neglect, or refusal of another to arbitrate under a written agreement for arbitration."

Arbitration received increasing visibility after World War II with its expansion into the labor-management arena. In 1947, Congress passed the Labor-Management Relations Act (LMRA). Section 301 of the Act, popularly known as the Taft-Hartley Act, gives federal courts jurisdiction of civil suits over violations of collective bargaining agreements, contracts that frequently contain arbitration provisions. Four Supreme Court cases decided between 1957 and 1960 firmly established the favored position that arbitration would enjoy in effectuating national labor policy. Three out of the four cases arose under Section 301 of the Labor Management Relations Act.

In *Textile Workers Union v. Lincoln Mills*, 353 U.S. 448, 77 S.Ct. 912, 1 L.Ed.2d 972 (1957), the Supreme Court held that an employer's promise to arbitrate grievances in a collective bargaining agreement was specifically enforceable under the federal common law of collective bargaining. The Court considered grievance arbitration provisions to be the *quid pro quo* for unions' non-strike agreements, and then connected labor arbitration to industrial harmony:

Viewed in this light, the legislation does more than confer jurisdiction in the federal courts over labor organizations. It expresses a federal policy that federal courts should enforce these agreements on behalf of or against labor organizations and that industrial peace can be best obtained only in that way.

Three years later, in a series of cases, known as the "Steelworkers Trilogy," the Court gave more concrete shape to its policy of giving solemn deference to labor arbitration awards. The first Trilogy case, *United Steelworkers v. American Manufacturing Company*, 363 U.S. 564, 80 S.Ct. 1343, 4 L.Ed.2d 1403 (1960) established the predominant role that arbitrators would play in the resolution of labor disputes:

The function of the court is very limited when the parties have agreed to submit all questions of contract interpretation to the arbitrator. It is confined to ascertaining whether the party seeking arbitration is making a claim which on its face is governed by the contract. Whether the moving party is right or wrong is a question of contract interpretation for the arbitrator.

In the second Trilogy case, *United Steelworkers v. Warrior & Gulf Navigation Co.*, 363 U.S. 574, 80

S.Ct. 1347, 4 L.Ed.2d 1409 (1960) the Court continued to reflect a strong congressional policy favoring the resolution of labor disputes through the arbitration process. Consistent with this policy, the courts were to have a limited role interpreting the collective bargaining agreement:

> ... the judicial inquiry under Section 301 must be strictly confined to the question whether the reluctant party did agree to arbitrate.... An order to arbitrate the particular grievance should not be denied unless it may be said with positive assurance that the arbitration clause is not susceptible of an interpretation that covers the asserted dispute.

Finally, in *United Steelworkers v. Enterprise Wheel & Car Corp.*, 363 U.S. 593, 80 S.Ct. 1358, 4 L.Ed.2d 1424 (1960) the Court again emphasized the preeminent role of arbitrators in interpreting the collective bargaining agreement. Courts would have no business second-guessing an arbitrator as long as the arbitration award "draws its essence from the collective bargaining agreement."

Until the early 1970's, arbitration jurisprudence developed chiefly from the use of arbitration in commercial transactions and labor agreements. Today, the subject matter of arbitration encompasses a much broader subject area to include: employment, prisoners' rights, medical malpractice, consumer rights, intellectual property rights, and antitrust. The expansion of arbitration into these new contexts raises significant questions in civil justice reform and challenges policy-makers to effect these changes without diminishing the quality of justice.

III. THE TRADITIONAL MODEL OF ARBITRATION

The doctrine of freedom of contact is the driving force in American arbitration law and practice. The traditional model of arbitration contemplates a *voluntary* process where parties submit a dispute to a neutral person for a decision. It results from a contractual arrangement in which parties agree in advance of a dispute, or after a dispute has arisen, that arbitration will substitute for formal judicial proceedings. The Supreme Court emphasized the voluntariness principle in *Volt Info. Sciences, Inc. v. Board of Trustees of Leland Stanford Junior Univ.*, 489 U.S. 468, 109 S.Ct. 1248, 103 L.Ed.2d 488 (1989):

> The FAA does not require parties to arbitrate when they have not agreed to do so.... It simply requires courts to enforce privately negotiated agreements to arbitrate, like other contracts, in accordance with their terms... Arbitration under the Act is a matter of consent, not coercion,....

In theory, traditional arbitration has numerous advantages over the litigation process, not necessarily because it is a superior form of justice, but simply because it uncomplicates the path to justice. Arbitration is generally considered a more efficient process than litigation because it is quicker and less expensive. Arbitration also offers greater flexibility of process and procedure than litigation. It is a private process over which disputing parties have considerable latitude because its foundation rests in the principle of freedom of contract. The parties choose the arbitrators and exercise control over the relevant procedures. They decide the degree of formality that will govern, and the extent to which the trappings of litigation, from pre-trial motions to discovery, are relevant.

Arbitrators typically have more expertise in the specific subject matter of the dispute than do judges. They also have greater flexibility in decision-making than judges because they are not bound by the principle of *stare decisis* in rendering a decision.

In practice, however, arbitration has been criticized on a number of grounds. First, efficiency may be lost when arbitration is conducted by a panel of arbitrators whose scheduling problems increase delay and costs. Second, some commentators argue that efficiency is achieved at the expense of the quality of justice and that the difficulty of appealing an arbitral award may give arbitrators a license to do injustice. Finally, in some areas, particularly labor relations cases, the increasing formality of arbitration hearings resembles aspects of the judicial system.

IV. COMPULSORY ARBITRATION

The growth of compulsory arbitration in the United States is not surprising given the current penchant for the arbitration process. The notion of *requiring* parties to arbitrate, however, is the antithesis of traditional arbitration with its emphasis on the voluntary agreement of the parties. Some of the most visible growth areas for mandatory arbitration are public sector employment disputes, nonunionized employment disputes, consumer disputes, court-annexed programs and medical malpractice disputes.

1. Public Sector Arbitration

Critical public sector employees such as the police, teachers and firefighters, are usually not permitted to participate in strikes as part of their labor negotiations. A majority of states, therefore, have enacted legislation requiring compulsory arbitration as the final step in negotiating the terms of a collective bargaining agreement between municipalities and their critical employees. These statutes typically provide for the arbitration of interest disputes by a tripartite panel of arbitrators who decide such issues as wages, hours and working conditions.

Judicial review of compulsory arbitration awards differs from review of traditional arbitration awards since there is usually a record of the arbitration hearing and a written decision from the arbitrator. Courts are therefore able to examine the awards to determine whether they are supported by substantial evidence in the record.

A major constitutional concern with compulsory arbitration statutes is that they delegate legislative power to independent arbitrators who are not accountable to the public for their decisions. This is a significant concern because many issues decided by these arbitrators ultimately involve political or legislative questions. While some state laws have been invalidated on the grounds of impermissible delegation of legislative power, the majority of courts have upheld the constitutionality of these statutes where there are reasonable criteria for the arbitration award.

2.　Court–Annexed Arbitration

Several state and federal district courts have adopted court-annexed arbitration systems in an effort to reduce the delay and expense associated with the disposition of civil litigation. Court-annexed systems, also known as judicial arbitration, generally operate by diverting specific categories of civil cases to mandatory, arbitration. Some systems, however, are permissive and litigants are simply offered the option of arbitration. The arbitrations are usually conducted by attorneys or retired judges who have quasi-judicial powers.

3.　Medical Malpractice Arbitration

One response to the rising costs of medical malpractice lawsuits has been the diversion of these cases from tort litigation to compulsory arbitration. A great number of states have enacted statutes requiring the arbitration of medical malpractice disputes. Statutory approaches vary. Some states provide for mandatory non-binding arbitration as a pre-requisite for bringing a case to court. Often, as an adjunct to this process, parties are required to submit their cases to a screening panel, sometimes known as an arbitration board, whose function is to weed out frivolous lawsuits. Parties have the right to demand a trial *de novo* in state court if they find the arbitrator's award unacceptable.

Other states provide for voluntary but binding arbitration agreements that patients sign before receiving medical treatment. The arbitrator's award is final in these situations. Thus, it is important to show that the patient had knowledge that he or she was agreeing to arbitration. Otherwise, an arbitration agreement will be struck down as unconscionable.

4. Employment Arbitration

Beginning with the Supreme Court's decision in *Gilmer v. Interstate/Johnson Lane Corp.*, 500 U.S. 20, 111 S.Ct. 1647, 114 L.Ed.2d 26 (1991), a case discussed more fully later in this Chapter, courts have looked favorably upon employment arbitration in the non-unionized context. In *Gilmer* the Court held that claims arising under the Age Discrimination in Employment Act (ADEA) could be subjected to compulsory arbitration pursuant to the FAA. Employment arbitration continued to receive favorable support in *Circuit City Stores v. Adams*, 532 U.S. 105, 121 S.Ct. 1302, 149 L.Ed.2d 234 (2001) wherein Supreme Court limited the employment contract exclusion in Section One of the FAA to the contracts of interstate transportation workers. All other employees could be required to submit employment related disputes to arbitration. However, the Supreme Court's strong endorsement of employment arbitration does not preclude government agencies from seeking separate forms of relief for employment discrimination. In *EEOC v. Waffle House, Inc.*, 534 U.S. 279, 122 S.Ct. 754, 151 L.Ed.2d 755 (2002), the Court held that despite an agreement between an employer and an employee to arbitrate workplace disputes, the EEOC was not barred from obtaining either injunctive or victim-specific relief.

V. ARBITRATION DEFINITIONS

1. Interest and Rights Arbitration

Arbitration in the labor-management area can be classified into two basic categories: "interests" arbitration and "rights" or grievance arbitration. "Interests" arbitration involves settling the terms of a contract between the parties. When impasse occurs, and parties are unable to agree on the terms of a contract, an arbitrator decides the terms. The use of "interests" arbitration is most common in public sector collective bargaining.

"Rights" arbitration, also known as grievance arbitration, concerns the violation or interpretation of an existing contract. The arbitrator issues a final decision regarding the meaning of the contract terms.

2.   Administered and Non-Administered Arbitration

Both terms refer to the types of services offered by arbitration providers. In "administered" arbitration, the organization providing the arbitration services handles the procedural aspects of the process. These services would include: providing rules that parties could adopt in pre-dispute agreements or in existing disputes; offering panels of arbitrators; scheduling, etc. Some examples of institutions that provide administered arbitration services are the American Arbitration Association (AAA), The National Arbitration Forum, and JAMS (formerly the Judicial Arbitration and Mediation Service). At the international level, examples include the International Chamber of Commerce (ICC) and the London Court of International Arbitration (LCIA).

In "non-administered" or ad hoc arbitration, the arbitrator and the parties' attorneys generally perform the functions of the administering organizations. The Non-Administered Arbitration Rules developed by the CPR International Institute for Conflict Prevention and Resolution are an example of rules that would govern a non-administered arbitration. See www.cpradr.org.

3.   Final Offer Arbitration

There is a general assumption that arbitrators are susceptible of making compromise decisions in an effort to remain acceptable to both parties. Final offer arbitration militates against this tendency by requiring that parties submit their "final offer" to the arbitrator who may choose only one. This device gives each party an incentive to make a reasonable offer or risk that the arbitrator will accept the other party's offer. Final offer arbitration is used in baseball salary disputes and in public sector collective bargaining.

A variation of "final offer" arbitration is the "high-low" agreement where the parties limit the amount they can both recover and lose. These agreements reduce risk for both parties.

4. Tripartite Arbitration

Instead of having one arbitrator, parties may decide upon a panel of three neutral arbitrators. A variation of three neutral arbitrators is a panel where each side selects an arbitrator and then the two party-appointed arbitrators select a neutral person to chair the panel. The ABA/AAA Code of Ethics for Arbitrators in Commercial Disputes (2004) (Appendix) contains extensive rules to govern the behavior of party-appointed arbitrators. In international commercial arbitration, a tripartite model is generally followed.

VI. LEGAL ISSUES

1. Arbitrability

The question of arbitrability focuses on whether a particular dispute is properly the subject of arbitration. There are two dimensions to this question: substantive and procedural. *Substantive* arbitrability is concerned with questions related to contract formation and whether a particular subject matter was intended by the parties to be covered by their arbitration agreement. The parties' agreement is critical. Because the traditional model of arbitration assumes a voluntary undertaking, a party cannot be required to submit a dispute to arbitration. *Procedural* arbitrability is concerned with whether the procedural requirements for arbitration, such as timeliness and specificity, have been satisfied.

(i) Substantive Arbitrability

The Court's language from the *Steelworkers Trilogy,* suggests a limited judicial role for courts in determining substantive arbitrability. In deciding whether to order or prevent an arbitration, the court's inquiry is limited "to ascertaining whether the party seeking arbitration is making a claim which on its face is governed by the contract." The court must order arbitration "unless it may be said with positive assurance that the arbitration clause is not susceptible of an interpretation that covers the asserted dispute."

As the law of arbitration between private parties has developed, a difference in perspective has evolved between arbitration in commercial matters and arbitration in labor relations. Since the "Steelworkers Trilogy" in 1960, courts have recognized a presumption of arbitrability in labor disputes. In

AT & T Technologies, Inc. v. Communications Workers of America, 475 U.S. 643, 106 S.Ct. 1415, 89 L.Ed.2d 648 (1986) the Court stated that this approach acknowledges the "greater institutional competence of arbitrators in interpreting collective bargaining agreements, [and] 'furthers the national labor policy of peaceful resolution of labor disputes and thus best accords with the parties' presumed objectives in pursuing collective bargaining.' " In *Wright v. Universal Maritime Service Corp.*, 525 U.S. 70, 119 S.Ct. 391, 142 L.Ed.2d 361 (1998), the Supreme Court justified *Warrior & Gulf*'s presumption of arbitrability because "arbitrators are in a better position than courts to *interpret the terms of a* [collective-bargaining agreement.]"

On the other hand, the traditional rule with respect to commercial contracts does not recognize a presumption of arbitrability. Rather, the agreement to arbitrate must expressly and unequivocally encompass the subject matter of a particular dispute before a party can be forced to submit to arbitration. Some courts however, are beginning to apply a presumption of arbitrability in commercial contracts cases. In *Mitsubishi Motors Corporation v. Soler Chrysler–Plymouth, Inc.*, 723 F.2d 155 (1st Cir.1983), a commercial contract case, the court cited familiar language from the *Steelworkers Trilogy* favoring a presumption of arbitration: "... all doubts are resolved in favor of arbitration; arbitration will be ordered 'unless it may be said with positive assurance that the arbitration clause is not susceptible of an interpretation that covers the asserted dispute.' "

Labor management relations in the public sector raise somewhat different considerations on the question of arbitrability. Collective bargaining agreements between a public employer and employees are sufficiently different from private commercial and labor agreements that they cannot be categorized under either one of those headings. In the field of public employment, the public policy favoring arbitration does not yet carry the same historical or general acceptance as exists in the private sector.

In recent years, substantive arbitrability has been a fertile source of litigation, particularly where statutory claims are involved. The Supreme Court has signaled strong support for the integrity of the arbitration process by upholding the enforceability of arbitration agreements arising under a wide range of federal statutes. The Court's rationale for its strong endorsement of arbitration is expressed in *Mitsubishi Motors Corp. v. Soler Chrysler–Plymouth, Inc.*, 473 U.S. 614, 105 S.Ct. 3346, 87 L.Ed.2d 444 (1985), a Sherman Act case in which the Court upheld the arbitrability of antitrust claims arising in an international commercial transaction:

> By agreeing to arbitrate a statutory claim, a party does not forego the substantive rights afforded by the statute; it only submits to their resolution in an arbitral, rather than a judicial, forum. It trades the procedures and opportunity for review

of the courtroom for the simplicity, informality, and expedition of arbitration.

In *Shearson/American Express v. McMahon*, 482 U.S. 220, 107 S.Ct. 2332, 96 L.Ed.2d 185 (1987) the Court upheld the arbitrability of claims arising under the Securities Exchange Act of 1934 and the civil provisions of the Racketeer Influenced and Corrupt Organizations Act (RICO). *Shearson* marked a significant departure from the Court's anti-arbitration orientation exemplified in *Wilko v. Swan*, 346 U.S. 427, 74 S.Ct. 182, 98 L.Ed. 168 (1953). *Wilko,* one of the earliest cases to address the arbitrability of statutory claims and a frequently cited precedent for rejecting arbitrability, held that claims arising under section 12(2) of the Securities Act of 1933 were not subject to compulsory arbitration. The *Wilko* court's mistrust of the arbitration process was based on several considerations: arbitrators were incapable of understanding the legal and factual complexities of claims arising under the Securities Act; arbitrators did not have to offer any reasons for their awards; the power to vacate an award is limited; and, an arbitrator's error in interpretation of law is not subject to judicial review.

The precedential value of *Wilko* was considerably weakened in *Shearson,* when the Court observed that the reasons for judicial hostility towards arbitration have subsequently been rejected by the court as a basis for holding statutory claims nonarbitrable. The *Shearson* Court established the following framework for analysis in determining the enforceability of arbitration agreements under the FAA. The FAA requires enforcement of arbitration agreements. Congress can override this mandate by precluding waiver of the judicial forum for the exercise of the specific statutory right at issue. But, the party opposing arbitration, has the burden of demonstrating that Congress intended to preclude waiver. Congressional intent may be found in the text or legislative history of the statute, or the "inherent conflict between arbitration and the statute's underlying purposes." The parties in *Shearson* failed to demonstrate that Congress intended to except from the FAA's coverage claims arising under RICO and the Exchange Act.

Wilko was finally overruled two years later, in *Rodriguez de Quijas v. Shearson/American Express, Inc.*, 490 U.S. 477, 109 S.Ct. 1917, 104 L.Ed.2d 526 (1989) when the Supreme Court upheld the enforceability of predispute agreements to arbitrate claims arising under the Securities Act of 1933. Writing for the majority, Justice Kennedy stated that "It also would be undesirable for the decisions in *Wilko* and *Shearson* to continue to exist side by side."

The Supreme Court's enthusiastic endorsement of arbitration continued beyond the commercial context to employment arbitration in the non-unionized context in *Gilmer v. Interstate/Johnson Lane Corp.*, 500 U.S. 20, 111 S.Ct. 1647, 114 L.Ed.2d 26 (1991). In Gilmer, the Court held that claims arising under the Age Discrimination in Employment Act (ADEA) can be subjected to compulsory arbitration pursuant to the FAA. Relying on the test enunciated in *Shearson,* the Court stated that a party would be held to his bargain to arbitrate unless he could show that Congress intended to preclude a waiver of a judicial forum for ADEA claims.

Robert Gilmer had been hired as a manager of financial services in 1981. In 1987, at the age of 62, his employment was terminated. As a condition of his employment, Gilmer had been required to sign an agreement to arbitrate any disputes between himself and his employer arising out of his employment or its termination. He argued that compulsory arbitration of ADEA claims was inconsistent with the purposes of the ADEA. The Court, however, was not persuaded. In the Court's view, there is no inconsistency between the social policies furthered by the ADEA and enforcing agreements to arbitrate age discrimination claims. Just as arbitration focuses on specific disputes between the parties, so too does judicial dispute resolution. Both processes can further broader social purposes. The court noted that other laws such as the Sherman Act, the Securities Exchange Act of 1934, RICO and the Securities Act of 1933 are designed to further important public policies but claims under them are appropriate for arbitration.

Gilmer claimed that compulsory arbitration deprived claimants of the judicial forum provided for by the ADEA. The court rejected this argument noting that "Congress ... did not explicitly preclude arbitration or other non judicial resolution of claims, even in its recent amendments to the

ADEA." The Court likewise rejected Gilmer's challenge to the adequacy of arbitration procedures—the lack of written opinions, biased arbitration panels, limited discovery, noting that it had rejected most of these generalized attacks in its recent arbitration cases because they rested on an outmoded suspicion of the arbitral process.

Gilmer also claimed that unequal bargaining power between employers and employees is sufficient reason not to enforce arbitration agreements related to ADEA claims. The Court responded, however, that "Mere inequality in bargaining power, . . . is not a sufficient reason to hold that arbitration agreements are never enforceable in the employment context." In any event, the court found no indication of unfair bargaining power in this case and stated that such an argument was best left for resolution in specific cases.

Finally, Gilmer argued that three earlier employment decisions, *Alexander v. Gardner–Denver Co.*, 415 U.S. 36, 94 S.Ct. 1011, 39 L.Ed.2d 147 (1974) and its progeny, *Barrentine v. Arkansas–Best Freight System, Inc.*, 450 U.S. 728, 101 S.Ct. 1437, 67 L.Ed.2d 641 (1981) and *McDonald v. City of West Branch*, 466 U.S. 284, 104 S.Ct. 1799, 80 L.Ed.2d 302 (1984) (discussed in section VI *infra*) precluded arbitration of employment discrimination claims. The Court distinguished these cases on several grounds: they arose in the collective bargaining context; they involved contractual rights unlike this case which involved individual statutory rights; the issue in those cases related to the preclusive effects of an arbitration award and not the enforceability of an agreement to arbitrate statutory claims; and, finally, those cases were not decided under the FAA which has a liberal federal policy favoring arbitration.

In the aftermath of *Gilmer*, case law has generally been supportive of mandatory arbitration of statutorily-based claims in employment cases. Nevertheless, *Gilmer* generated considerable criticism by scholars who argued that the public interest in enforcement of some statutory claims in employment cases precluded enforcement of agreements to arbitrate and that in cases of unequal bargaining power such agreements should not be enforced. As a result of the criticism, considerable efforts have been undertaken to insure that the arbitration of statutory employment disputes satisfy standards of fairness. A significant effort in this regard, *A Due Process Protocol For Mediation and Arbitration of Statutory Disputes Arising Out Of The Employment Relationship* (1995), is reprinted in the Appendix. Courts have referred to this protocol in considering issues of fairness in arbitration. See *Cole v. Burns Int'l Sec. Servs.*, 105 F.3d 1465, 323 U.S.App.D.C. 133 (D.C.Cir.1997).

The Supreme Court again addressed the issue of substantive arbitrability in *First Options of Chicago, Inc. v. Kaplan*, 514 U.S. 938, 115 S.Ct. 1920, 131 L.Ed.2d 985 (1995), although it did not use the "substantive" "procedural" terminology. Emphasizing that arbitration is a contractual matter between the parties, the Court held that whether arbitrators or the courts have the power to decide substantive arbitrability depends upon the content of the parties' agreement. If the parties decided to submit the arbitrability question to an arbitrator, then their agreement governs. Otherwise, the court decides questions of arbitrability. See also *Pacificare Health Systems, Inc. v. Book,* 538 U.S. 401, 123 S.Ct. 1531, 155 L.Ed.2d 578 (2003).

(ii) Procedural Arbitrability

Questions related to procedural arbitrability such as those concerning defenses or waivers, are reserved to arbitrators. Generally, these questions are closely connected to the substantive merits of the dispute and it makes little sense to have them decided in a different forum. Thus, arbitrators' decisions on procedural questions will receive the same judicial deference as their decisions on the merits of the dispute.

The Supreme Court specifically addressed the question of procedural arbitrability in *John Wiley & Sons, Inc. v. Livingston*, 376 U.S. 543, 84 S.Ct. 909, 11 L.Ed.2d 898 (1964), and acknowledged the specialized competence of arbitrators to resolve procedural issues. *Wiley* involved an action under Section 301 of the Labor Management Relations Act, to compel arbitration under a collective bargaining agreement. The specific question before the Court was whether the court or an arbitrator should decide if arbitration provisions in a collective-bargaining contract survived a corporate merger so as to bind the surviving corporation. The Court had "no doubt" that this question should be decided by the courts but held that once the court makes a determination that the parties are obligated to submit a dispute to arbitration, then "procedural" questions arising out of the dispute should be left to the arbitrator.

In recent years the Supreme Court has expanded the scope of procedural arbitrability by granting arbitrators increased powers. In *Howsam v. Dean Witter Reynolds, Inc.*, 537 U.S. 79, 123 S.Ct. 588, 154 L.Ed.2d 491 (2002), the Court held that questions related to the statute of limitations should be decided by the arbitrator rather than the court. One year later, in *Green Tree Financial Corp. v. Bazzle,* 539 U.S. 444, 123 S.Ct. 2402, 156 L.Ed.2d 414 (2003), the Court again expanded the power of arbitrators, holding that the arbitrator, rather than the court, should determine whether class action arbitration is permissible when the parties' contract is silent on this issue.

2. Separability

The separability doctrine holds that the agreement to arbitrate is separate from the main contract. The issue of separability arises when there is a challenge to the validity of an arbitration clause because the overall contract is invalid. The claim may be that the entire contract is void because of such defects as fraud in the inducement, lack of a meeting of the minds, or lack of mutuality of consideration. The crucial question raised by such claims is whether the court or the arbitrator should resolve them?

The federal rule of separability enunciated by the Supreme Court in *Prima Paint Corp. v. Flood & Conklin Mfg. Co.*, 388 U.S. 395, 87 S.Ct. 1801, 18 L.Ed.2d 1270 (1967), allows arbitrators to resolve such claims unless they are related to the arbitration clause itself. *Prima Paint* involved a claim of fraud in the inducement of a contract governed by the FAA. Flood & Conklin (F & C) agreed both to perform consulting services for and not compete with Prima Paint. The contract contained a broad arbitration clause which provided that " '[a]ny controversy or claim arising out of or relating to this Agreement . . . shall be settled by arbitration in the City of New York, . . .' " F & C sent Prima Paint a notice requesting arbitration on the grounds that Prima had failed to make a payment under the contract. Prima brought an action in federal court to rescind the entire agreement on the grounds of fraud. The alleged fraud consisted of F & C's misrepresentation at the time the contract was made, that it was solvent, when in fact, it was insolvent. F & C moved to stay Prima's lawsuit pending arbitration of the fraud issue. The lower courts held that the action should be stayed to permit arbitration of the issue. The Second Circuit Court of Appeals held that a claim of fraud in the inducement is not for the court, but for the arbitrator to decide and called this a rule of "national substantive law." The Supreme Court adopted a broad view of severability:

> [A]rbitration clauses as a matter of federal law are 'separable' from the contracts in which they are embedded, and . . . where no claim is made

that fraud was directed to the arbitration clause itself, a broad arbitration clause will be held to encompass arbitration of the claim that the contract itself was induced by fraud.

The Court's holding in *Prima Paint* extended only to the specific issue of fraud in the inducement. Federal courts and a majority of state courts, however, have expanded its principle to include other defects, consistent with a liberal regard for the federal policy favoring arbitration. More recently, in *Buckeye Check Cashing, Inc. v. Cardegna,* 546 U.S. 440, 126 S.Ct. 1204, 163 L.Ed.2d 1038 (2006), which is discussed more fully later in this Chapter, the Supreme Court affirmed the validity of *Prima Paint,* holding that as a matter of substantive federal law, an arbitration provision is severable from the remainder of a contract, and a challenge to the validity of the contract as a whole, and not specifically to the arbitration clause within it, should be for the arbitrator, not the court, to decide.

Kompetenz-Kompetenz

Closely related to separability is the *kompetenz-kompetenz* doctrine that gives arbitrators the power to rule on jurisdictional challenges. In essence, it gives arbitrators the power to decide their own jurisdiction. One of the benefits of *kompetenz-kompetenz* provisions is that they prevent dilatory tactics by parties who can cause extensive delays in getting a case to arbitration. Although such provisions are not recognized under the FAA, they may be permissible under the Court's holding in *First*

Options of Chicago, Inc. v. Kaplan that permits parties to delegate the determination of jurisdictional questions to arbitrators.

3. Federalism Concerns

One of the unique features of the American arbitration system is the co-existence of both state and federal arbitration laws. Questions regarding the relationship between state and federal law have generated a growing arbitration jurisprudence. The FAA was enacted during the era of *Swift v. Tyson* when federal courts were free to fashion general federal common law for questions not governed by state statutes. It left open several issues about the role of state law in arbitration proceedings. After the Supreme Court's decision in *Erie Railroad Co. v. Tompkins* in 1938, a number of questions arose regarding the application of the *Erie* doctrine to the FAA. Many of these questions related to whether the FAA should be treated as substantive law under *Erie*. Other issues arose regarding the preemptive effect of the FAA. The following section identifies the leading Supreme Court cases in this area:

(a) ***Bernhardt v. Polygraphic Co.***, 350 U.S. 198, 76 S.Ct. 273, 100 L.Ed. 199 (1956). This was a diversity case that involved an application for a stay of litigation pending arbitration. The Supreme Court made it clear that enforcement of arbitration clauses under Section 2 of the FAA was substantive for purposes of the *Erie* doctrine. *Bernhardt* was an action for damages resulting from discharge under an employment contract made in New York between a New York corporation and a New York resident. The petitioner later became a resident of Vermont where he was to perform his duties.

The contract provided that in case of any dispute the parties would submit the matter to arbitration under New York law. The district court ruled that under *Erie*, the arbitration provision of the contract was governed by Vermont law which held that arbitration contracts were revocable at any time prior to the issuance of an arbitral award. The Supreme Court ruled that the arbitration contract at issue fell outside the provisions of section 2 of the FAA because the contract was neither a maritime transaction nor a transaction in commerce.

(b) *Prima Paint Corp. v. Flood & Conklin Mfg. Co.*, 388 U.S. 395, 87 S.Ct. 1801, 18 L.Ed.2d 1270 (1967). The facts of this case are discussed in the previous section on separability. With respect to federalism issues, one of the arguments which had been raised in *Prima Paint* was that under the *Erie* doctrine, federal courts were bound to follow state law which called for a different result on the disputed issue in that case. The Supreme Court responded as follows:

> The question in this case, however, is not whether Congress may fashion federal substantive rules to govern questions arising in simple diversity cases ... Rather, the question is

whether Congress may prescribe how federal courts are to conduct themselves with respect to the subject matter over which Congress plainly has power to legislate. The answer to that can only be in the affirmative.

(c) ***Moses H. Cone Memorial Hospital v. Mercury Construction Corp.***, 460 U.S. 1, 103 S.Ct. 927, 74 L.Ed.2d 765 (1983). The Supreme Court stated in *Moses H. Cone* that the substantive law created by the FAA was applicable in state and federal courts. The factual background of this case involved a contract dispute between a hospital and a building contractor. Their agreement provided that disputes could be submitted by either party to binding arbitration. After a dispute arose, the hospital filed an action in state court seeking a declaratory judgment that the contractor had no right to arbitration. In response, the contractor filed a diversity suit in federal district court seeking an order compelling arbitration under Section 4 of the FAA. The district court stayed the action out of deference to the parallel state court litigation. The Fourth Circuit reversed and remanded the case with instructions to order arbitration.

The Supreme Court considered the propriety of the district court's decision to stay the federal suit and found no showing of "exceptional circumstances" to justify the stay. The Court concluded, therefore, that the stay frustrated the FAA's policy of "rapid and unobstructed enforcement of arbitration agreements." The language of

Moses H. Cone clearly expresses what had simply been implied in *Prima Paint* that:

> Section 2 is a congressional declaration of a liberal federal policy favoring arbitration agreements, notwithstanding any state substantive or procedural policies to the contrary. The effect of the section is to create a body of federal substantive law of arbitrability, applicable to any arbitration agreement within the coverage of the Act.

(d) ***Southland Corp. v. Keating***, 465 U.S. 1, 104 S.Ct. 852, 79 L.Ed.2d 1 (1984). The Supreme Court invalidated a state law that undercut the enforceability of arbitration agreements. The facts in *Southland Corp.* involved the constitutionality of a section of the California Franchise Investment Law that invalidated certain arbitration agreements covered by the FAA. Southland Corp., the owner and franchiser of 7-eleven convenience stores and several 7-Eleven franchisees had an agreement with a clause requiring arbitration of any controversy or claim arising out of or relating to the franchise agreement. Several of the franchisees filed actions against Southland in the California Superior Court, alleging fraud, misrepresentation, breach of contract, breach of fiduciary duty, and violation of the disclosure requirements of the California Franchise Investment Law. These actions were consolidated into a class action and Southland moved to compel arbitration in accordance with the contract. The California Superior Court ordered arbitration of all claims except those based upon the Franchise Investment Law. The appeals court reversed and the California Supreme Court upheld the decision.

Relying on its earlier pronouncements in *Prima Paint,* and *Moses H. Cone,* that the FAA created a body of federal substantive law applicable in both state and federal courts, the Court held that the California law violated the Supremacy clause and was therefore, invalid. More recently in *Buckeye Check Cashing, Inc. v. Cardegna,* 546 U.S. 440, 126 S.Ct. 1204, 163 L.Ed.2d 1038 (2006) the Court affirmed its holding in Southland that substantive federal arbitration law applies in state as well as federal courts.

(e) ***Dean Witter Reynolds, Inc. v. Byrd***, 470 U.S. 213, 105 S.Ct. 1238, 84 L.Ed.2d 158 (1985). In this case the Supreme Court held that the FAA requires federal courts to enforce agreements to arbitrate, even if this results in "piecemeal litigation." The facts of this case involved an investor who signed a Customer's Agreement with Dean Witter Reynolds which provided that any controversy would be settled by arbitration. After the value of his account declined substantially, the investor filed a complaint against Dean Witter in federal court alleging various violations of the Securities Exchange Act of 1934 and of various state law provisions. Dean Witter filed a motion for an order severing the pendent state law claims, compelling their arbitration, and staying arbitration of those claims pending resolution of the federal-court action. The district court denied the motion to sever and the appeals court affirmed.

The Court's opinion in *Dean Witter* makes it clear that the FAA is not simply a quick fix dispute resolution vehicle but rather a mechanism for the enforcement of private arbitration agreements:

> The preeminent concern of Congress in passing the Act was to enforce private agreements into which parties had entered, and that concern requires that we rigorously enforce agreements to arbitrate, even if the result is "piecemeal" litigation, at least absent a countervailing policy manifested in another federal statute.... By compelling arbitration of state-law claims, a district court successfully protects the contractual rights of the parties and their rights under the Arbitration Act.

(f) ***Perry v. Thomas***, 482 U.S. 483, 107 S.Ct. 2520, 96 L.Ed.2d 426 (1987). The Supreme Court considered whether § 2 of the FAA preempted a provision of the California Labor Code's proscription on arbitration. An employee had filed an action in California state court seeking payment of commissions he claimed were owed him by his former employer in the securities industry. His employer sought to compel arbitration. The Supreme Court found an "unmistakable conflict" between the state law guarantee of a judicial forum and § 2 of the FAA and concluded that "under the Supremacy Clause, the state statute must give way."

(g) ***Volt Information Sciences, Inc. v. Board of Trustees of Leland Stanford Junior University***, 489 U.S. 468, 109 S.Ct. 1248, 103 L.Ed.2d 488 (1989). *Volt* marks a detour in the expansive judicial interpretation of the FAA with the Court's refusal to extend federal arbitration law where the parties had agreed to be governed by state arbitration rules. The case arose out of a construction contract between a university and a contractor. One of the contract provisions called for arbitration of all disputes between the parties "arising out of or relating to this contract or the breach thereof." The contract also had a choice-of-law clause providing that "the Contract shall be governed by the law of the place where the Project is located." A dispute over compensation arose and the contractor made a formal demand for arbitration. The university responded by filing an action against the contractor in California Supreme Court alleging fraud and breach of contract and seeking indemnification from two other companies involved in the project, with whom it did not have arbitration agreements. The contractor moved to compel arbitration and the university moved to stay the arbitration pursuant to a California rule which permits a court to stay arbitration pending resolution of related litigation between a party to the arbitration agreement and third parties not bound by it.

The Supreme Court acknowledged its prior holdings on the preemptive effect of the FAA, but held that in this case the FAA did not preempt California law since the parties had agreed to abide by state rules on arbitration. California law, which the parties had agreed would govern, permits a court to stay arbitration pending resolution of related litigation involving third parties not bound by the arbitration agreement.

(h) *Allied-Bruce Terminix Companies, Inc. v. Dobson*, 513 U.S. 265, 115 S.Ct. 834, 130 L.Ed.2d 753 (1995). The Supreme Court considered the applicability of the FAA to a provision of an Alabama consumer protection statute that made predispute arbitration agreements invalid and unenforceable and reaffirmed the principles established in *Southland* regarding the broad reach of the FAA in state as well as federal courts. The plaintiff, a purchaser of Terminex termite protection services, argued that the FAA was applicable only where the parties contemplated interstate commerce. The Supreme Court rejected the plaintiff's narrow interpretation and held that the FAA reached all transactions that Congress could have regulated under its power to regulate interstate commerce. Thus, the plaintiff who sought to sue the termite exterminator for breach of contract, was required to arbitrate.

(i) *Mastrobuono v. Shearson Lehman Hutton, Inc.*, 514 U.S. 52, 115 S.Ct. 1212, 131 L.Ed.2d 76 (1995). This case involved an agreement that included both a state choice of law clause (New York) and an arbitration provision stating that disputes would be resolved under the rules of the National Association of Securities Dealers (NASD). While the NASD rules allow an award of punitive damages by arbitrators, New York state law does not. The Court limited the reach of *Volt*, holding that the agreement did not preclude an award of punitive damages and concluded in a significant passage:

At most, the choice-of-law clause introduces an ambiguity into an arbitration agreement that would otherwise allow punitive damage awards ... [W]hen a court interprets such provisions in an agreement covered by the FAA, "due regard must be given to the federal policy favoring arbitration, and ambiguities as to the scope of the arbitration clause itself resolved in favor of arbitration." ... We think the best way to harmonize the choice-of-law provision with the arbitration provision is to read "the laws of the State of New York" to encompass substantive principles that New York courts would apply, but not to include special rules limiting the authority of arbitrators. Thus, the choice-of-law provision covers the rights and duties of the parties, while the arbitration clause covers arbitration; neither sentence intrudes upon the other.

(j) ***Doctor's Associates, Inc. v. Casarotto***, 517 U.S. 681, 116 S.Ct. 1652, 134 L.Ed.2d 902 (1996). In this case the Supreme Court continued its endorsement of a contractual approach to arbitration law and invalidated a Montana statute that conditioned the enforceability of arbitration agreements on compliance with special notice requirements that were not applicable to contracts generally. The statute required that an arbitration clause be printed on the first page of the contract in underlined capital letters. The Court observed that while arbitration agreements could still be invalidated under "generally applicable contract defenses" such as fraud and unconscionability, courts and state legislatures could not focus on arbitration agreements and hold them to a higher level of scrutiny.

(k) **Buckeye Check Cashing, Inc. v. Cardegna**, 546 U.S. 440, 126 S.Ct. 1204, 163 L.Ed.2d 1038 (2006). In *Buckeye* the Supreme Court reaffirmed the strong federal policy favoring enforcement of arbitration agreements, recognizing the supremacy of the FAA over state laws on arbitration. The plaintiffs in Buckeye brought a class action suit against Buckeye Check Cashing claiming that its deferred-payment check cashing procedures were usurious loans that violated Florida law. The defendant Buckeye Check Cashing attempted to compel arbitration and to stay the court proceedings according to the arbitration provision in the Agreement signed by the plaintiffs. The plaintiffs argued that the court should not enforce the arbitration agreement because it was part of an illegal scheme. The case navigated from the trial court which denied Buckeye's motion to compel arbitration, to a state appellate

court, to the Florida Supreme Court which held
that enforcing an arbitration agreement in a contract challenged as unlawful would violate state
public policy and contract law. In addition to
upholding the supremacy of the FAA over state
law, the Court also reaffirmed the severability
rule of *Prima Paint,* and held that unless the
challenge is to the arbitration clause itself, the
issue of the contract's validity should be considered by the arbitrator in the first instance.

The Supreme Court recently re-affirmed its holding in *Buckeye* in *Preston v. Ferrer,* 552 U.S. ___,
128 S.Ct. 978 (2008).

Thus, it is clear from the Supreme Court's expansive interpretations in these cases that the FAA is a
source of substantive federal law that preempts all
conflicting state laws. A state statute can override
the strong pro-arbitration policy of the FAA only
where a choice of law provision in the parties'
underlying contact clearly expresses a mutual intent by them that the arbitration process is to be
controlled by the law of a particular state. Otherwise states may regulate arbitration contracts only
under general contract law principles and they may
do so only to the extent that arbitration contracts
are treated similarly to other contracts.

4. Adhesion and Unconscionability

The issues of adhesion and unconscionability
arise when a standardized contract, prepared by a
party with superior bargaining strength, is given
to another party on a "take it or leave it" basis.
The weaker party usually has very little choice re-

garding its terms. Such contracts lack true voluntariness and thus offend the traditional model of arbitration which requires that parties voluntarily assume a contractual undertaking to arbitrate their disputes.

Unequal bargaining power may exist in a variety of arbitration contexts including pre-dispute employment agreements, clauses requiring arbitration before biased panels and in contracts containing arbitration provisions involving sellers and consumers, franchiser and franchisees, physicians and patients, etc. Arbitration agreements with true adhesive characteristics will be set aside unless they satisfy what one court has labeled "minimum levels of integrity." For example, in *Graham v. Scissor–Tail, Inc.*, 28 Cal.3d 807, 171 Cal.Rptr. 604, 623 P.2d 165 (1981), the Supreme Court of California invalidated a standardized contract between a music promoter and musical group where one of the contract provisions required arbitration of disputes before the musician's union. The court considered the union to be presumptively biased in favor of one party and held the contract unconscionable and unenforceable.

Litigants may have difficulty, however, avoiding predispute arbitration agreements solely on the grounds of unequal bargaining power. In *Gilmer v. Interstate/Johnson Lane Corp.*, the Supreme Court stated that "Mere inequality of bargaining power, however, is not a sufficient reason to hold that arbitration agreements are never enforceable in the employment context." The Court cited its earlier holdings in *Rodriguez de Quijas* and *Shearson* that upheld the arbitrability of agreements between securities dealers and investors even though the relationship between those parties "... may involve unequal bargaining power." Relying on *Mitsubishi*, the Court indicated that in order for arbitration agreements to be set aside, litigants would have to establish "... well-supported claims that the agreement to arbitrate resulted from the sort of fraud or overwhelming economic power that would provide grounds 'for the revocation of any contract.' "

Scholars have criticized the lack of fairness in many consumer and employment arbitration contracts and several broad-based coalitions representing the interests of employers and employees, consumers, arbitrators and provider organizations have adopted protocols to insure procedural and substantive fairness in arbitration proceedings. See e.g., *Due Process Protocol for Mediation and Arbitration of Consumer Disputes* (1998), available at www.adr. org; *A Due Process Protocol For Mediation And Arbitration Of Statutory Disputes Arising Out Of The Employment Relationship* (1995) (Appendix). The Supreme Court has taken a strict position with respect to the issue of whether steep costs for consumer could invalidate an arbitration agreement. In *Green Tree Financial Corp.–Alabama v. Randolph*, 531 U.S. 79, 121 S.Ct. 513, 148 L.Ed.2d 373 (2000), the Court held that where a party claims that an arbitration agreement should be invalidated because arbitration costs would be prohibitively expensive, that party must "bear the burden of showing the likelihood of incurring such costs."

VII. THE ARBITRATION PROCEEDING

1. Provisional Relief

Provisional relief is a short-term remedy ordered by a court before a case is finally adjudicated on the merits. It is not uncommon for parties to a commercial arbitration agreement to seek such remedies as an injunction or attachment in order to maintain the status quo pending arbitration. The value of provisional relief in disputes was recognized by the Supreme Court in *Boys Markets, Inc. v. Retail Clerks Union, Local 770*, 398 U.S. 235, 90 S.Ct. 1583, 26 L.Ed.2d 199 (1970), a case arising under Section 301 of the Labor Management Relations Act (LMRA):

> [t]he injunction ... is so important a remedial device, particularly in the arbitration context, that its availability or non-availability in various courts will not only produce rampant forum shopping and maneuvering from one court to another but will also greatly frustrate any relative uniformity in the enforcement of arbitration agreements.

It should be noted that in Section 4 of the Norris-LaGuardia Act, 29 U.S.C.A. § 104, there is an explicit ban against preliminary injunctions pending arbitration of labor disputes. The Supreme Court's decision in *Boys Market* recognized that Section 301 of the LMRA contains a narrow exception to Section 4 of the Norris–LaGuardia Act.

The FAA gives little guidance on the availability of provisional remedies. Section 8 of the Federal Arbitration Act permits admiralty arbitration to begin by libel and seizure of the ship or other property of the opposing party. Otherwise, however, the FAA is silent regarding the ancillary power of a federal court to act, once it determines that a dispute is arbitrable. The UAA upon which many state arbitration statutes is based, omits any reference to allowing courts to order prejudgment relief.

In order to remedy this gap, the RUAA, Section 8 (Appendix), permits courts to grant provisional relief before an arbitrator is appointed in order to protect the effectiveness of the arbitration proceeding.

Most courts permit provisional relief to maintain the status quo pending arbitration. E.g., *Salvucci v. Sheehan*, 349 Mass. 659, 212 N.E.2d 243 (1965); *Merrill Lynch v. Salvano*, 999 F.2d 211 (7th Cir. 1993). Courts have adopted a variety of approaches when determining whether to grant injunctions pending arbitration. Some courts apply traditional equitable analysis, examining the four factors that are used for all other preliminary injunctions. The plaintiff must demonstrate: (1) irreparable harm if injunctive relief is not granted; (2) likelihood of success on the merits; (3) that the potential harm to the plaintiff outweighs the harm suffered by the defendant; and (4) that the public interest will not be harmed if the court grants the injunction. See *Teradyne, Inc. v. Mostek Corporation*, 797 F.2d 43 (1st Cir.1986).

Other courts analyze the language of the contract containing the arbitration clause and grant a preliminary injunction only if the language requires the parties to maintain the status quo pending the resolution of any disputes. E.g., *RGI, Inc. v. Tucker & Associates, Inc.*, 858 F.2d 227 (5th Cir.1988). Still, other courts grant preliminary injunctions if arbitration would not be able to compensate the parties for any injury incurred before the arbitrator rendered a decision. E.g., *Merrill Lynch, Pierce, Fenner & Smith, Inc. v. Bradley*, 756 F.2d 1048 (4th Cir.1985).

2. Initiating Arbitration

Arbitration may be initiated pursuant to a contractual provision or as a result of an ad hoc agreement to arbitrate. The agreement may be quite specific and provide for such concerns as the selection of the arbitrator, administration of the hearing, procedural rules and substantive law. If these details are not covered in the agreement or there is an ad hoc agreement to arbitrate, the parties may turn to specific agencies that administer arbitration.

Generally, a party would notify another party of her intent to arbitrate by sending a written demand for arbitration (Appendix). The RUAA, section 9 (Appendix), requires that this notice be given to all parties to the arbitration agreement and not simply to the party against whom an arbitration claim is filed. The demand would identify the parties, describe the dispute and the type of relief that is claimed. While the demand need not comply with the formalities of a complaint in a civil action, it must be sufficiently clear to inform the opposing party of the specific issues to be arbitrated. The opposing party would usually respond in writing, indicating whether it believed the dispute was arbitrable.

3.   Selection of Arbitrators

Assuming the disputing parties agree that their dispute is arbitrable, they will begin the arbitrator selection process. Generally, arbitrations are conducted by one arbitrator. It is not uncommon however, to have a panel of three arbitrators, two of whom would be chosen by the parties and a third who would be appointed by a joint decision of the party-selected arbitrators. Other methods for selecting arbitrators are included in the UAA, RUAA, FAA and various state arbitration statutes and agency rules. In the labor field, parties to a collective bargaining agreement might designate a permanent arbitrator in their original contract.

(i) Qualifications of the Arbitrator

The personal qualifications of arbitrators include: honesty, integrity, impartiality and general competence in the subject matter of the dispute. Beyond these general requirements, arbitration practice is generally an open field. Some systems however, such as court-annexed arbitration, require that attorneys serve as arbitrators.

(ii) Arbitral Immunity

Both state and federal courts recognize that arbitrators enjoy quasi-judicial immunity from civil liability for actions taken in their arbitral capacity. This principle has also been observed in the international commercial setting. Arbitral immunity is justified with the same policy considerations that apply to judicial immunity namely, that arbitrators perform an important societal function and therefore need to be protected from reprisals that could have a negative impact on their adjudicatory powers. The rationale for this principle, expressed long ago by the Massachusetts Supreme Judicial Court in *Hoosac Tunnel Dock & Elevator Co. v. O'Brien*, 137 Mass. 424 (Mass.1884), continues to influence the courts today:

> An arbitrator is a quasi judicial officer, under our laws, exercising judicial functions. There is as much reason in his case for protecting and insuring his impartiality, independence, and freedom from undue influences, as in the case of a judge or juror. The same considerations of public policy apply, and we are of opinion that the same immunity extends to him.

(iii) *Testimonial Immunity*

As a general rule, an arbitrator enjoys testimonial immunity and may not be required to testify regarding the merits of an award. There are, however, exceptions to this rule. For example, an arbitrator's testimony is permitted to show the fact that particular issues were submitted to arbitration for a decision. An arbitrator may also testify as to wrongful acts by one of the parties to the arbitration or even by other arbitrators on the panel.

4. The Arbitration Hearing

The requirements for the arbitration hearing vary from state to state but generally the hearing is similar in many respects to a trial. Both parties make opening statements and present their case to a neutral third party. Case presentations may include witnesses, documentation, and site inspections. The parties make closing arguments and may be required to submit briefs and memoranda in support of their position before the neutral renders a decision. The form of the hearings is essentially decided by the parties. Typically, the parties agree to abide by the rules of the agency that is administering the arbitration.

The arbitration process is different from the formality of litigation and trial in a number of respects. Arbitral factfinding is generally not equivalent to judicial factfinding. The record of the arbitration proceedings is not as complete. Written transcripts are usually unnecessary unless the parties decide to order them. The usual evidentiary rules are not applicable as the arbitrator has considerable discretion in the admission of evidence. Finally, rights such as discovery, compulsory process, cross-examination, and testimony under oath, are often limited.

5. Law Applied by the Arbitrator

The extent to which arbitrators should follow and apply substantive law remains unclear. The UAA, FAA and state statutes are silent on the application of law by the arbitrator. This is not surprising for, as the Supreme Court has observed, the majority of arbitrators are not lawyers and the specialized competence of arbitrators relates to "the law of the shop not the law of the land."

Certainly, the parties are free to specify in the arbitration clause, what rules of law will be applicable. In such cases, the arbitrator is bound to honor their request. Without such direction however, arbitrators are not bound by any uniform approach but only by their sense of justice. A study of commercial arbitration conducted several years ago by Professor Soia Mentschikoff attests to this approach. In her study, arbitrators were asked about their use of substantive rules of law in deciding cases. Eighty per cent of the arbitrators responded that they thought they should exercise decision-making power within the context of the principles of substantive law. At the same time, however, more than ninety per cent of these same arbitrators, thought that they could ignore substantive law if the interests of justice required it.

6.   Arbitration Ethics

Arbitrators act in a quasi-judicial capacity and therefore, they are held to the same high standards of impartiality by which judges are bound. In general, this means that arbitrators must avoid both the appearance and reality of conflict of interest and uphold the integrity and fairness of the arbitration process. It is important that potential arbitrators make a reasonable inquiry to determine whether any existing or prior financial, professional, family or social relationships might create an appearance of bias. If so, they should disclose this information in order to preserve the integrity of the arbitration process. As Justice White observed in his concurring opinion in *Commonwealth Coatings Corp. v. Continental Casualty Co.*, 393 U.S. 145, 89 S.Ct. 337, 21 L.Ed.2d 301 (1968): Arbitrators "should err on the side of disclosure" because "it is far better that the relationship be disclosed at the outset when the parties are free to reject the arbitrator or accept him with knowledge of the relationship." For a more recent court opinion that discusses the extent of an arbitrator's duty of disclosure, see *Positive Software Solutions, Inc. v. New Century Mortgage Corp.*, 436 F.3d 495 (5th Cir.2006).

In addition to disclosure issues, lawyers who work as arbitrators should also be mindful of ABA Model

Rule 1.12 that governs the circumstances under which former judges, arbitrators, mediators or other third-party neutrals may engage in future representation. Rule 1.12 is reprinted in the Appendix.

Two primary codes that provide ethical guidelines to individuals serving as commercial and labor arbitrators are: the Code of Professional Responsibility for Arbitrators of Labor-Management Disputes (amended 2007), available at www.naarb.org and the ABA/AAA Code of Ethics for Arbitrators in Commercial Disputes (2004) (Appendix). In the international context, ethical guidance is available to arbitrators in the IBA Guidelines on Conflicts of Interest in International Arbitration, approved by the International Bar Association on May 22, 2004.

The ethical obligations of organizations that provide arbitration services have been the subject of recent attention as arbitration practice has grown dramatically. In 2002, the CPR–Georgetown Commission on Ethics and Standards of Practice in alternative dispute resolution (ADR) published standards for ADR Provider Organizations, including arbitration providers. The standards are available at www.cpradr.org Some of the same standards that apply to individual arbitrators, such fairness, impartiality and, disclosure of conflicts of interest, also apply to provider organizations.

Ethical Responsibilities of Lawyers

Attorneys who represent clients in binding arbitration procedures should be mindful of the requirements of Model Rule 3.3, "Candor Toward the

Tribunal," which is reprinted in the Appendix. The term "tribunal" is defined in Model Rule 1.0 to include an arbitrator in a binding arbitration procedure.

VIII. THE ARBITRATION AWARD

An arbitration award is not self-executing. A party must bring a motion to confirm the award and it must be confirmed by the appropriate court before sanctions may be imposed for a party's failure to comply with it. Voluntary compliance with arbitral awards is usually high. Where parties are not satisfied with an award however, they have two options. First, they can refuse to comply with the award in which case the successful party must petition the court for confirmation of the award pursuant to FAA, Section 9. Alternatively, they can request that the appropriate court vacate the award pursuant to Section 10 or modify it pursuant to Section 11.

Traditionally, the courts have taken a narrow view of their role in reviewing arbitration awards and have focused their review on the limited vacatur standards established in the FAA. In an effort to expand judicial review, some parties have included "opt-in" provisions in their arbitration agreements in which they agree for judicial review of the merits of the awards. In essence, the parties are relying on the fundamental principle of freedom of contract that underlies arbitration law to vary the law. The courts have been divided on the merits of this practice. Relying on the Supreme Court's contractual view of the commercial arbitration process expressed in *Volt, Mastrobuono* and *First Options of Chicago*, some courts have upheld contractual provisions providing for increased judicial review of arbitral awards on grounds beyond those provided by the FAA. See e.g., *Gateway Technologies, Inc. v. MCI Telecommunications Corp.*, 64 F.3d 993 (5th Cir.1995). Other courts have opposed the practice. See e.g., *Hall Street Associates LLC v. Mattel, Inc.*, 196 Fed.Appx. 476 (9th Cir.2006).

1. Judicial Review of the Arbitration Award under the FAA

The FAA, Section 10(a) lists four grounds on which an award may be vacated:

(a) Where the award was procured by corruption, fraud, or undue means.

(b) Where there was evident partiality or corruption in the arbitrators, or either of them.

(c) Where the arbitrators were guilty of misconduct in refusing to postpone the hearing, upon sufficient cause shown, or in refusing to hear evidence pertinent and material to the controversy; or of any other misbehavior by which the rights of any party have been prejudiced.

(d) Where the arbitrators exceeded their powers, or so imperfectly executed them that a mutual, final, and definite award upon the subject matter submitted was not made.

Manifest Disregard of the Law

Case law has offered additional limited grounds for vacating an arbitrators' award. Dictum from the now overruled Supreme Court decision, *Wilko v. Swan*, 346 U.S. 427, 74 S.Ct. 182, 98 L.Ed. 168 (1953) suggests that an award may be set aside if it is in "manifest disregard" of the law. This term was never defined by the Supreme Court but a useful definition appears in *Merrill Lynch, Pierce, Fenner & Smith, Inc. v. Bobker*, 808 F.2d 930 (2nd Cir. 1986):

> The [arbitrator's] error must have been obvious and capable of being readily and instantly perceived by the average person qualified to serve as an arbitrator. Moreover, the term "disregard" implies that the arbitrator appreciates the existence of a clearly governing legal principle but decides to ignore or pay no attention to it.

Several federal courts have recognized the "manifest disregard of the law" standard in reviewing arbitration awards under the FAA and the Supreme Court has signaled its approval of this nonstatutory ground with a statement in *First Options of Chicago* that "parties [are] bound by [an] arbitrator's decision not in 'manifest disregard' of the law." More recently, some federal courts have taken a more expansive view and recognized manifest disregard of the evidence as a ground for vacating arbitration awards. See e.g. *Halligan v. Piper Jaffray, Inc.*, 148 F.3d 197 (2nd Cir.1998), cert. denied Piper Jaffray, Inc. v. Halligan, 526 U.S. 1034, 119 S.Ct. 1286, 143 L.Ed.2d 378 (1999).

Public Policy

In addition to the "manifest disregard" of the law nonstatutory ground for vacatur, arbitration awards may also be vacated on public policy grounds. The scope of review in such cases is limited to well defined policy based on legal precedent and is not simply based on speculative interests. The Supreme Court emphasized its commitment to this rule in *United Paperworkers International Union v. Misco, Inc.*, 484 U.S. 29, 108 S.Ct. 364, 98 L.Ed.2d 286 (1987) when it reversed a federal court decision that set aside an arbitrator's award on public policy grounds.

> A court's refusal to enforce an arbitrator's *interpretation* of a collective bargaining agreement is limited to situations where the contract as interpreted would violate "some explicit public policy" that is "well defined and dominant, and is to be ascertained by reference to the laws and legal precedents and not from general considerations of supposed public interests." [authorities omitted.]

Knowledge of the factual background in *Misco* is useful in understanding the depth of the Court's ruling. A Misco employee, Isiah Cooper, was discharged for allegedly violating his employer's drug rules. The employee had been found in the back seat of an automobile belonging to another person with a lighted marijuana cigarette in the front seat ashtray. The employee was then fired for violating the company rule against marijuana use on plant premise and he filed a grievance. Shortly before the arbitration hearing, the employer learned that the police searched the employee's car on the same day he had been found in the car with the marijuana cigarette and found gleanings of marijuana.

After a hearing the arbitrator upheld the grievance and directed the employer to reinstate the employee with back pay and full seniority. The arbitrator refused to accept into evidence the fact that marijuana had been found in the employee's car on company property because the employer did not know of this fact when the employee was discharged and thus did not rely on it as a basis for the discharge.

The Company filed an action in district court seeking to vacate the arbitration award on several grounds, one of which was that ordering reinstatement of Cooper was contrary to public policy. The district court vacated the arbitration award and the Court of Appeals affirmed. The Supreme Court reversed, holding that the Court of Appeals' public policy formulation was inadequate. Even if it were acceptable however, the Court concluded that no violation of that policy was demonstrated in this case.

Even though *Misco* involved labor arbitration, the Court's holding has been applied to all forms of arbitration. The Court reaffirmed the *Misco* doctrine in *Eastern Associated Coal Corp. v. United Mine Workers,* 531 U.S. 57, 121 S.Ct. 462, 148 L.Ed.2d 354 (2000) where it noted that in *Misco:*

The U.S. Supreme Court has made clear that a court's refusal to enforce an arbitrator's interpretation of a contract is limited to situations where the contract as interpreted would violate some explicit public policy that is well defined and dominant, and is to be ascertained by reference to the law and legal precedents, and not from general considerations of supposed public interests. [check quote]

2. Venue

The Supreme Court has taken a permissive view of the venue provisions in Sections 9 through 11 of the FAA. In *Cortez Byrd Chips, Inc. v. Bill Harbert Construction Co.*, 529 U.S. 193, 120 S.Ct. 1331, 146 L.Ed.2d 171 (2000) the Court held that the FAA's venue provisions are permissive rather than mandatory. Thus, a motion to confirm, vacate or modify an arbitration award may be brought either in the district where the award was made or in any district proper under the general venue statute.

3. Punitive Damages

Punitive or exemplary damages may be defined as those that exceed compensatory damages and that are awarded to punish a person for outrageous conduct. Public policy disfavors granting punitive awards that in most states requires a finding of some type of moral culpability.

Generally, punitive damages are disfavored in labor arbitration unless the collective bargaining agreement specifically provides for them. Labor arbitration usually involves parties who have an ongoing relationship, and it is thought that awarding punitive damages in this context could undercut the parties' confidence in the arbitration process.

Judicial review of an arbitrator's award of punitive damages in commercial arbitration cases depends upon the jurisdiction in which the award is granted. The courts have adopted three approaches. Several courts have upheld an arbitrator's power to award punitive damages unless this power is specifically excluded in the contract. A second approach permits the award of punitive damages only if the parties' agreement to arbitrate specifically provided for punitive damage awards. A minority of states, led by New York, hold that arbitrators have no power to award punitive damages even if they are agreed to by the parties. The rationale for this view as expressed by the New York Court of Appeals in *Garrity v. Lyle Stuart, Inc.*, 40 N.Y.2d 354, 386 N.Y.S.2d 831, 353 N.E.2d 793 (1976), rejected Belko v. AVX Corp., 251 Cal.Rptr. 557 (1988) is that giving such powers to arbitrators displaces the Court's power. The Supreme Court diluted the impact of *Garrity* in *Mastrobuono v. Shearson Lehman Hutton, Inc.*, 514 U.S. 52, 115 S.Ct. 1212, 131 L.Ed.2d 76 (1995) when it upheld an arbitration award of punitive damages by an NASD panel even though the parties had a New York choice-of-law provision in the pre-dispute arbitration agreement. The continuing vitality of *Garrity* is also questionable in light of the New York Appellate Division's decision in *Mulder v. Donaldson, Lufkin & Jenrette*, 224 A.D.2d 125, 648 N.Y.S.2d 535 (N.Y.A.D. 1 Dept. 1996).

Judicial review of punitive damages awards under present law is limited to the same statutory standards for vacatur of other arbitration awards. An aggrieved party would have to establish that in awarding punitive damages, the arbitrators were guilty of corruption, fraud, undue means, evident partiality, misconduct or exceeding their powers. An award will also be vacated if a party has failed to receive a fundamentally fair hearing or if it is not consistent with the substantive state law governing the arbitration.

4. Res Judicata, Collateral Estoppel and Arbitration

Arbitration's significant expansion raises critical questions concerning the preclusive effects of an arbitrator's decision in litigation arising from disputes that have been resolved in a prior arbitration. Under the doctrine of res judicata, also known as claim preclusion, a final judgment on the merits of an action precludes the parties or their privies from relitigating issues that were or could have been raised in that action. Collateral estoppel, also known as issue preclusion, applies to a subsequent suit between the parties on a different cause of action. Once a court has decided an issue of fact or law necessary to its judgment, that decision may preclude relitigation of the issue in a suit on a different cause of action involving a party to the first case. These doctrines developed at common law to relieve parties of the transaction costs associated with multiple lawsuits, and to promote finality and judicial economy by bringing an end to litigation.

It is well-settled that the doctrines of res judicata and collateral estoppel apply to arbitration awards. Section 84 of the *Restatement (Second) of Judgments* provides:

(1) . . . a valid and final award by arbitration has the same effects under the rules of res judicata, subject to the same exceptions and qualifications, as a judgment of a court.

(2) An award by arbitration with respect to a claim does not preclude relitigation of the same or a related claim based on the same transaction if a scheme of remedies permits assertion of the second claim notwithstanding the award regarding the first claim.

(3) A determination of an issue in arbitration does not preclude relitigation of that issue if:

(a) According preclusive effect to determination of the issue would be incompatible with a legal policy or contractual provision that the tribunal in which the issue subsequently arises be free to make an independent determination of the issue in question, or with a purpose of the arbitration agreement that the arbitration be specially expeditious; or

(b) The procedure leading to the award lacked the elements of adjudicatory procedure prescribed in § 83(2).

(4) If the terms of an agreement to arbitrate limit the binding effect of the award in another adjudication or arbitration proceeding, the extent to which the award has conclusive effect is determined in accordance with that limitation.

In recent years the Supreme Court has limited the claim and issue preclusion effects of arbitral awards where employees' federal statutory rights have been implicated under Title VII of the 1964 Civil Rights Act, the Fair Labor Standards Act and 42 U.S.C.A. § 1983. The major cases in this area are discussed below:

(a) In *Alexander v. Gardner–Denver Co.*, 415 U.S. 36, 94 S.Ct. 1011, 39 L.Ed.2d 147 (1974) the Court considered the preclusive effect of an arbitral award in connection with an employee's statutory right to a trial de novo under Title VII. The factual background involved a discharged employee who filed a grievance under a collective-bargaining agreement that contained a broad arbitration clause. The employee also claimed that his discharge resulted from racial discrimination and he filed a racial discrimination complaint with the Colorado Civil Rights Commission. This was referred to the Equal Employment Opportunity Commission. Following an arbitration hearing at which the arbitrator held that his discharge was for cause and an EEOC determination that there was no reasonable ground to believe that a Title VII violation had occurred, the employee brought an action in district court alleging that his discharge resulted from racial discrimination. The district court granted Gardner-Denver's motion for summary judgment holding that the employee was bound by the prior arbitral decision and had no right to sue under Title VIII. The Court of Appeals affirmed. The Supreme Court reversed and declined to adopt a preclusion rule on the theory that the employee was asserting a statutory right "independent" of the arbitration process and was not seeking review of the arbitrator's decision.

Writing for the majority, Justice Powell opined that while the informality of arbitration procedures are well-suited to resolve contractual disputes, they are "inappropriate" to resolve Title VII rights. Arbitration was considered by the Court to be inferior to the judicial process in resolving Title VII claims because of the familiar laundry list of arbitration deficiencies:

> ... the specialized competence of arbitrators pertains primarily to the law of the shop, not the law of the land ... authorities omitted ... the factfinding process in arbitration usually is not equivalent to judicial factfinding. The record of the arbitration proceedings is not as complete; the usual rules of evidence do not apply; and rights and procedures common to civil trials, such as discovery, compulsory process, cross-examination, and testimony under oath, are often severely limited or unavailable.

Postscript on Alexander

In *Gilmer v. Interstate/Johnson Lane Corp.*, 500
U.S. 20, 111 S.Ct. 1647, 114 L.Ed.2d 26 (1991), the
Court retracted its statement regarding the inferi-
ority of arbitration to the judicial process for resolving statutory claims. The factual background of
Gilmer involved a nonunion workplace setting and
the Court permitted a prospective waiver of a judicial forum for claims arising under the federal Age
Discrimination in Employment Act (ADEA). This
holding seemed to be in conflict with *Alexander*
wherein the Court held that statutory rights were
not subject to prospective waiver. In *Wright v. Universal Maritime Service Corp.*, 525 U.S. 70, 119
S.Ct. 391, 142 L.Ed.2d 361 (1998), a case arising
under the Americans with Disability Act of 1990
(ADA), the Supreme Court recognized the tension
between *Gilmer* and *Alexander* but did not resolve
the differences between the two cases.

The issue in *Wright* was whether an employee's
collective bargaining agreement that provided for
arbitration precluded a judicial forum for his claim
under the ADA. The Court held that an employee
must be allowed to present statutory claims in court
unless there is a clear waiver of this right. The
Court declined, however, to decide the validity of
the union-negotiated waiver in *Wright* because it
concluded that the provision in the contract before
it, establishing a grievance procedure including arbitration for "[m]atters under dispute which cannot
be promptly settled" was not a "clear and unmis-

takable" waiver of the right to a judicial forum for resolving statutory employment disputes.

(b) In *Barrentine v. Arkansas–Best Freight System, Inc.*, 450 U.S. 728, 101 S.Ct. 1437, 67 L.Ed.2d 641 (1981) the Supreme Court again declined to defer to an arbitral decision where an employee's claim was based on rights arising out of the Fair Labor Standards Act [FLSA], a statute that was designed to provide minimum substantive protections to individual workers. The Court offered two rationales to support its denial of preclusion in this case. First, even if the employee had a meritorious claim, his union might decide for good reason not to support the claim strongly in arbitration. Second, even assuming that the union fairly presents the employee's wage claims, statutory rights might still not be adequately protected. Since arbitrators must follow the intent of the parties, rather than enforce the statute, they could issue rulings that were against the public policy underlying the FLSA.

(c) In *McDonald v. City of West Branch*, 466 U.S. 284, 104 S.Ct. 1799, 80 L.Ed.2d 302 (1984) the Supreme Court relied on its earlier holdings in *Alexander v. Gardner–Denver Co.* and *Barrentine v. Arkansas–Best Freight System, Inc.* and denied preclusive effect to an unappealed arbitration award in an action arising under 42 U.S.C.A. § 1983. Gary McDonald was discharged from the police force and filed a grievance pursuant to the collective bargaining agreement between the City of West Branch and the union, contending that there was "no proper cause" for his discharge. The grievance was taken to arbitration and the arbitrator ruled against Mc-Donald. Subsequently, McDonald filed an action under 42 U.S.C.A. § 1983 against the city and certain officials including the Chief of Police, alleging that he was discharged for exercising his First Amendment rights. A jury returned a verdict against the Chief of Police which was reversed by the Court of Appeals. The Court of Appeals found that the arbitration process had not been abused and that McDonald's First Amendment claims were barred by res judicata and collateral estoppel.

The Supreme Court reversed the Court of Appeals and offered four reasons why judicial dispute resolution was preferable to arbitration in section 1983 cases. First, an arbitrator may not have the expertise to resolve the complex legal questions that arise in these cases. Second, an arbitrator may not have the authority to enforce section 1983 because his authority is derived solely from the contract. Third, the union may not make a vigorous presentation of the employee's case in arbitration. Finally, arbitral factfinding is less comprehensive than judicial factfinding.

IX. INTERNATIONAL ARBITRATION

Arbitration is a favored method of resolving international commercial disputes for the same reason that it is appealing on the domestic front: speed, low cost, privacy, expertise of the decisionmaker and procedural flexibility. At the international level, arbitration has additional advantages that include avoiding the unknown in a foreign courtroom and obtaining jurisdiction over foreign parties. In practice, however, international arbitration may be more expensive and protracted than domestic arbitration.

Parties may participate in administered arbitration where they seek administrative assistance from organizations such as the American Arbitration Association (AAA) and the International Chamber of Commerce (ICC), both of which provide detailed rules for arbitration proceedings. Or they may prefer to conduct the arbitration themselves on an "ad hoc" basis. More recently, specialized forums for resolving disputes through arbitration have been established. The International Center for Settlement of Investment Disputes (ICSID) was established to provide foreign investors with a forum for resolving investment disputes. With the growth of Bilateral Investment Treaties (BITS) there has been a significant increase in arbitrations conducted under ICSID.

International arbitration law in the United States is governed by both state and federal statutes. At the federal level, the FAA applies to contracts involving interstate and foreign commerce, as well as maritime transactions. Chapter 2 of the FAA has provisions that implement the United Nations Convention on the Recognition and Enforcement of Foreign Arbitral Awards, also known as the "New York Convention." This significant international agreement to which the United States is a party, provides for the recognition of arbitration agreements and for the enforcement of foreign arbitral awards. Article III provides:

[e]ach Contracting State shall recognize arbitral awards as binding and enforce them in accordance with the rules of procedure of the territory where the award is relied upon, under the conditions laid down in the following articles. There shall not be imposed substantially more onerous conditions or higher fees or charges on the recognition or enforcement of arbitral awards to which this Convention applies than are imposed on the recognition or enforcement of domestic arbitral awards.

At the state level, every state has enacted its own arbitration statute that applies to intrastate arbitrations. In recent years, a number of states have enacted laws specifically governing international arbitration in an effort to create a hospitable climate for international commerce and trade. Many of these statutes are much more detailed than the FAA and include provisions for such items as jurisdiction, choice of law, grounds for challenging the arbitrators, and arbitrator appointment procedure. Some states have drafted their statutes in accordance with the UNCITRAL Model Law on International Commercial Arbitration.

Arbitration Bibliography

J.J. Barcelo III, *Who Decides the Arbitrator's Jurisdiction? Separability and Competence–Competence in Transnational Perspective,* 36 Vand. J. Transnat'l L. 1115 (2003);

T. Carbonneau, *Cases and Materials on Arbitration* Law and Practice, 4th edition (2007);

L. Cooper, D. Nolan & R. Bales, *ADR in the Workplace*, 2nd edition (2005);

F. Elkouri et al., ed., *How Arbitration Works: Elkouri & Elkouri* (6th ed. 2003);

S. Goldberg, F. Sander, N. Rogers, S. Cole, *Dispute Resolution: Negotiation, Mediation, and Other Processes,* 5th ed. (2007);

P. Haagen, Editor, *Arbitration Now: Opportunities for Fairness, Process Renewal and Invigoration*, (ABA Section of Dispute Resolution 1999);

S. Hayford, *Reining in the "Manifest Disregard" of the Law Standard: The Key to Restoring Order to the Law of Vacatur*, 1998 J. Disp. Resol. 117;

S. Hayford, *Law in Disarray: Judicial Standards for Vacatur of Commercial Arbitration Awards*, 30 Ga. L. Rev. 731 (1996);

L. Hirshman, *The Second Arbitration Trilogy: The Federalization of Arbitration Law*, 71 Va. L. Rev. 1305 (1985);

R. Holtzman, *Arbitrator Ethics in the 21st Century*, in P. Haagen, Editor, *Arbitration Now: Opportunities for Fairness, Process Renewal and Invigoration* 159 (ABA Section of Dispute Resolution 1999);

S. Huber & M. Weston, *Arbitration: Cases and Materials*, 2nd edition (2006);

L. Kanowitz, *Alternative Dispute Resolution and the Public Interest: The Arbitration Experience*, 38 Hastings L. J. 239 (1987);

C. Katsoris, *Punitive Damages in Securities Arbitration: The Tower of Babel Revisited*, 18 Fordham Urb. L. J. 573 (1991);

I. MacNeil, R. Speidel and T. Stipanowich, *Federal Arbitration Law: Agreements, Awards, and Remedies Under the Federal Arbitration Act* (1994);

S. Mentschikoff, *Commercial Arbitration,* 61 Colum. L. Rev. 846 (1961);

D. Nolan, *Labor and Employment Arbitration in a Nutshell*, 2nd edition (2006);

A. Rau, E. Sherman and S. Peppet, *Processes of Dispute Resolution: The Role of Lawyers,* 4th edition (2006);

D. Schwartz, *Enforcing Small Print to Protect Big Business: Employee and Consumer Rights Claims in an Age of Compelled Arbitration*, 1997 Wis. L. Rev. 33;

T. Stipanowich, *Punitive Damages and the Consumerization of Arbitration*, 92 Nw. U. L. Rev. 1 (1997);

S. Ware, *Arbitration and Unconscionability After Doctor's Associates, Inc. v. Casarotto*, 31 Wake Forest L. Rev. 1001 (1996);

G. M. Wilner, *Domke on Commercial Arbitration* (3rd edition 2003).

CHAPTER 5

DISPUTE RESOLUTION IN THE COURT SYSTEM

The growing popularity of ADR within the justice system offers litigants the opportunity to resolve disputes in a broader systems framework than the traditional litigation process. Courts today are making greater use of the primary dispute resolution processes of negotiation, mediation and arbitration, in addition to the traditional judicial settlement conference. Mediation is now the most common form of court-connected ADR in federal district courts.

Hybrid mechanisms such as the summary jury trial and early neutral evaluation programs have been established in most courts, using third parties to facilitate negotiation and help manage cases in an efficient and responsive manner. Finally, one of the most significant developments in court ADR is the expanding use of magistrates, special masters and neutral experts. In short, the full panoply of judicial ADR developments shows that federal and state court systems are struggling to meet the demands for qualitative and quantitative justice.

One of the most important pieces of legislation to integrate ADR in the court system is the Alternative Dispute Resolution Act of 1998, 28 U.S.C.A. § 652 (ADRA). The Act, which follows in the wake of the Civil Justice Reform Act of 1990, requires that every federal district court implement an ADR program at the local level and offer at least one ADR process to litigants. Federal courts are authorized to mandate participation in mediation and early neutral evaluation but they must obtain the parties' consent for court-annexed arbitration. One of the difficulties with ADRA is that no procedural guidelines were established to assist courts in implementing ADR programs. Thus, important issues such as confidentiality are left to the discretion of individual courts.

The institutionalization of ADR within the court system has not been without criticism. As courts focus more on settlement than adjudication, scholars and public policy advocates have expressed concern that judges may neglect their adjudicative roles and that the flexibility and informality of ADR processes may be at odds with parties' due process rights. Additionally, evaluations of court annexed ADR programs have yielded mixed results regarding the effectiveness of ADR in reducing cost and delay.

I. COURT–ANNEXED ARBITRATION

The diversion of specified cases to arbitration is expected to result in expeditious settlements. In some cases, this may happen where the diversion acts as an incentive to a pre-hearing settlement. In other situations, the parties may accept the arbitrator's award or, the arbitrator's decision may act as a stimulus to negotiations between the parties. Attorneys are required to participate in good faith and risk sanctions for their failure to do so.

Court-annexed arbitration differs from the traditional arbitration model in a number of respects. It operates under the court's supervision and thus lacks the private and consensual attributes of traditional arbitration. Litigants have the right to a trial *de novo* if they are not satisfied with the arbitrator's award. In some systems, however, litigants must pay court costs or arbitrators' fees if they do not better their position at trial. This of course is a disincentive to exercising a right to trial *de novo*.

Court-annexed programs have survived seventh amendment challenges as long as there are no substantial restrictions placed on the right to a jury trial. Courts typically find that the burden imposed on parties by compulsory arbitration is usually outweighed by the benefits of a speedy, less expensive and more efficient trial system. The leading case upholding the constitutionality of compulsory arbitration is *Application of Smith*, 381 Pa. 223, 112 A.2d 625 (1955). A local court rule authorized compulsory arbitration in all cases involving claims less than $10,000.00. Responding to a challenge based on Pennsylvania's constitutional provisions for the right to a jury trial, the Pennsylvania Supreme Court held that:

> [t]he only purpose of the constitutional provision is to secure the right of trial by jury before rights of person or property are *finally* determined. All

that is required is that the right of appeal for the purpose of presenting the issue to a jury must not be burdened by the imposition of onerous conditions, restrictions or regulations which would make the right practically unavailable.

A number of studies have been conducted on the effect of court-annexed arbitration on the quality of the justice system. While litigants generally perceive the system to be beneficial and fair, there is some dispute as to whether court-annexed arbitration significantly reduces judicial time and public costs. In fact, some commentators believe that the growing formality of these programs may actually increase costs and delays.

II. COURT–ANNEXED MEDIATION

In recent years, mediation has become the most favored ADR option in the courts, and not surprisingly, lawyers play a dominant role in it. Typically, court mediation programs establish rules that define the types of cases subject to mediation, procedures to refer cases to mediation, and certification of mediators. Court programs are both voluntary and mandatory, and sanctions may be imposed on parties who refuse to participate in mediation. The subject of mandatory mediation is a topic of ongoing concern as scholars criticize statutes that require good faith participation in mediation. While court mediation programs have been advanced as a way to save time and reduce costs, studies vary on the validity of these claims. Empirical research does show, however, that timing is a relevant factor in determining whether mediation reduces costs. The earlier a case is referred to mediation, the greater the likelihood that settlement will occur.

Appellate courts have also developed mediation programs following the lead of the U.S. Court of Appeals for the Second Circuit with its Civil Appeals Management Plan (CAMP). Appeals are mediated by attorneys. Courts differ on whether the focus is case management or settlement and whether clients are allowed to participate.

III.   THE SUMMARY JURY TRIAL

1.   Overview

The summary jury trial (SJT) facilitates settlement by giving lawyers and their clients an advance assessment of what a jury might do in a given case. It is a nonbinding process in which lawyers present a brief synopsis of their case to a jury which then renders a non-binding, advisory decision. After attending the SJT, parties with settlement authority try to reach an agreement. If settlement is not reached, the parties are still entitled to a full trial in court. Although the majority of federal district courts authorize the use of the SJT, in recent years actual usage has been low.

The SJT was developed by Judge Thomas Lambros of the United States District Court for the Northern District of Ohio in an effort to alleviate overcrowded dockets in the civil justice system. Judge Lambros theorized that disputing parties would be more willing to settle cases and forego trials if they had a reasonable prediction of what a jury would do in their case. He relied on Rule 16 FRCP (Appendix) for authority to convene the SJT.

The 1993 amendments to Rule 16 expanded the authority of federal courts to explore settlement possibilities through the SJT. According to the Revised Drafter's notes: "Even if a case cannot immediately be settled, the judge and attorneys can explore possible use of alternative procedures such as . . . summary jury trials . . . that can lead to consensual resolution of the dispute without a full trial on the merits." The extent to which courts will do this is unclear, however, given the omission of summary jury trials from the list of permissible mandatory dispute resolution processes in the Alternative Dispute Resolution Act of 1998, 28 U.S.C.A. Sec. 652(a):

> Any district court that elects to require the use of alternative dispute resolution in certain cases may do so only with respect to mediation, early neutral evaluation, and, if the parties consent, arbitration.

2. Governing Principles

Traditional settlement discussions often fail when the parties' perceptions of the merits of a case are significantly different from those of their adversary. Differing views of the merits of a case result from a number of factors. Lawyers may assess a potential outcome on a key issue erroneously. The parties may have an unrealistic assessment of what the potential outcome will be at trial, where they have an exaggerated sense of the worth of their case. This may result from poor client counseling on the part of their lawyers or from their own expectations. For example, the severely injured victim in a product liability case would not be willing to settle for one million dollars if he thinks that a jury will award him three million dollars. After learning that SJT jurors had awarded him $500,000.00 in damages following the SJT, the injured victim and his lawyer might be more inclined to settle the case for one million dollars.

The SJT is useful for cases that will probably not settle in traditional settlement negotiations where parties usually rely on the lawyer's or judge's sense of case evaluation. Based on prior experience, each side and the judge come up with a set of numbers. When this occurs, the parties cannot come to a meeting of the minds because of differing expectations about the value of a case. The SJT acts as the agent of reality and the tie-breaker. On the other hand, the SJT may not be advisable where the credibility of a witness is the critical issue in the case. Given the inherent time constraints of the process, it is generally not possible to subject witnesses to the full examination of trial. But parties have employed live witness testimony and cross examination in SJT's when necessary to resolve a factual issue. Finally, where a question of law is unsettled and needs to be resolved by a court, the SJT is usually not appropriate.

3. The Summary Jury Trial Process

The SJT usually takes place after discovery has been substantially completed and pending motions have been resolved. Where parties target their discovery toward critical or key issues focused on settlement, the SJT can be conducted at an earlier time while reserving complex discovery for any trial that may occur. Because it is designed to be a flexible device, procedures vary in different courts. Under the Lambros model, the trial is conducted in a courtroom with either a judge or magistrate presiding. Lawyers for each side submit a trial brief on the issues of law as well as proposed jury instructions.

A six member advisory jury is selected from the regular jury panel through an abbreviated voir dire examination. Each side is allowed two peremptory challenges. In most cases the jurors are not told that their verdict is nonbinding until the SJT is completed. Clients are required to attend the trial and corporate clients must be represented by an agent with settlement authority.

Lawyers make opening statements and then make summary presentations of their cases. The summarizations must be based on admissible evidence. Formal objections are discouraged. Some courts have allowed live witness testimony. Following rebuttal and closing arguments by counsel, the court charges the jury on the law and the jury then renders a consensus verdict. If jurors are unable to reach consensus, they may return individual verdicts describing each juror's opinion on liability and damages.

Post-trial proceedings begin with a debriefing session in which counsel for both parties have an opportunity to question the jurors after the verdict is rendered. This session gives the parties valuable insight on the individual juror's reaction to their cases. What evidence worked? Which arguments fell flat? Which facts were deemed weak? What swayed the jurors? The parties with settlement authority then meet privately to conduct settlement discussions in light of the jury's verdict. Regardless of the outcome of the SJT, the parties retain the right to a full trial on the merits.

The total hearing usually lasts for one day but it may be longer. Parties who use the SJT generally seek the same degree of confidentiality that settlement negotiations enjoy. The proceedings generally are not recorded. No statements, communications or jury findings from the SJT are admissible at a later trial on the merits.

4.   Major Advantages of the Summary Jury Trial

The SJT simulates an actual trial from voir dire to jury instruction thereby giving parties who want their day in court a taste of the real thing without the risks and costs of a full blown trial. The major advantages of the SJT are the predictive feature of the advisory jury verdict combined with the wide range of settlement possibilities that parties can pursue in the negotiation phase without being bound by any decision of a jury. When the parties have advance notice of what a jury is likely to do, they have a more reasonable understanding of the parameters of the settlement range. Clients have a realistic incentive to settle because they have learned first-hand from watching the SJT the strengths and weaknesses of their case.

Another advantage of the SJT is the savings in time and money which would have been spent on a full trial. Attorneys' fees are considerably reduced because the proceeding is short. Even if the SJT does not result in settlement, the lawyers' time and effort in preparing for the SJT has not been wasted. The parties have organized their cases, the issues have been refined and the resulting trial should be a more efficient process.

The SJT also benefits the courts by providing new case management options in appropriate situations. Every case does not have to run the full nine yards for the litigants to experience a just resolution of their cases. Anecdotal reports show a great time savings to the courts. For example, in *McKay v. Ashland Oil, Inc.*, 120 F.R.D. 43 (E.D.Ky.1988), the court wrote: "In my own experience summary jury trials have netted me a savings in time of about 60 days and I have only used the procedure five times. It settled two of these cases that were set for 30–day trials." Judge Lambros reports that he has used the procedure successfully in over 1,000 mass toxic tort cases. In general, reports show that the SJT has been used successfully in a wide range of actions including: negligence, products liability, toxic tort, personal injury, contract, discrimination, admiralty and antitrust. Certainly there is room for more empirical studies of the SJT before a final assessment of its value can be made.

5. Criticisms of the Summary Jury Trial

Some judges and lawyers have raised several concerns about the value of SJTs. First, some critics argue that because lawyers make the major case presentations, there is no cross-examination of witnesses, and therefore, the SJT fails to assess the credibility of witnesses. Unless credibility is the central issue however, parties can test credibility through the use of documentary evidence and abbreviated cross-examination. A second criticism argues that the transaction costs of preparing for the SJT may actually increase the cost of litigation if the process does not result in settlement. Such preparation, however, can also reduce the costs of the eventual trial. Finally, there are concerns with protecting confidentiality. Critics argue that compelling parties to participate in the SJT may result in disclosure of privileged information. While some courts do compel use, others require voluntary agreements if the process is employed. Moreover, the evidence is subject to court admissibility standards.

6. Case Law Development

(i) Power to Compel Parties to Participate

The SJT has spurned considerable cases and commentary related to the legal power of a federal court to order parties to participate in the process. Supporters of the SJT believe that the authority for requiring parties to participate in SJTs derives from two sources: the inherent power of the court to manage its calendar and the pre-trial powers of a court pursuant to Rule 16 of the Federal Rules of Civil Procedure (Appendix). Rule 16 gives judges substantial pre-trial authority.

Most courts that have considered the compulsion issue, have held, however, that mandating participation in a SJT is a permissible exercise of judicial power, e.g., *McKay v. Ashland Oil, Inc.*, 120 F.R.D. 43 (E.D.Ky.1988). A few courts, notably, *Strandell v. Jackson County*, 838 F.2d 884 (7th Cir.1987), have held that the use of mandatory summary jury trials is an unwarranted extension of judicial power. *Strandell* involved a criminal contempt charge against an attorney who represented a civil rights plaintiff. The attorney refused to participate in a SJT after being ordered to do so by the court because he believed that it required him to reveal privileged information. This would result in giving his opponents an unfair advantage. The Seventh Circuit Court of Appeals vacated his contempt judgment holding that the pre-trial conference of Rule 16 was intended simply to generate settlement discussions and not "to require that an unwilling litigant be sidetracked from the normal course of litigation." See also *In re NLO, Inc.*, 5 F.3d 154 (6th Cir.1993).

(ii) Right of Access

Use of the SJT has also raised First Amendment questions, specifically, whether the right of press access into the courtroom attaches to the SJT. In *Cincinnati Gas & Electric Co. v. General Electric Co.*, 854 F.2d 900 (6th Cir.1988) the Sixth Circuit Court of Appeals held that the First Amendment right of access does not apply to the SJT on the theory that the "summary jury trial does not present any matter for adjudication by the court." The court also observed that the SJT is similar to a settlement discussion which historically has been considered a private proceeding and concluded that public access to this proceeding would not add anything to its effectiveness.

(iii) Authority of the Court to Empanel the Advisory Jury

A court's authority to empanel advisory jurors was sharply questioned in *Hume v. M & C Management*, 129 F.R.D. 506 (N.D.Ohio 1990) wherein a federal district court judge wrote that courts "... have no authority to summon citizens to serve as settlement advisors, just as they would have no authority to summon citizens to serve as hand servants for themselves, lawyers or litigants."

Both parties in *Hume* asked the court to convene a SJT according to the Lambros model following unsuccessful settlement discussions in a Fair Housing case. The court denied the motion on the grounds that federal judges lacked authority to require citizens to serve as jurors in the SJT. The court based its holding on a provision in the Jury Selection and Service Act of 1968 that requires citizens to serve only on "grand" and "petit" juries. In a footnote reference to Judge Posner's criticisms of the SJT, the court noted that SJT's could compromise the integrity of the jury system.

IV. EARLY NEUTRAL EVALUATION

1. Overview

Early Neutral Evaluation (ENE) originated as a form of judicial, court-annexed ADR that involved early, systematic case assessment by a private attorney experienced in the substantive area of the dispute. The objective analysis by a neutral evaluator forces attorneys and their clients to confront their own and their opponent's case at an early juncture in the litigation process before adversarial pre-trial battles blind them to opportunities for settlement.

The first ENE program began on an experimental basis in the Northern District of California in 1985. As a result of the program's success, it became a permanent feature of that court in 1988. ENE programs have now expanded to other federal districts and to the private sector. Based on the limited empirical studies to date, the extent to which ENE programs actually assist settlement and reduce cost is unclear. Nevertheless, many judges are enthusiastic about ENE programs because of their value in narrowing issues and helping parties to become more realistic.

2.   How ENE Operates

An ENE procedure based on the Northern District of California model operates generally in the following manner. After the first status conference, parties are required to attend a confidential evaluation session directed by a court-appointed lawyer who is experienced in the substantive area of the dispute. At least seven days before the evaluation session, the parties must submit written statements identifying significant issues, the type of discovery which would be helpful in shaping settlement and the names of any representatives of the opposing party whose presence would assist in settlement. The court orders the client to attend the evaluation session.

A typical session begins with an opening statement by the neutral evaluator. The parties then present a narrative of their case and exchange detailed information. The rules of evidence do not apply and there is no formal examination or cross-examination of witnesses. All communications at the evaluation session are protected from disclosure.

Following the parties' case presentation, the neutral offers assistance in a number of ways: by helping the parties identify their areas of agreement and entering into stipulations where appropriate; by assessing the strengths and weakness of the parties' arguments and evidence; by estimating, where feasible, the likelihood of liability and the dollar range of damages as a spur to settlement; and by helping the parties make a plan for conducting discovery. It may well be, however, that the parties are willing to share more information after the presentations and therefore, extensive discovery will not be necessary. The evaluator may also assist in mediating settlement discussions arising from the evaluation.

3. On the Merits

ENE bears some resemblance to the mini-trial and the judicial status conference but there are definite differences. Compared to the mini-trial, ENE is a less complicated procedure. The parties and their lawyers are required to attend the evaluation session and the neutral evaluator is chosen by the court, not the parties. Proponents of ENE suggest that it is more productive than the typical judicial status conference because the neutral evaluator is not bound by the ethical and time constraints imposed upon judges and can therefore probe more deeply into the dispute than judges are able to do. Discussions are more focused and the parties therefore have a better understanding of the parameters of the dispute.

The key to successful use of ENE as with all ADR processes, lies in identification of the appropriate cases. Experience thus far suggests that the type of cases that can benefit from ENE are commercial contract and tort cases where there are obvious, clear-cut differences between the parties regarding the valuation of the case. In some situations, ENE may be appropriate for only some issues such as differences over the amount of damages, while other issues may more suited for mediation, arbitration or litigation.

V. MAGISTRATES, SPECIAL MASTERS, AND NEUTRAL EXPERTS

The growth of multi-party, complex litigation such as the asbestos, Dalkon Shield and Agent Orange cases, has strained judicial resources and forced the civil justice system to develop new and more efficient methods of case management. Towards this end, the courts have made increased use of magistrates, special masters, and neutral experts to assist with settlement efforts and to develop claims facilities in mass tort and other complex cases. The individuals appointed in these cases are usually either retired judges, lawyers with technical expertise or lawyers with specialized knowledge in a substantive area such as environmental law or toxic torts. As judicial adjuncts, they are not constrained by the limitations imposed on Article III judges. Theoretically, they have more time to spend on managing cases and are therefore more accessible to the litigants. They are also more free to explore settlement techniques than the assigned judges who may have to try the case if settlement attempts fail and, therefore, cannot get deeply embroiled in mediation attempts.

Of course, there can be some negative results with the use of this judicial support system if the masters, magistrates and experts are not selected carefully. Ineffective masters and magistrates, for example, could prolong the discovery process, increase motion practice and undermine confidence in the judicial system.

1. Magistrates

Federal magistrates are appointed by the court pursuant to the Federal Magistrates Act, 28 U.S.C.A. § 631 et seq. that was enacted in 1968. In accordance with the Act, judges from each district may appoint magistrates to perform specified statutory functions and "additional duties as are not inconsistent with the Constitution and laws of the United States." One example of appropriate "additional duties" for a magistrate is described in *Mathews v. Weber*, 423 U.S. 261, 96 S.Ct. 549, 46 L.Ed.2d 483 (1976), an action challenging a district court rule that referred all social security appeals to a magistrate for initial review. The rule directed the magistrate to conduct hearings and prepare a written proposed order with proposed findings of fact and conclusions of law. The Supreme Court held that the preliminary review assignment given to the magistrate in this case was one of the "additional duties" contemplated by the Act.

Magistrates aid district court judges in a variety of ways including conducting discovery in mass tort cases, conducting Early Neutral Evaluation (ENE) conferences and hosting judicial settlement conferences. There is a growing tendency to assign greater case management and settlement responsibilities to magistrates as federal district courts implement ADR programs.

2. Special Masters

Courts have inherent authority as well as authority under Rule 53 of the Federal Rules of Civil Procedure to appoint special masters. Rule 53 provides in relevant part:

Rule 53. Masters

(c) Master's Authority. Unless the appointing order expressly directs otherwise, a master has authority to regulate all proceedings and take all appropriate measures to perform fairly and efficiently the assigned duties. The master may by order impose upon a party any contempt sanction provided by Rule 37 or 45, and may recommend a contempt sanction against a party and sanctions against a nonparty.

The court may appoint a special master when exceptional conditions are present in a case or because the complexity of litigation requires additional assistance. For example, in *United States v. Su-*

quamish Indian Tribe, 901 F.2d 772 (9th Cir.1990), the Ninth Circuit Court of Appeals upheld the referral to a special master the issue of determining whether the Suquamish Indian tribe could assert the fishing rights of another tribe as a successor in interest.

It is useful if the litigants and judge agree on the appointment of a specific person as a master. Where the litigants have confidence and trust in the master's ability to manage a case and facilitate settlement, there is a greater opportunity for a collaborative effort to settle the case.

The traditional role of masters has largely been ministerial and adjudicatory, i.e., render accountings, preside over hearings and make findings of fact and recommendations. More recently, however, masters are functioning as facilitators and as special master mediators in the settlement of complex disputes. Special master mediation has proved to be successful in complex disputes under the following conditions: where traditional settlement attempts have failed; where sufficient discovery has been completed so that both sides are educated about the case; and, where the parties are willing to participate in the mediation process.

Another special master model that has been used successfully, uses prominent attorneys to serve as settlement masters. Under this approach, the master examines cases filed on the civil docket on a regular basis and seeks cases for settlement where the subject matter of the dispute is within the legal expertise of the master. Assuming that the parties have an interest in settlement and that they can afford the master's fee, the court refers the case to the settlement master.

One of the most publicized uses of a special master as settlement facilitator involved a complex dispute over fishing rights in the Great Lakes. *United States v. Michigan*, 471 F.Supp. 192 (W.D.Mich.1979), remanded 623 F.2d 448 (6th Cir. 1980), modified 653 F.2d 277 (6th Cir.1981), cert. denied Michigan v. United States, 454 U.S. 1124, 102 S.Ct. 971, 71 L.Ed.2d 110 (1981). This case had a twelve year litigation history and numerous parties including several tribes of Indians and various federal government officials. The parties all had deeply held political beliefs that seemed to resist compromise.

Judge Richard A. Enslen appointed a law professor, Frances McGovern, as a special master in the case and authorized him to oversee pre-trial developments and to conduct settlement discussions. The judge was insulated from any of the details of the settlement discussions. Professor McGovern writes that the case presented a classic example of polycentric issues which could not be easily resolved in an adjudication process:

> The solution to any given question concerning resource division was dependent upon the solutions reached on the other questions: no issues were independent. This complex interrelationship of issues created difficulties which were com-

pounded by the lack of any—much less clear—
legal standards. The court was being asked to
make extremely complex management decisions
by using policy differences unreflected in the substantive law—"reasonable living standards,"
"subsistence," "maximizing value," and "equal
distribution."

McGovern, *Toward A Functional Approach for
Managing Complex Litigation,* 53 U.Chi.L.Rev. 440,
459 (1986).

After establishing an abbreviated discovery schedule, the master focused on facilitating a settlement.
Using a computer-assisted negotiation model, the
master helped the parties arrive at an agreement
after only three days of negotiations. Only one tribe
refused to be bound by the agreement and proceed-
ed with litigation.

The most recent and highly publicized use of a
Special Master occurred in connection with the September 11 Victims Compensation Fund. The congressional legislation that established the Fund, the
Air Transportation Safety and System Stabilization
Act, delegated management of the Fund to a Special
Master who would be responsible for managing the
claims of victims following the tragic events of
September 11, 2001. Attorney Kenneth Feinberg
was appointed Special Master to develop a system
for awarding fair compensation to claimants who
satisfied the Fund's criteria. He was given broad
power to create procedural and substantive rules
and to adjudicate claims. Claimants were required

to choose one of two options: litigate their claims against the airlines and others or accept the relief that would be offered by the government.

3.   Neutral Experts

Neutral fact-finding is an informal process in which a neutral third party studies a particular issue and reports findings on that issue. The court may appoint neutral experts in accordance with Rule 706 of the Federal Rules of Evidence which provides in part:

Rule 706. Court Appointed Experts

(a) *Appointment.* The court may on its own motion or on the motion of any party enter an order to show cause why expert witnesses should not be appointed, and may request the parties to submit nominations. The court may appoint any expert witnesses agreed upon by the parties, and may appoint expert witnesses of its own selection.... A witness so appointed shall advise the parties of the witness' findings, if any; the witness' deposition may be taken by any party; and the witness may be called to testify by the court or any party. The witness shall be subject to cross-examination by each party, including a party calling the witness.

The courts enjoy broad discretion in deciding whether to appoint a neutral witness and individual parties cannot require that the court do so. Generally, a judge would wait until discovery has been substantially developed before determining the need for an expert. In cases involving complex technical or scientific issues, use of a neutral expert may be the most efficient means of resolving a dispute.

The conclusions of the expert witness may take the form of an oral or written report to the court or to the parties. Alternatively, the expert may be required to testify and be subject to cross-examination.

Just as magistrates and masters are assuming increased importance in settlement negotiations, so too are court-appointed experts. Because of their technical expertise in areas such as patent infringement, copyright, trade secret violations, antitrust cases, these experts bring greater understanding to the substantive aspects of complex disputes and are often better able to fashion creative solutions than are judges.

VI. RESTORATIVE JUSTICE: ADR IN THE CRIMINAL LAW CONTEXTS

The use of ADR in the criminal law context has developed significantly with the growth of the restorative justice movement. Instead of a retributive justice approach that emphasizes guilt and punishment for criminal offenders, restorative justice focuses on healing and reconciliation for the offender, the victim of crime and the community. Offenders are held accountable while the process focuses on the victim. One of the most well-known restorative justice processes, developed by Mark Umbreit, is victim-offender mediation (VOM) a process in which criminal offenders, frequently juveniles, engage in the mediation process with victims and then make restitution agreements. Other popular examples of restorative justice mechanisms include family group conferencing and community sentencing circles.

Bibliography

R. Ackerman, *The September 11th Victim Compensation Fund: An Effective Administrative Response to National Tragedy,* 10 Harv. Negot. L. Rev. 135 (2005);

E. Berkowitz, *The Problematic Role of the Special Master: Undermining the Legitimacy of the September 11th Victim Compensation Fund,* 24 Yale L. & Pol'y Rev 1 (2006);

W. Brazil, *Early Neutral Evaluation or Mediation? When Might ENE Deliver More Value?* 14 Dispute Resol. Mag. 10 (Fall 2007);

W. Brazil, *"Judicial Adjuncts: Special Masters and Court-Appointed Experts,"* Chapter 5 in *ADR and the Courts: A Manual for Judges and Lawyers, CPR Legal Program* (Butterworth Publications 1987);

S. Cole, C. McEwen and N. Rogers, *Mediation: Law, Policy, Practice* (2nd edition) (2006 Supp.);

K. Feinberg, *Creative Use of ADR: The Court-Appointed Special Settlement Master,* 59 Alb. L. Rev. 881 (1996);

J. Fitzhugh, *Report Card On ENE: Early Neutral Evaluation in the Vermont Federal District Court,* 24 Vt. B. J. & L. Dig. 44 (September 1998);

T. Lambros, *The Summary Jury Trial and Other Alternative Methods of Dispute Resolution: A Report to the Judicial Conference of the United States, Committee on the Operation of the Jury System,* 103 F.R.D. 461 (1984);

F. McGovern, *Toward A Functional Approach for Managing Complex Litigation,* 53 U.Chi.L.Rev. 440 (1986);

T. Metzloff, *Improving the Summary Jury Trial,* 77 Judicature 9 (1993);

E. Plapinger & D. Steinstra, *ADR and Settlement in the Federal District Courts: A Sourcebook for Judges and Lawyers* 5 (1996);

L. Ponte, *Putting Mandatory Summary Jury Trial Back on the Docket: Recommendations on the Exercise of Judicial Authority,* 63 Fordham L. Rev. 1069 (1995);

R. Posner, *The Summary Jury Trial and Other Methods of Alternative Dispute Resolution: Some Cautionary Observations,* 53 U.Chi.L.Rev. 366 (1986);

J. Resnik, *Managerial Judges,* 96 Harv. L. Rev. 374 (1982);

R. Reuben, *Constitutional Gravity: A Unitary Theory of Alternative Dispute Resolution and Public Civil Justice,* 47 UCLA L. Rev. 949 (2000);

R. Reuban, *Tort Reform Renews Debate Over Mandatory Mediation,* 13 Disp Resol. Mag. 13 (Winter 2007);

J. Rosenberg & H. J. Folberg, *Alternative Dispute Resolution: An Empirical Analysis,* 46 Stan. L. Rev. 1487 (1994);

F. Sander, *Another View of Mandatory Mediation,* 13 Disp. Resol. Mag 13 (Winter 2007);

M. Umbreit, *The Handbook of Victim Offender Mediation* (2001);

R. Wissler, *Court-Connected Mediation in General Civil Cases: What We Know From Empirical Research,* 17 Ohio St. J. Disp. Resol. 641;

Woodley, *Saving the Summary Jury Trial: A Proposal To Halt the Flow of Litigation and End the Uncertainties,* 1995 J. Disp. Res. 213;

H. Zehr, *The Little Book of Restorative Justice* (2002).

CHAPTER 6

HYBRID DISPUTE RESOLUTION PROCEDURES

The continued growth of the ADR movement has resulted in several innovative combinations of negotiation, mediation and arbitration, the primary dispute resolution processes. Facilitated negotiation combines with mediation in the mini-trial and it blends with regulatory rule-making in the "neg-reg" process. Mediation connects with arbitration in the "med-arb" and arb-med processes. Three other processes, conciliation, reference and ombuds procedures, while not new, are being used with much more frequency today than in the past. Private adjudication comprises the essence of reference or "rent-a-judge" procedures. Finally, the role of conciliator and ombudsperson involves aspects of mediation and fact-finding.

I. THE MINI-TRIAL

1. Definition

The mini-trial is not really a trial in any meaningful sense of that word. Rather, it is a structured settlement process that can blend together some components of negotiation, mediation and adversarial case presentation. A mutually agreeable neutral advisor usually presides over the proceeding but it may also be conducted without a neutral advisor. The trial has two phases. First, counsel for each side make abbreviated but adversarial presentations of their "best" cases to senior management executives with full settlement authority. Then, following the hearing, the business executives discuss settlement. The process is private and voluntary.

The phrase "mini-trial" was coined by a New York Times journalist in 1977 to describe successful settlement negotiations in a complex patent infringement case between TRW Inc. and Telecredit, Inc. involving millions of dollars. The hypnotic power of those words have attached to this process ever since that time.

2. The Structure of a Mini–Trial

The mini-trial is a flexible procedure that may be tailored to meet individual litigant needs. Therefore, the format for individual hearings varies. In general, parties would initiate the mini-trial by entering into an agreement describing the procedures that would govern the process. A typical agreement would include provisions for conducting discovery, selection of the neutral adviser, exchange of position papers, identifying the individuals from each organization who will serve on the mini-trial panel and confidentiality provisions. Sample procedures for a mini-trial appear at the end of this section.

There are essentially three structural phases of the mini-trial: a discovery phase, the actual hearing and post-hearing settlement discussions by the parties.

Discovery is usually brief but it must be sufficient for each side to appreciate the key issues involved in the case. At a minimum, the parties would exchange key exhibits, introductory statements and a summary of witnesses' testimony.

At the hearing, which is also referred to as the "information exchange," counsel for each party make summary presentations of their cases to senior management representatives. The legal and factual issues have been distilled by this time so that these presentations are able to focus on the underlying merits of the dispute. It is important that the management representatives have settlement authority. Otherwise, the full impact of the face-to-face presentations is diluted.

The hearing is intended to be informal and the rules of evidence and civil procedure are typically waived but it is structured around adversarial presentation and rebuttal of positions. The neutral advisor, usually an attorney or retired judge, may comment on the arguments or evidence, and question the witnesses or counsel. Hearing this commentary and questioning helps the executives hearing the case to appreciate the strength and weaknesses of their own cases and the opponents' cases. Following the information exchange between counsel, the parties may request that the neutral advisor evaluate the case and offer an opinion as to the probable outcome if the case were tried in court. The neutral's opinion can have a significant impact on the parties' decision to settle, particularly where the neutral is a retired judge or a seasoned trial attorney with experience in the type of case involved in the dispute. The neutral may also be asked to mediate during the settlement discussions.

In some situations, the parties may decide not to use a neutral advisor to conduct the information exchange. Following the hearing, the parties would simply attempt to negotiate a settlement on their own with the assistance of their attorneys.

3.   The Settlement Discussions

Senior management representatives who have attended the information exchange enter into post-hearing negotiation discussions with a view towards reaching an out-of-court settlement. While the mini-trial usually takes one day, it may take a few weeks to reach an agreement.

Settlement discussions following a mini-trial differ from traditional negotiation in a number of respects. First, the discussions are more focused after a mini-trial. The summary presentations by counsel have cut away the "fat" and honed in on the critical issues in dispute. The parties have a much better sense of the strengths and weaknesses of their cases. More realistic dialogue is possible because discussion is not between the initial parties to the dispute or the lawyers who continued to press the dispute, but between high level executive personnel who, theoretically, are removed from the emotional aspects of disputing.

If the parties are still unable to settle the case on their own during the post-hearing settlement talks, they may agree that the neutral advisor will act as a mediator. Even if the case does not settle, the mini-trial is still considered an efficient process because the time spent in preparing for the information exchange helps organize the courtroom trial.

4. Appropriate Use of the Mini–Trial

The mini-trial has proved to be successful in complex civil cases where there are mixed questions of law and fact. It has been used successfully in cases involving patent infringement, government contracts, products liability, antitrust, construction and contract enforcement. On the other hand, there are inherent limitations to this process. Where one of the parties needs the cathartic effect of trial, the short-hand version of a trial will probably prove unsatisfactory. If one of the parties has no serious desire to settle, the mini-trial is probably a waste of time. The following guidelines are representative of the procedures that would be used at a mini-trial administered by the American Arbitration Association. Guidelines for non-administered mini-trial procedures are available from the CPR Institute for Dispute Resolution in New York City (http://www.cpradr.org).

AMERICAN ARBITRATION ASSOCIATION
MINI–TRIAL PROCEDURES

1. The mini-trial process may be initiated by the written or oral request of either party, made to any regional office of the AAA, but will not be pursued unless both parties agree to resolve their dispute by means of a mini-trial.

2. The course of the mini-trial process shall be governed by a written agreement between the parties.

3. The mini-trial shall consist of an information exchange and settlement negotiation.

4. Each party is represented throughout the mini-trial process by legal counsel whose role is to prepare and present the party's "best case" at the information exchange.

5. Each party shall have in attendance throughout the information exchange and settlement negotiation a senior executive with settlement authority.

6. A neutral advisor shall be present at the information exchange to decide questions of procedure and to render advice to the party representatives when requested by them.

7. The neutral advisor shall be selected by mutual agreement of the parties, who may consult with the AAA for recommendations. To facilitate the selection process, the AAA will make available to the parties a list of individuals to serve as neutral advisors. If the parties fail to agree upon the selection of a neutral advisor, they shall ask that the

AAA appoint an advisor from the panel it has compiled for this purpose.

8.   Discovery between the parties may take place prior to the information exchange, in accordance with the agreement between the parties.

9.   Prior to the information exchange, the parties shall exchange written statements summarizing the issues in the case, and copies of all documents they intend to present at the information exchange.

10.   Federal or state rules of evidence do not apply to presentations made at the information exchange. Any limitation on the scope of the evidence offered at the information exchange shall be determined by mutual agreement of the parties prior to the exchange and shall be enforced by the neutral advisor.

11.   After the information exchange, the senior executives shall meet and attempt, in good faith, to formulate a voluntary settlement of the dispute.

12.   If the senior executives are unable to settle the dispute, the neutral advisor shall render an advisory opinion as to the likely outcome of the case if it were litigated in a court of law. The neutral advisor's opinion shall identify the issues of law and fact which are critical to the disposition of the case and give the reasons for the opinion that is offered.

13.   After the neutral advisor has rendered an advisory opinion, the senior executives shall meet for a second time in an attempt to resolve the dispute. If they are unable to reach a settlement at

this time, they may either abandon the proceeding or submit to the neutral advisor written offers of settlement. If the parties elect to make such written offers, the neutral advisor shall make a recommendation for settlement based on those offers. If the parties reject the recommendation of the neutral advisor, either party may declare the mini-trial terminated and resolve the dispute by other means.

14. Mini-trial proceedings are confidential; no written or oral statement made by any participant in the proceeding may be used as evidence or in admission in any other proceeding.

15. The fees and expenses of the neutral advisor shall be borne equally by the parties, and each party is responsible for its own costs, including legal fees, incurred in connection with the mini-trial. The parties may, however, in their written agreement alter the allocation of fees and expenses.

16. Neither the AAA nor any neutral advisor serving in a mini-trial proceeding governed by these procedures shall be liable to any party for any act or omission in connection with the mini-trial. The parties shall indemnify the AAA and the neutral advisor for any liability to third parties arising out of the mini-trial process.

Administrative Fee

Parties initiating a mini-trial under these procedures will make arrangements with the local AAA office for administrative fees and neutral-advisor compensation.

II. REFERENCE PROCEDURES

Almost every state permits cases to be referred to private judges whose authority is equivalent to that of the public judiciary. Reference procedures, also known as "private judging" or "rent-a-judge," vary in each state in the amount of power given to the referee, the effect of the referee's decision, the amount of public involvement in the process and the extent to which it has the force of public adjudication. The litigants select and pay for the referee who is often a retired judge. In some states the decision of the referee has the force and effect of a trial court judgment.

The major benefit of using a reference procedure is speed. In by-passing the traditional court structure, litigants avoid the systemic weaknesses of the judicial system, specifically, the long wait for a day in court. Other advantages of reference procedures over public judging are privacy and the ability to select the referee. Unlike the arbitration process to which it bears similarities, litigants have the right of full review of the referee's decision.

Reference systems have been criticized on public policy grounds for their lack of public accountability and for creating a two-tiered system of justice where the wealthy who can afford to, use personally selected private judges and the poor are relegated to the public system of justice. However, the full due process system available in the regular courts to any litigant, weakens this criticism. Private judging has also been criticized for luring talented public judges off the bench to the private sector where they earn high hourly rates for judging. There is, however, little empirical evidence to support this claim.

III. MED–ARB

Combining mediation and arbitration in a sequential process can be an efficient and cost-effective method of resolving many disputes. In effect, the third party neutral functions as a catalyst for the settlement process because the presence of the neutral who may ultimately have to make a decision in the case gives the parties a realistic incentive to settle. The med-arb process originated in the collective bargaining context where it has been referred to as "muscle" mediation. Today, the med-arb process has been adopted in some commercial cases and in court-annexed programs.

In some variations of the med-arb process, the mediator acts simply as an advisory arbitrator. When the parties are informed as to what the arbitrator's decision would be, they may be induced to settle on their own. In other models, the mediator recommends to the court how the dispute should be resolved.

Med-arb is considered a more efficient process than straight mediation followed by arbitration with a different person because the parties may be able to narrow the issues in dispute during the mediation and leave unresolved issues to arbitration. Moreover, if the mediation process does not result in an agreement, it will not be necessary for the parties to begin their story all over again with a new arbitrator. There are obvious savings here in transaction costs associated with beginning again.

There are, however, some disadvantages. First, when neutrals mix roles, there may be ambiguity with respect to liability if questions of malpractice arise. Second, ethical issues may arise when one individual serves as both a mediator and arbitrator in the same dispute. Parties may be unwilling to share information about their true interests and needs with a mediator who will have decisional authority if no agreement is reached. Likewise, it may be difficult, if not impossible for the neutral who learned confidential information as a mediator to render an objective decision as an arbitrator. For example, assume that a neutral learns in a private mediation caucus that the plaintiff in a $100,000.00 products liability case is really willing to settle the case for $35,000.00 (even though the case is worth at least $65,000.00.) If the case does not settle in mediation and the same neutral awards $35,000.00 to the plaintiff in arbitration, there are serious concerns about the fairness of that award. In order to insure fairness, parties should give informed consent before entering into the med-arb process where the same neutral serves as both a mediator and arbitrator in the same dispute.

Arb-Med

In the arb-med process the sequence described above is reversed. The third party neutral begins as an arbitrator and then shifts roles to the mediation process. Scholars have argued that the major benefit of arb-med is that it encourages parties to resolve disputes themselves. Further research is needed to assess the benefits of arb-med.

IV. NEGOTIATED RULEMAKING

Growing discontent with the delays and court challenges attached to the traditional federal rulemaking process led regulatory reformers to propose negotiation as a preferred method of rulemaking. The concept of negotiated rulemaking, also known as "neg-reg," or regulatory negotiation, describes the use of negotiation by an administrative agency in any decision-making procedures. It involves direct participation in rulemaking by public agency regulators and the private business and advocacy groups affected by the regulations. The goal of the process is to reach consensus.

Negotiated rulemaking avoids the adversarial approach of traditional notice and comment rulemaking where a final draft of a regulation is given to affected parties for comment. Special interest concerns would invariably cause many regulations to be challenged and time-consuming court battles would be initiated. Face-to-face negotiations at the initial drafting stages promotes a problem-solving approach which is likely to leave the affected parties more satisfied with the result.

Advocates of negotiated rulemaking refer to its potential to make rules more acceptable to affected parties and thus less likely to be challenged in court. By direct participation and collaborative efforts, the affected parties invest in the rulemaking process and therefore, claim some ownership of the substantive result. Thus, there is greater cooperation between state agencies, the community and public interest groups.

Negotiated rulemaking has been used successfully by a number of federal agencies and the benefits of the process were officially recognized in the Negotiated Rulemaking Act of 1990, an amendment to the Administrative Procedure Act. It was permanently reauthorized in the Administrative Dispute Resolution Act of 1996. Section 2 of the Act reflects Congress' findings that negotiated rulemaking can provide significant advantages over current adversarial rulemaking procedures that "may discourage the affected parties from meeting and communicating with each other, and may cause parties with different interests to assume conflicting and antagonistic positions and to engage in expensive and time-consuming litigation over agency rules." Section 5 of the Act notes that on the other hand, "negotiated rulemaking can increase the acceptability and improve the substance of rules, making it less likely that the affected parties will resist enforcement or challenge such rules in court."

Under the scheme established in the Act, a federal agency may establish a negotiated rulemaking committee if the head of the agency determines that such a procedure would be in the public interest. The statute lists several factors that would go into this determination including need, adequate resources and reasonable likelihood that there could be a committee with balanced representation of persons. If the agency does decide to convene a committee, notice of this intent must be published in the Federal Register and appropriate trade magazines. After considering comments, the agency may or may not decide to establish a negotiated rulemaking committee. The committee terminates upon the promulgation of the final rule under consideration.

Following the popularity of negotiated rulemaking in federal administrative agencies and its endorsement by the Executive Branch, several states have adopted neg-reg statutes. Recent criticism of the neg-reg process, however, has challenged its claim to efficiency. Whether the trend toward consensus-based rulemaking process continues, may depend in large measure upon the manner in which neg-reg processes are administered.

V. OMBUDSPERSON

An ombudsperson is a neutral individual employed by a company to assist employees in resolving workplace disputes. Also referred to as an ombuds or ombudsman, these individuals hear complaints, engage in fact finding, and generally promote the resolution of disputes through informal methods such as mediation and counseling.

The traditional notion of an "ombudsman" derives from the Scandinavian countries where a public official would be designated to listen to the public's complaints and attempt to respond to them. In the United States, however, ombudspersons are often employed by private organizations to act as in-house neutrals in responding to employment-related problems. In many corporations, hospitals and universities for example, the office of ombudsperson functions as an official "complaint department" with clout. Employees can engage in the venting process and be assured of respect and fair dealing while the ombudsperson may be able to make constructive recommendations for change to management. One of the concerns that has arisen with the use of the ombudsman is maintaining the confidentiality of communications. At least one federal court has refused to recognize a confidentiality privilege for a corporate ombudsman who investigates and mediates workplace disputes. See *Carman v. McDonnell Douglas Corp.*, 114 F.3d 790 (8th Cir. 1997).

Ethical guidance for ombudspersons is available from the American Bar Association (ABA) Standards for the Establishment and Operation of Ombuds Offices (Feb. 2004) and the International Ombudsman's Association's Code of Ethics and Standards of Practice. The ABA Standards describes four categories of ombuds, classical ombuds, organizational ombuds, advocate ombuds and executive ombuds and they identify three core characteristics of an ombuds office: independence, impartiality, and confidentiality.

VI. CONCILIATION

Conciliation is an informal process, similar to mediation but less structured than the mediation process. In conciliation, a neutral third party intervenes in a conflict in order to assist parties in arriving at a resolution. It is commonly used in high conflict situations where parties are unable or unwilling to participate in negotiations. The neutral third party engages in a variety of techniques to reduce tensions between the parties, improve communications, and understand and interpret issues and positions.

In the international commercial context, the term "conciliation" is used interchangeably with "mediation." See UNCITRAL Model Law on International Conciliation (2002), available at www.uncitral.org.

VII. ONLINE DISPUTE RESOLUTION

The dramatic growth of cyberspace commerce has brought about increased interest in the development of online dispute resolution (ODR), also referred to as EDR (electronic dispute resolution). ODR includes traditional ADR processes that incorporate information technology such as the Internet, websites, e-mail communications, and streaming media, as well as more innovative techniques such as double blind bidding and auctions. Disputes that may be appropriate for resolution through ODR include those that are created by the Internet such as domain names, as well as those related to commercial transactions that use the Internet.

ODR provides for virtual communications between parties in cyberspace and thus eliminates the transaction costs of traditional dispute resolution, whether that means going to courts in different jurisdictions to initiate lawsuits or participating in traditional ADR with face-to-face meetings.

Despite the appeal of cyberspace dispute resolution, there are a number of policy and regulatory issues that need to be addressed in connection with commercial transactions. Towards this end, the American Bar Association appointed a task force, the ABA Task Force on E–Commerce and ADR, to study issues raised by multi-jurisdictional business–to-business (B2B) and business-to-consumer (B2C) transactions. In 2002, the Task Force published a report on protocols, guidelines and standards that can be implemented by parties to online transactions and by online providers. The report is available at www.abanet.org/dispute/webpolicy.html.

VIII. CONSENSUS BUILDING

Consensus building is a deliberative process that uses a neutral facilitator or mediator to bring together stakeholders so that they can jointly seek solutions to a problem. In the *Consensus Building Handbook,* Professor Lawrence Susskind identifies five steps in the consensus building process: (1) convening; (2) clarifying responsibilities; (3) deliberation; (4) decisionmaking; (5) implementation of agreement.

The goal of consensus building is to reach an informed consensus, an outcome that requires an understanding of all stakeholders' underlying needs and interests. Thus, all parties with a stake in the outcome of the dispute should be included in the consensus building process.

IX. DISPUTE REVIEW BOARDS

Dispute Review Boards (DRB) are preventive ADR mechanisms identified primarily with the construction industry. The DRB hears disputes and makes non-binding recommendations based on the facts and the panel members' expertise. The board is composed of three members with construction industry expertise—the contractor and owner each select a board member and both of them select the third member. The costs of the DRB are typically shared by owners and contractors. DRB members usually visit the construction site periodically and familiarize themselves with the parties and the project. Unlike other ADR processes that are initiated after a dispute arises, DRBs are established at the pre-construction phase of a project and hear ongoing disputes.

Bibliography

T. Brewer & L. Mills, *Combining Mediation & Arbitration,* Dispute Resol. J., November 1999 at 32;

R. Chernick et al., *Private Judging: Privatizing Civil Justice* (1997);

C. Coglianese, *Assessing Consensus: The Promise and Performance of Negotiated Rulemaking,* 46 Duke L. J. 1255 (1997);

L. Fuller, *Collective Bargaining and the Arbitrator,* Proceedings, Fifteenth Annual Meeting, National Academy of Arbitrators, Washington, D.C.: Bureau of National Affairs (1962);

S. Goldberg, *The Mediation of Grievances Under a Collective Bargaining Contract: An Alternative to Arbitration,* 77 Nw.U.L.Rev. 270 (1982);

K. M. J. Harmon, *Construction Conflicts and Dispute Review Boards: Attitudes and Opinions of Construction Industry Members*, Dispute Resolution Journal, (Jan. 2003);

P. Harter, *Negotiating Regulations: A Cure for Malaise,* 71 Geo.L.J. 1, 6 (1982);

P. Harter, *Negotiating Rules and Other Policies: Pay Close Heed to Structure for Success,* Disp. Res. Mag. 15 (ABA Section of Dispute Resolution) (Fall 1997);

E. Katsh & J. Rifkin, *Online Dispute Resolution* (2001);

R. M. Matyas et al., *Construction Dispute Review Board Manual* (1996);

F. McGovern, *Toward a Functional Approach for Managing Complex Litigation,* 53 U. Chi. L. Rev. 440 459 (1986);

National Institute for Dispute Resolution, *Report of the Ad Hoc Panel on Dispute Resolution and Public Policy* (1983);

Note, *The California Rent–A–Judge Experiment: Constitutional and Policy Considerations of Pay As You Go Courts,* 94 Harv.L.Rev. 1592 (1981);

M. Rowe, *The Ombudsman's Role in a Dispute Resolution System,* 7 Neg.J. 353 (1991);

L. Singer, *Settling Disputes* (2d ed. 1994);

L. Susskind, S. McKearnan, J. Thomas–Larmer, *The Consensus Building Handbook: A Comprehensive Guide to Reaching Agreement* (1999);

L. E. Susskind & J. L. Cruikshank, *Breaking Robert's Rules: The New Way To Run Your Meeting, Build Consensus, and Get Results* (2006).

*

APPENDICES

Appendices

App.

A. Federal Rules of Evidence, Rule 408
B. Federal Rules of Civil Procedure, Rule 16
C. Federal Rules of Civil Procedure, Rule 68
D. Model Standards of Practice for Family and Divorce Mediation (August 2000)
E. The Model Standards of Conduct for Mediators (September 2005)
F. American Arbitration Association Commercial Arbitration Rules and Commercial Mediation Procedures (2007)
G. Mandated Participation and Settlement Coercion: Dispute Resolution as it Relates to the Courts
H. Ethical Standards of Professional Responsibility for the Society of Professionals in Dispute Resolution
I. The Uniform Arbitration Act
J. Federal Arbitration Act
K. Revised Uniform Arbitration Act (August 2000)
L. Demand for Arbitration (American Arbitration Association)
M. Task Force on Alternative Dispute Resolution in Employment, Due Process Protocol
N. The Code of Ethics for Arbitrators in Commercial Disputes (2004)
O. Model Rules of Professional Conduct, Client-Lawyer Relationship, Rule 1.12
P. Model Rules of Professional Conduct, Advocate, Rule 3.3
Q. Model Rules of Professional Conduct, Law Firms and Associations, Rule 5.5
R. Uniform Mediation Act

APPENDIX A

FEDERAL RULES OF EVIDENCE—RULE 408

COMPROMISE AND OFFERS TO COMPROMISE

(a) Prohibited uses.—Evidence of the following is not admissible on behalf of any party, when offered to prove liability for, invalidity of, or amount of a claim that was disputed as to validity or amount, or to impeach through a prior inconsistent statement or contradiction:

(1) furnishing or offering or promising to furnish—or accepting or offering or promising to accept—a valuable consideration in compromising or attempting to compromise the claim; and

(2) conduct or statements made in compromise negotiations regarding the claim, except when offered in a criminal case and the negotiations related to a claim by a public office or agency in the exercise of regulatory, investigative, or enforcement authority.

(b) Permitted uses.—This rule does not require exclusion if the evidence is offered for purposes not prohibited by subdivision (a). Examples of permissible purposes include proving a witness's bias or prejudice; negating a contention of undue delay; and proving an effort to obstruct a criminal investigation or prosecution.

APPENDIX B

FEDERAL RULES OF CIVIL PROCEDURE—RULE 16

PRETRIAL CONFERENCE; SCHEDULING; MANAGEMENT

(a) Purposes of a Pretrial Conference. In any action, the court may order the attorneys and any unrepresented parties to appear for one or more pretrial conferences for such purposes as:

(1) expediting disposition of the action;

(2) establishing early and continuing control so that the case will not be protracted because of lack of management;

(3) discouraging wasteful pretrial activities;

(4) improving the quality of the trial through more thorough preparation; and

(5) facilitating settlement.

(b) Scheduling.

(1) *Scheduling Order.* Except in categories of actions exempted by local rule, the district judge—or a magistrate judge when authorized by local rule—must issue a scheduling order:

(A) after receiving the parties' report under Rule 26(f); or

(B) after consulting with the parties' attorneys and any unrepresented parties at a scheduling conference or by telephone, mail, or other means.

(2) *Time to Issue.* The judge must issue the scheduling order as soon as practicable, but in any event within the earlier of 120 days after any defendant has been served with the complaint or 90 days after any defendant has appeared.

(3) *Contents of the Order.*

(A) *Required Contents.* The scheduling order must limit the time to join other parties, amend the pleadings, complete discovery, and file motions.

(B) *Permitted Contents.* The scheduling order may:

(i) modify the timing of disclosures under Rules 26(a) and 26(e)(1);

(ii) modify the extent of discovery;

(iii) provide for disclosure or discovery of electronically stored information;

(iv) include any agreements the parties reach for asserting claims of privilege or of protection as trial-preparation material after information is produced;

(v) set dates for pretrial conferences and for trial; and

(vi) include other appropriate matters.

(4) *Modifying a Schedule.* A schedule may be modified only for good cause and with the judge's consent.

(c) Attendance and Matters for Consideration at a Pretrial Conference.

(1) *Attendance.* A represented party must authorize at least one of its attorneys to make stipulations and admissions about all matters that can reasonably be anticipated for discussion at a pretrial conference. If appropriate, the court may require that a party or its representative be present or reasonably available by other means to consider possible settlement.

(2) *Matters for Consideration.* At any pretrial conference, the court may consider and take appropriate action on the following matters:

(A) formulating and simplifying the issues, and eliminating frivolous claims or defenses;

(B) amending the pleadings if necessary or desirable;

(C) obtaining admissions and stipulations about facts and documents to avoid unnecessary proof, and ruling in advance on the admissibility of evidence;

(D) avoiding unnecessary proof and cumulative evidence, and limiting the use of testimony under Federal Rule of Evidence 702;

(E) determining the appropriateness and timing of summary adjudication under Rule 56;

(F) controlling and scheduling discovery, including orders affecting disclosures and discovery under Rule 26 and Rules 29 through 37;

(G) identifying witnesses and documents, scheduling the filing and exchange of any pretrial briefs, and setting dates for further conferences and for trial;

(H) referring matters to a magistrate judge or a master;

(I) settling the case and using special procedures to assist in resolving the dispute when authorized by statute or local rule;

(J) determining the form and content of the pretrial order;

(K) disposing of pending motions;

(L) adopting special procedures for managing potentially difficult or protracted actions that may involve complex issues, multiple parties, difficult legal questions, or unusual proof problems;

(M) ordering a separate trial under Rule 42(b) of a claim, counterclaim, crossclaim, third-party claim, or particular issue;

(N) ordering the presentation of evidence early in the trial on a manageable issue that might, on the evidence, be the basis for a judgment as a matter of law under Rule 50(a) or a judgment on partial findings under Rule 52(c);

(O) establishing a reasonable limit on the time allowed to present evidence; and

(P) facilitating in other ways the just, speedy, and inexpensive disposition of the action.

(d) Pretrial Orders. After any conference under this rule, the court should issue an order reciting the action taken. This order controls the course of the action unless the court modifies it.

(e) Final Pretrial Conference and Orders. The court may hold a final pretrial conference to formulate a trial plan, including a plan to facilitate the admission of evidence. The conference must be held as close to the start of trial as is reasonable, and must be attended by at least one attorney who will conduct the trial for each party and by any unrepresented party. The court may modify the order issued after a final pretrial conference only to prevent manifest injustice.

(f) Sanctions.

(1) *In General.* On motion or on its own, the court may issue any just orders, including those authorized by Rule 37(b)(2)(A)(ii)-(vii), if a party or its attorney:

(A) fails to appear at a scheduling or other pretrial conference;

(B) is substantially unprepared to participate—or does not participate in good faith—in the conference; or

(C) fails to obey a scheduling or other pretrial order.

(2) *Imposing Fees and Costs.* Instead of or in addition to any other sanction, the court must order the party, its attorney, or both to pay the reasonable expenses—including attorney's fees—incurred because of any noncompliance with this rule, unless the noncompliance was substantially justified or other circumstances make an award of expenses unjust.

APPENDIX C

FEDERAL RULES OF CIVIL PROCEDURE—RULE 68

OFFER OF JUDGMENT

(a) Making an Offer; Judgment on an Accepted Offer. More than 10 days before the trial begins, a party defending against a claim may serve on an opposing party an offer to allow judgment on specified terms, with the costs then accrued. If, within 10 days after being served, the opposing party serves written notice accepting the offer, either party may then file the offer and notice of acceptance, plus proof of service. The clerk must then enter judgment.

(b) Unaccepted Offer. An unaccepted offer is considered withdrawn, but it does not preclude a later offer. Evidence of an unaccepted offer is not admissible except in a proceeding to determine costs.

(c) Offer After Liability Is Determined. When one party's liability to another has been determined but the extent of liability remains to be determined by further proceedings, the party held liable may make an offer of judgment. It must be served within a reasonable time—but at least 10 days—before a hearing to determine the extent of liability.

(d) Paying Costs After an Unaccepted Offer. If the judgment that the offeree finally obtains is not more favorable than the unaccepted offer, the offeree must pay the costs incurred after the offer was made.

APPENDIX D

MODEL STANDARDS OF PRACTICE FOR FAMILY AND DIVORCE MEDIATION (AUGUST 2000)

Overview and Definitions[1]

Family and divorce mediation ("family mediation" or "mediation") is a process in which a mediator, an impartial third party, facilitates the resolution of family disputes by promoting the participants' voluntary agreement. The family mediator assists communication, encourages understanding and focuses the participants on their individual and common interests. The family mediator works with the participants to explore options, make decisions and reach their own agreements.

1. These standards were developed by the Symposium on Standards of Practice, which represents a collaborative effort of the Association of Family and Conciliation Courts (AFCC), the Family Law Section of the American Bar Association, the National Council of Dispute Resolution Organizations, as well as prominent individuals in the mediation field. They represent the family mediation community's definition of the role of mediation in the dispute resolution system in the twenty-first century and are intended to create a unified set of standards that will replace existing ones, including the ABA Standards of Practice for LawyerMediators in Family Disputes (1984).

Family mediation is not a substitute for the need for family members to obtain independent legal advice or counseling or therapy. Nor is it appropriate for all families. However, experience has established that family mediation is a valuable option for many families because it can:

1. increase the self-determination of participants and their ability to communicator;

2. promote the best interests of children; and

3. reduce the economic and emotional costs associated with the resolution of family disputes.

Effective mediation requires that the family mediator be qualified by training, experience and temperament; that the mediator be impartial; that the participants reach their decisions voluntarily; that their decisions be based on sufficient factual data; that the mediator be aware of the impact of culture and diversity; and that the best interests of children be taken into account. Further, the mediator should also be prepared to identify families whose history includes domestic abuse or child abuse.

These *Model Standards of Practice for Family and Divorce Mediation* (*"Model Standards"*) aim to perform three major functions:

1. To serve as a guide for the conduct of family mediators;

2. To inform the mediating participants of what they can expect; and

3. To promote public confidence in mediation as a process for resolving family disputes.

The *Model Standards* are aspirational in character. They describe good practices for family mediators. They are not intended to create legal rules or standards of liability.

The *Model Standards* include different levels of guidance:

1. Use of the term "may" in Standard is the lowest strength of guidance and indicates a practice that the family mediator should consider adopting but which can be deviated from in the exercise of good professional judgment.

2. Most of the *Standards* employ the term "should" which indicates that the practice described in the *Standard* is highly desirable and should be departed from only with very strong reason.

3. The rarer use of the term "shall" in a Standard is a higher level of guidance to the family mediator, indicating that the mediator should not have discretion to depart from the practice described.

Standard I

A family mediator shall recognize that mediation is based on the principle of self-determination by the participants.

A. Self-determination is the fundamental principle of family mediation. The mediation process relies upon the ability of participants to make their own voluntary and informed decisions.

B. The primary role of family mediator is to assist the participants to gain a better understanding of their own needs and interests and the needs and interest of others and to facilitated agreement among the participants.

C. A family mediator should inform the participants that they may seek information and advice from a variety of sources during the mediation process.

D. A family mediator shall inform the participants that they may withdraw from family mediation at any time and are not required to reach an agreement in mediation.

E. The family mediator's commitment shall be to the participants and the process. Pressure from outside of the mediation process shall never influence the mediator to coerce participants to settle.

Standard II

A family mediator shall be qualified by education and training to undertake the mediation.

A. To perform the family mediator's role a mediator should:

   1. have knowledge of family law;

2. have knowledge of and training in the impact of family conflict on parents, children and other participants, including knowledge of child development, domestic abuse and child abuse and neglect;

3. have education and training specific to the process of mediation;

4. Be able to recognize the impact of culture and diversity.

B. Family mediators should provide information to the participant about the mediator's relevant training education and expertise.

Standard III

A family mediator shall facilitate the participants' understanding of what mediation is and assess their capacity to mediate before the participants reach an agreement to mediate.

A. Before family mediation begins a mediator should provide the participants with an overview of the process and its purposes, including:

1. informing the participants that reaching an agreement in family mediation is consensual in nature, that a mediator is an impartial facilitator, and that a mediator may not impose or force any settlement on the parties;

2. distinguishing family mediation from other processes designed to address family issues and disputes;

3. informing the participants that any agreements reached will be reviewed by the court when court approval is required;

4. informing the participants that they may obtain independent advice from attorneys, counsel, advocates, accountants, therapists or other professional during the mediation process;

5. advising the participants, in appropriate cases, that they can seek the advice of religious figures, elders or other significant persons in their community whose opinions they value;

6. discussing, if applicable, the issue of separate sessions with the participants, a description of the circumstances in which the mediator may meet alone with any of the participants, or with any third party and the conditions of confidentiality concerning these separate sessions;

7. informing the participants that the presence or absence of other persons at a mediation including attorneys, counselors or advocates, depends on the agreement of the participants and the mediator, unless a statute or regulation otherwise requires or the mediator believes that the presence of another person is required or may be beneficial because of a history or threat of violence or other serious coercive activity by a participant;

8. describing the obligations of the mediator to maintain the confidentiality of the mediation

process and its results as well as any exceptions to confidentiality;

9. advising the participants of the circumstances under which the mediator may suspend or terminate the mediation process and that a participant has a right to suspend or terminate mediation at any time.

B. The participants should sign a written agreement to mediate their dispute and the terms and conditions thereof within a reasonable time after first consulting the family mediator.

C. The family mediator should be alert to the capacity and willingness of the participants to mediate before proceeding with the mediation and throughout the process. A mediator should not agree to conduct the mediation if the mediator reasonably believes one or more of the participants is unable or unwilling to participate.

D. Family mediators should not accept a dispute for mediation if they cannot satisfy the expectations of the participants concerning the timing of the process.

Standard IV

A family mediator shall conduct the mediation process in an impartial manner. A family mediator shall disclose all actual and potential grounds of bias and conflicts of interest reasonably known to the mediator. The participants shall be free to retain the mediator by an informed, written waiver of the conflicts of interest. However, if a bias or conflict of interest clearly impairs a mediator's impartiality, the mediator shall withdraw regardless of the express agreement of the participants.

A. Impartiality means freedom from favoritism or bias in word, action or appearance, and includes a commitment to assist all participants as opposed to any one individual.

B. Conflict of interest means any relationship between the mediator, any participant or the subject matter of the dispute, that compromises or appears to compromise the mediator's impartiality.

C. A family mediator should not accept a dispute for mediation if the family mediator cannot be impartial.

D. A family mediator should identify and disclose potential grounds of bias or conflict of interest upon which a mediator's impartiality might reasonably be questioned. Such disclosure should be made prior to the start of a mediation and in time to allow the participants to select an alternate mediator.

E. A family mediator should resolve all doubts in favor of disclosure. All disclosure should be made as soon as practical after the mediator becomes aware of the bias or potential conflict of interest. The duty to disclosure is a continuing duty.

F. A family mediator should guard against bias or partiality based on the participants' personal characteristics, background or performance at the mediation.

G. A family mediator should avoid conflicts of interest in recommending the services of other professionals.

H. A family mediator shall not use information about participants obtained in a mediation for personal gain or advantage.

I. A family mediator should withdraw pursuant to Standard IX if the mediator believes the mediator's impartiality has been compromised or a conflict of interest has been identified and has not been waived by the participants.

Standard V

A family mediator shall fully disclose and explain the basis of any compensation, fees and charges to the participants.

A. The participants should be provided with sufficient information about fees at the outset of mediation to determine if they wish to retain the services of the mediator.

B. The participants' written agreement to mediate their dispute should include a description of their fee arrangement with the mediator.

C. A mediator should not enter into a fee agreement that is contingent upon the results of the mediation or the amount of the settlement.

D. A mediator should not accept a fee for referral of a matter to another mediator or to any other person.

E. Upon termination of mediation a mediator should return any unearned fee to the participants.

Standard VI

A family mediator shall structure the mediation process so that the participants make decisions based on sufficient information and knowledge.

A. The mediator should facilitate full and accurate disclosure and the acquisition and development of information during mediation so that the participants can make informed decisions. This may be accomplished by encouraging participants to consult appropriate experts.

B. Consistent with standards of impartiality and preserving participant self-determination, a mediator may provide the participants with information that the mediator is qualified by training or experience to provide. The mediator shall not provide therapy or legal advice.

C. The mediator should recommend that the participants obtain independent legal representation before concluding an agreement.

D. If the participants so desire, the mediator should allow attorneys, counsel or advocates for the participants to be present at the mediation sessions.

E. With the agreement of the participants, the mediator may document the participants' resolution of their dispute. The mediator should inform the participants that any agreement should be reviewed by an independent attorney before it is signed.

Standard VII

A family mediator shall maintain the confidentiality of all information acquired in the mediation process, unless the mediator is permitted or required to reveal the information by law or agreement of the participants.

A. The mediator should discuss the participants' expectations of confidentiality with them prior to undertaking the mediation. The written agreement to mediate should include provisions concerning confidentiality.

B. Prior to undertaking the mediation the mediator should inform the participants of the limitations of confidentiality such as statutory, judicially or ethically mandated reporting.

C. The mediator shall disclose a participant's threat of suicide or violence against any person to the threatened person and the appropriate authorities if the mediator believes such threat is likely to be acted upon as permitted by law.

D. If the mediator holds private sessions with a participant, the obligations of confidentiality concerning those sessions should be discussed and agreed upon prior to the sessions.

E. If subpoenaed or otherwise noticed to testify or to produce documents the mediator should inform the participants immediately. The mediator should not testify or provide documents in response to a subpoena without an order of the court if the mediator reasonably believes doing so would violate an obligation of confidentiality to the participants.

Standard VIII

A family mediator shall assist participants in determining how to promote the best interests of children.

A. The mediator should encourage the participants to explore the range of options available for separation or post divorce parenting arrangements and their respective costs and benefits. Referral to a specialist in child development may be appropriate for these purposes. The topics for discussion may include, among others:

1. information about community resources and programs that can help the participants and their children cope with the consequences of family reorganization and family violence;

2. problems that continuing conflict creates for children's development and what steps might be taken to ameliorate the effects of conflict on the children;

3. development of a parenting plan that covers the children's physical residence and decision-

making responsibilities for the children, with appropriate levels of detail as agreed to be the participants;

4. the possible need to revise parenting plans as the developmental needs of the children evolve over time; and

5. encouragement to the participants to develop appropriate dispute resolution mechanisms to facilitate future revisions of the parenting plan.

B. The mediator should be sensitive to the impact of culture and religion on parenting philosophy and other decisions.

C. The mediator shall inform any court-appointed representative for the children of the mediation. If a representative for the children participants, the mediator should, at the outset, discuss the effect of that participation on the mediation process and the confidentiality of the mediation with the participants. Whether the representative of the children participates or not, the mediator shall provide the representative with the resulting agreements insofar as they relate to the children.

D. Except in extraordinary circumstances, the children should not participate in the mediation process without the consent of both parents and the children's court-appointed representative.

E. Prior to including the children in the mediation process, the mediator should consult with the parents and the children's court-appointed representative about whether the children should participants in the mediation process and the form of that participation.

F. The mediator should inform all concerned about the available options for the children's participation (which may include personal participation, an interview with a mental health professional, or the mediator reporting to the parents, or a videotape statement by the child) and discuss the costs and benefits of each with the participants.

Standard IX

A family mediator shall recognize a family situation involving child abuse or neglect and take appropriate steps to shape the mediation process accordingly.

A. As used in these Standards, child abuse or neglect is defined by applicable state law.

B. A mediator shall not undertake a mediation in which the family situation has been assessed to involve child abuse or neglect without appropriate and adequate training.

C. If the mediator has reasonable grounds to believe that a child of the participants is abused or neglected within the meaning of the jurisdiction's child abuse and neglect laws, the mediator shall comply with applicable child protection laws.

1. The mediator should encourage the participants to explore appropriate services for the family.

2. The mediator should consider the appropriateness of suspending or terminating the mediation process in light of the allegations.

Standard X

A family mediator shall recognize a family situation involving domestic abuse and take appropriate steps to shape the mediation process accordingly.

A. As used in these Standards, domestic abuse includes domestic violence as defined by applicable state law and issues of control and intimidation.

B. A mediator shall not undertake a mediation in which the family situation has been assessed to involve domestic abuse without appropriate and adequate training.

C. Some cases are not suitable for mediation because of safety, control or intimidation issues. A mediator should make a reasonable effort to screen for the existence of domestic abuse prior to entering into an agreement to mediate. The mediator should continue to assess for domestic abuse throughout the mediation process.

D. If domestic abuse appears to be present the mediator shall consider taking measures to insure the safety of participants and the mediator including among others:

1. establishing appropriate security arrangements;

2. holding separate sessions with the participants even without the agreement of all participants;

3. allowing a friend, representative, advocate, counsel or attorney to attend the mediation sessions;

4. encouraging the participants to be represented by an attorney, counsel or an advocate throughout the mediation process;

5. referring the participants to appropriate community resources;

6. suspending or terminating the mediation sessions, with appropriate steps to protect the safety of the participants.

E. The mediator should facilitate the participants' formulation of parenting plans that protect the physical safety and psychological well-being of themselves and their children.

Standard XI

A family mediator shall suspend or terminate the mediation process when the mediator reasonably believes that a participant is unable to effectively participate or for other compelling reason.

A. Circumstances under which a mediator should consider suspending or terminating the mediation, may include, among others:

1. the safety of a participant or well-being of a child is threatened;

2. a participant has or is threatening to abduct a child;

3. a participant is unable to participate due to the influence of drugs, alcohol, or physical or mental condition;

4. the participants are about to enter into an agreement that the mediator reasonably believes to be unconscionable;

5. a participant is using the mediation to further illegal conduct;

6. a participant is using the mediation process to gain an unfair advantage;

7. if the mediator believes the mediator's impartiality has been compromised in accordance with *Standard IV.*

B. If the mediator does suspend or terminate the mediation, the mediator should take all reasonable steps to minimize prejudice or inconvenience to the participants which may result.

Standard XII

A family mediator shall be truthful in the advertisement and solicitation for mediation.

A. Mediators should refrain from promises and guarantees of results. A mediator should not advertise statistical settlement data or settlement rates.

B. Mediators should accurately represent their qualifications. In an advertisement or other communication, a mediator may make reference to meeting state, national, or private organizational qualifications only if the entity referred to has a procedure for qualifying mediators and the mediator has been duly granted the requisite status.

Standard XIII

A family mediator shall acquire and maintain professional competence in mediation.

A. Mediators should continuously improve their professional skills and abilities by, among other activities, participating in relevant continuing education programs and should regularly engage in self-assessment.

B. Mediators should participate in programs of peer consultation and should help train and mentor the work of less experienced mediators.

C. Mediators should continuously strive to understand the impact of culture and diversity on the mediator's practice.

Appendix: Special Policy Considerations for State Regulation of Family Mediators and Court Affiliated Programs

The *Model Standards* recognize the *National Standards for Court Connected Dispute Resolution Programs* (1992). There are also state and local regulations governing such programs and family mediators. The following principles of organization and practice, however, are especially important for regulation of mediators and court-connected family mediation programs. They are worthy of separate mention.

A. Individual states or local courts should set standards and qualifications for family mediators including procedures for evaluations and handling grievances against mediators. In developing these standards and qualifications, regulators should consult with appropriate professional groups, including professional associations of family mediators.

B. When family mediators are appointed by a court or other institution, the appointing agency should make reasonable efforts to insure that each mediator is qualified for the appointment. If a list of family mediators qualified for court appointment exists, the requirements for being included on the list should be made public and available to all interested persons.

C. Confidentiality should not be construed to limit or prohibit the effective monitoring, research or evaluation of mediation programs by responsible individuals or academic institutions provided that no identifying information about any person involved in the mediation is disclose without their prior written consent. Under appropriate circumstances, researchers may be permitted to obtain access to statistical data and, with the permission of the participants, to individual case files, observations of live mediations, and interviews with participants.

APPENDIX E

THE MODEL STANDARDS OF CONDUCT FOR MEDIATORS

September 2005

Note: *This material was published in 2005 by the Association for Conflict Resolution (ACR), the Section of Dispute Resolution of the American Bar Association (ABA), and the American Arbitration Association (AAA). It is reproduced here by permission of the Association for Conflict Resolution (ACR), a merged organization of AFM, CREnet, and SPIDR.www.ACRnet.org.*

Preamble

Mediation is used to resolve a broad range of conflicts within a variety of settings. These Standards are designed to serve as fundamental ethical guidelines for persons mediating in all practice contexts. They serve three primary goals: to guide the conduct of mediators; to inform the mediating parties; and to promote public confidence in mediation as a process for resolving disputes.

Mediation is a process in which an impartial third party facilitates communication and negotiation and promotes voluntary decision making by the parties to the dispute.

Mediation serves various purposes, including providing the opportunity for parties to define and clarify issues, understand different perspectives, identify interests, explore and assess possible solutions, and reach mutually satisfactory agreements, when desired.

Note on Construction

These Standards are to be read and construed in their entirety. There is no priority significance attached to the sequence in which the Standards appear.

The use of the term "shall" in a Standard indicates that the mediator must follow the practice described. The use of the term "should" indicates that the practice described in the standard is highly desirable, but not required, and is to be departed from only for very strong reasons and requires careful use of judgment and discretion.

The use of the term "mediator" is understood to be inclusive so that it applies to co-mediator models.

These Standards do not include specific temporal parameters when referencing mediation, and therefore, do not define the exact beginning or ending of mediation.

Various aspects of a mediation, including some matters covered by these Standards, may also be affected by applicable law, court rules, regulations, other applicable professional rules, mediation rules to which the parties have agreed and other agreements of the parties. These sources may create conflicts with, and may take precedence over, these Standards. However, a mediator should make every effort to comply with the spirit and intent of these Standards in resolving such conflicts. This effort should include honoring all remaining Standards not in conflict with these other sources.

These Standards, unless and until adopted by a court or other regulatory authority do not have the force of law. Nonetheless, the fact that these Standards have been adopted by the respective sponsoring entities, should alert mediators to the fact that the Standards might be viewed as establishing a standard of care for mediators.

STANDARD I. SELF–DETERMINATION

A. A mediator shall conduct a mediation based on the principle of party self-determination. Self-determination is the act of coming to a voluntary, uncoerced decision in which each party makes free and informed choices as to process and outcome. Parties may exercise self-determination at any stage of mediation, including mediator selection, process design, participation in or withdrawal from the process, and outcomes.

1. Although party self-determination for process design is a fundamental principle of mediation practice, a mediator may need to balance such party self-determination with a mediator's duty to conduct a quality process in accordance with these Standards.

2. A mediator cannot personally ensure that each party has made free and informed choices to reach particular decisions, but, where appropriate, a mediator should make the parties aware of the importance of consulting other professionals to help them make informed choices.

B. A mediator shall not undermine party self-determination by any party for reasons such as higher settlement rates, egos, increased fees, or outside pressures from court personnel, program administrators, provider organizations, the media or others.

STANDARD II. IMPARTIALITY

A. A mediator shall decline a mediation if the mediator cannot conduct it in an impartial manner. Impartiality means freedom from favoritism, bias or prejudice.

B. A mediator shall conduct a mediation in an impartial manner and avoid conduct that gives the appearance of partiality.

1. A mediator should not act with partiality or prejudice based on any participant's personal characteristics, background, values and beliefs, or performance at a mediation, or any other reason.

2. A mediator should neither give nor accept a gift, favor, loan or other item of value that raises a question as to the mediator's actual or perceived impartiality.

3. A mediator may accept or give de minimis gifts or incidental items or services that are pro-

vided to facilitate a mediation or respect cultural norms so long as such practices do not raise questions as to a mediator's actual or perceived impartiality.

C. If at any time a mediator is unable to conduct a mediation in an impartial manner, the mediator shall withdraw.

STANDARD III. CONFLICTS OF INTEREST

A. A mediator shall avoid a conflict of interest or the appearance of a conflict of interest during and after a mediation. A conflict of interest can arise from involvement by a mediator with the subject matter of the dispute or from any relationship between a mediator and any mediation participant, whether past or present, personal or professional, that reasonably raises a question of a mediator's impartiality.

B. A mediator shall make a reasonable inquiry to determine whether there are any facts that a reasonable individual would consider likely to create a potential or actual conflict of interest for a mediator. A mediator's actions necessary to accomplish a reasonable inquiry into potential conflicts of interest may vary based on practice context.

C. A mediator shall disclose, as soon as practicable, all actual and potential conflicts of interest that are reasonably known to the mediator and could reasonably be seen as raising a question about the mediator's impartiality. After disclosure, if all parties agree, the mediator may proceed with the mediation.

D.   If a mediator learns any fact after accepting a mediation that raises a question with respect to that mediator's service creating a potential or actual conflict of interest, the mediator shall disclose it as quickly as practicable. After disclosure, if all parties agree, the mediator may proceed with the mediation.

E.   If a mediator's conflict of interest might reasonably be viewed as undermining the integrity of the mediation, a mediator shall withdraw from or decline to proceed with the mediation regardless of the expressed desire or agreement of the parties to the contrary.

F.   Subsequent to a mediation, a mediator shall not establish another relationship with any of the participants in any matter that would raise questions about the integrity of the mediation. When a mediator develops personal or professional relationships with parties, other individuals or organizations following a mediation in which they were involved, the mediator should consider factors such as time elapsed following the mediation, the nature of the relationships established, and services offered when determining whether the relationships might create a perceived or actual conflict of interest.

STANDARD IV. COMPETENCE

A.   A mediator shall mediate only when the mediator has the necessary competence to satisfy the reasonable expectations of the parties.

1. Any person may be selected as a mediator, provided that the parties are satisfied with the mediator's competence and qualifications. Training, experience in mediation, skills, cultural understandings and other qualities are often necessary for mediator competence. A person who offers to serve as a mediator creates the expectation that the person is competent to mediate effectively.

2. A mediator should attend educational programs and related activities to maintain and enhance the mediator's knowledge and skills related to mediation.

3. A mediator should have available for the parties' information relevant to the mediator's training, education, experience and approach to conducting a mediation.

B. If a mediator, during the course of a mediation determines that the mediator cannot conduct the mediation competently, the mediator shall discuss that determination with the parties as soon as is practicable and take appropriate steps to address the situation, including, but not limited to, withdrawing or requesting appropriate assistance.

C. If a mediator's ability to conduct a mediation is impaired by drugs, alcohol, medication or otherwise, the mediator shall not conduct the mediation.

STANDARD V. CONFIDENTIALITY

A. A mediator shall maintain the confidentiality of all information obtained by the mediator in mediation, unless otherwise agreed to by the parties or required by applicable law.

1.   If the parties to a mediation agree that the mediator may disclose information obtained during the mediation, the mediator may do so.

2.   A mediator should not communicate to any non-participant information about how the parties acted in the mediation. A mediator may report, if required, whether parties appeared at a scheduled mediation and whether or not the parties reached a resolution.

3.   If a mediator participates in teaching, research or evaluation of mediation, the mediator should protect the anonymity of the parties and abide by their reasonable expectations regarding confidentiality.

B.   A mediator who meets with any persons in private session during a mediation shall not convey directly or indirectly to any other person, any information that was obtained during that private session without the consent of the disclosing person.

C.   A mediator shall promote understanding among the parties of the extent to which the parties will maintain confidentiality of information they obtain in a mediation.

D.   Depending on the circumstance of a mediation, the parties may have varying expectations regarding confidentiality that a mediator should address. The parties may make their own rules with respect to confidentiality, or the accepted practice of an individual mediator or institution may dictate a particular set of expectations.

STANDARD VI. QUALITY OF THE PROCESS

A. A mediator shall conduct a mediation in accordance with these Standards and in a manner that promotes diligence, timeliness, safety, presence of the appropriate participants, party participation, procedural fairness, party competency and mutual respect among all participants.

1. A mediator should agree to mediate only when the mediator is prepared to commit the attention essential to an effective mediation.

2. A mediator should only accept cases when the mediator can satisfy the reasonable expectation of the parties concerning the timing of a mediation.

3. The presence or absence of persons at a mediation depends on the agreement of the parties and the mediator. The parties and mediator may agree that others may be excluded from particular sessions or from all sessions.

4. A mediator should promote honesty and candor between and among all participants, and a mediator shall not knowingly misrepresent any material fact or circumstance in the course of a mediation.

5. The role of a mediator differs substantially from other professional roles. Mixing the role of a mediator and the role of another profession is problematic and thus, a mediator should distin-

guish between the roles. A mediator may provide information that the mediator is qualified by training or experience to provide, only if the mediator can do so consistent with these Standards.

6. A mediator shall not conduct a dispute resolution procedure other than mediation but label it mediation in an effort to gain the protection of rules, statutes, or other governing authorities pertaining to mediation.

7. A mediator may recommend, when appropriate, that parties consider resolving their dispute through arbitration, counseling, neutral evaluation or other processes.

8. A mediator shall not undertake an additional dispute resolution role in the same matter without the consent of the parties. Before providing such service, a mediator shall inform the parties of the implications of the change in process and obtain their consent to the change. A mediator who undertakes such role assumes different duties and responsibilities that may be governed by other standards.

9. If a mediation is being used to further criminal conduct, a mediator should take appropriate steps including, if necessary, postponing, withdrawing from or terminating the mediation.

10. If a party appears to have difficulty comprehending the process, issues, or settlement options, or difficulty participating in a mediation, the mediator should explore the circumstances

and potential accommodations, modifications or adjustments that would make possible the party's capacity to comprehend, participate and exercise self-determination.

B. If a mediator is made aware of domestic abuse or violence among the parties, the mediator shall take appropriate steps including, if necessary, postponing, withdrawing from or terminating the mediation.

C. If a mediator believes that participant conduct, including that of the mediator, jeopardizes conducting a mediation consistent with these Standards, a mediator shall take appropriate steps including, if necessary, postponing, withdrawing from or terminating the mediation.

STANDARD VII. ADVERTISING AND SOLICITATION

A. A mediator shall be truthful and not misleading when advertising, soliciting or otherwise communicating the mediator's qualifications, experience, services and fees.

1. A mediator should not include any promises as to outcome in communications, including business cards, stationery, or computer-based communications.

2. A mediator should only claim to meet the mediator qualifications of a governmental entity or private organization if that entity or organization has a recognized procedure for qualifying

mediators and it grants such status to the mediator.

B.   A mediator shall not solicit in a manner that gives an appearance of partiality for or against a party or otherwise undermines the integrity of the process.

C.   A mediator shall not communicate to others, in promotional materials or through other forms of communication, the names of persons served without their permission.

STANDARD VIII. FEES AND OTHER CHARGES

A.   A mediator shall provide each party or each party's representative true and complete information about mediation fees, expenses and any other actual or potential charges that may be incurred in connection with a mediation.

1.   If a mediator charges fees, the mediator should develop them in light of all relevant factors, including the type and complexity of the matter, the qualifications of the mediator, the time required and the rates customary for such mediation services.

2.   A mediator's fee arrangement should be in writing unless the parties request otherwise.

B.   A mediator shall not charge fees in a manner that impairs a mediator's impartiality.

1.   A mediator should not enter into a fee agreement which is contingent upon the result of the mediation or amount of the settlement.

2. While a mediator may accept unequal fee payments from the parties, a mediator should not use fee arrangements that adversely impact the mediator's ability to conduct a mediation in an impartial manner.

STANDARD IX. ADVANCEMENT OF MEDIATION PRACTICE

A. A mediator should act in a manner that advances the practice of mediation. A mediator promotes this Standard by engaging in some or all of the following:

1. Fostering diversity within the field of mediation.

2. Striving to make mediation accessible to those who elect to use it, including providing services at a reduced rate or on a pro bono basis as appropriate.

3. Participating in research when given the opportunity, including obtaining participant feedback when appropriate.

4. Participating in outreach and education efforts to assist the public in developing an improved understanding of, and appreciation for, mediation.

5. Assisting newer mediators through training, mentoring and networking.

B. A mediator should demonstrate respect for differing points of view within the field, seek to learn from other mediators and work together with other mediators to improve the profession and better serve people in conflict.

Note:

The updated version of the Model Standards of Conduct for Mediators (2005) is the result of a collaborative effort between the Association for Conflict Resolution (ACR), the Section of Dispute Resolution of the American Bar Association (ABA), and the American Arbitration Association (AAA). The Model Standards were originally drafted and adopted in 1994 by the ABA Section of Dispute Resolution, the AAA, and the Society of Professionals in Dispute Resolution (or SPIDR which merged with two other organizations in 2001 to form ACR).

APPENDIX F

AMERICAN ARBITRATION ASSOCIATION COMMERCIAL ARBITRATION RULES AND COMMERCIAL MEDIATION PROCEDURES

IMPORTANT NOTICE

These rules and any amendment of them shall apply in the form in effect at the time the administrative filing requirements are met for a demand for arbitration or submission agreement received by the AAA. To ensure that you have the most current information, see our Web Site at www.adr.org.

INTRODUCTION

Each year, many millions of business transactions take place. Occasionally, disagreements develop over these business transactions. Many of these disputes are resolved by arbitration, the voluntary submission of a dispute to an impartial person or persons for final and binding determination. Arbitration has proven to be an effective way to resolve these disputes privately, promptly, and economically.

The American Arbitration Association (AAA), a not-for-profit, public service organization, offers a broad range of dispute resolution services to business executives, attorneys, individuals, trade associations, unions, management, consumers, families, communities, and all levels of government. Services are available through AAA headquarters in New York and through offices located in major cities throughout the United States. Hearings may be held at locations convenient for the parties and are not limited to cities with AAA offices. In addition, the AAA serves as a center for education and training, issues specialized publications, and conducts research on all forms of out-of-court dispute settlement.

Standard Arbitration Clause

The parties can provide for arbitration of future disputes by inserting the following clause into their contracts:

Any controversy or claim arising out of or relating to this contract, or the breach thereof, shall be settled by arbitration administered by the American Arbitration Association under its Commercial Arbitration Rules, and judgment on the award rendered by the arbitrator(s) may be entered in any court having jurisdiction thereof.

Arbitration of existing disputes may be accomplished by use of the following:

We, the undersigned parties, hereby agree to submit to arbitration administered by the American Arbitration Association under its Commercial Arbitration Rules the following controversy: (describe briefly) We further agree that the above controversy be submitted to (one) (three) arbitrator(s). We further agree that we will faithfully observe this agreement and the rules, that we will abide by and perform any award rendered by the arbitrator(s), and that a judgment of any court having jurisdiction may be entered on the award.

In transactions likely to require emergency interim relief, the parties may wish to add to their clause the following language:

The parties also agree that the AAA Optional Rules for Emergency Measures of Protection shall apply to the proceedings.

These Optional Rules may be found below.

The services of the AAA are generally concluded with the transmittal of the award. Although there is voluntary compliance with the majority of awards, judgment on the award can be entered in a court having appropriate jurisdiction if necessary.

Administrative Fees

The AAA charges a filing fee based on the amount of the claim or counterclaim. This fee information, which is included with these rules, allows the parties to exercise control over their administrative fees.

The fees cover AAA administrative services; they do not cover arbitrator compensation or expenses, if any, reporting services, or any post-award charges incurred by the parties in enforcing the award.

Mediation

The parties might wish to submit their dispute to mediation prior to arbitration. In mediation, the neutral mediator assists the parties in reaching a settlement but does not have the authority to make a binding decision or award. Mediation is administered by the AAA in accordance with its Commercial Mediation Procedures. There is no additional administrative fee where parties to a pending arbitration attempt to mediate their dispute under the AAA's auspices.

If the parties want to adopt mediation as a part of their contractual dispute settlement procedure, they can insert the following mediation clause into their contract in conjunction with a standard arbitration provision:

If a dispute arises out of or relates to this contract, or the breach thereof, and if the dispute cannot be settled through negotiation, the parties agree first to try in good faith to settle the dispute by mediation administered by the American Arbitration Association under its Commercial Mediation Procedures before resorting to arbitration, litigation, or some other dispute resolution procedure.

If the parties want to use a mediator to resolve an existing dispute, they can enter into the following submission:

The parties hereby submit the following dispute to mediation administered by the American Arbitration Association under its Commercial Mediation Procedures. (The clause may also provide for the qualifications of the mediator(s), method of payment, locale of meetings, and any other item of concern to the parties.)

Large, Complex Cases

Unless the parties agree otherwise, the procedures for Large, Complex Commercial Disputes, which appear in this pamphlet, will be applied to all cases administered by the AAA under the Commercial Arbitration Rules in which the disclosed claim or counterclaim of any party is at least $500,000 exclusive of claimed interest, arbitration fees and costs.

The key features of these procedures include:

§ a highly qualified, trained Roster of Neutrals;

§ a mandatory preliminary hearing with the arbitrators, which may be conducted by teleconference;

§ broad arbitrator authority to order and control discovery, including depositions;

§ presumption that hearings will proceed on a consecutive or block basis.

COMMERCIAL MEDIATION PROCEDURES

M–1. Agreement of Parties

Whenever, by stipulation or in their contract, the parties have provided for mediation or conciliation of existing or future disputes under the auspices of the American Arbitration Association (AAA) or under these procedures, the parties and their representatives, unless agreed otherwise in writing, shall be deemed to have made these procedural guidelines, as amended and in effect as of the date of filing of a request for mediation, a part of their agreement and designate the AAA as the administrator of their mediation.

The parties by mutual agreement may vary any part of these procedures including, but not limited to, agreeing to conduct the mediation via telephone or other electronic or technical means.

M–2. Initiation of Mediation

Any party or parties to a dispute may initiate mediation under the AAA's auspices by making a request for mediation to any of the AAA's regional offices or case management centers via telephone, email, regular mail or fax. Requests for mediation may also be filed online via WebFile at **www.adr. org.**

The party initiating the mediation shall simultaneously notify the other party or parties of the request. The initiating party shall provide the following information to the AAA and the other party or parties as applicable:

a) A copy of the mediation provision of the parties' contract or the parties' stipulation to mediate.

b) The names, regular mail addresses, email addresses, and telephone numbers of all parties to the dispute and representatives, if any, in the mediation.

c) A brief statement of the nature of the dispute and the relief requested.

d) Any specific qualifications the mediator should possess.

Where there is no preexisting stipulation or contract by which the parties have provided for mediation of existing or future disputes under the auspices of the AAA, a party may request the AAA to invite another party to participate in "mediation by voluntary submission". Upon receipt of such a request, the AAA will contact the other party or parties involved in the dispute and attempt to obtain a submission to mediation.

M–3. Representation

Subject to any applicable law, any party may be represented by persons of the party's choice. The names and addresses of such persons shall be communicated in writing to all parties and to the AAA.

M–4. Appointment of the Mediator

Parties may search the online profiles of the AAA's Panel of Mediators at www.aaamediation. com in an effort to agree on a mediator. If the parties have not agreed to the appointment of a mediator and have not provided any other method of appointment, the mediator shall be appointed in the following manner:

a) Upon receipt of a request for mediation, the AAA will send to each party a list of mediators from the AAA's Panel of Mediators. The parties are encouraged to agree to a mediator from the submitted list and to advise the AAA of their agreement.

b) If the parties are unable to agree upon a mediator, each party shall strike unacceptable names from the list, number the remaining names in order of preference, and return the list to the AAA. If a party does not return the list within the time specified, all mediators on the list shall be deemed acceptable. From among the mediators who have been mutually approved by the parties, and in accordance with the designated order of mutual preference, the AAA shall invite a mediator to serve.

c) If the parties fail to agree on any of the mediators listed, or if acceptable mediators are unable to serve, or if for any other reason the appointment cannot be made from the submitted list, the AAA shall have the authority to make the appointment from among other members of the Panel of Mediators without the submission of additional lists.

M–5. Mediator's Impartiality and Duty to Disclose

AAA mediators are required to abide by the Model Standards of Conduct for Mediators in effect at the time a mediator is appointed to a case. Where there is a conflict between the Model Standards and any provision of these Mediation Procedures, these Mediation Procedures shall govern. The Standards require mediators to (i) decline a mediation if the mediator cannot conduct it in an impartial manner, and (ii) disclose, as soon as practicable, all actual and potential conflicts of interest that are reasonably known to the mediator and could reasonably be seen as raising a question about the mediator's impartiality.

Prior to accepting an appointment, AAA mediators are required to make a reasonable inquiry to determine whether there are any facts that a reasonable individual would consider likely to create a potential or actual conflict of interest for the mediator. AAA mediators are required to disclose any circumstance likely to create a presumption of bias or prevent a resolution of the parties' dispute within the time-frame desired by the parties. Upon receipt of such disclosures, the AAA shall immediately communicate the disclosures to the parties for their comments.

The parties may, upon receiving disclosure of actual or potential conflicts of interest of the mediator, waive such conflicts and proceed with the mediation. In the event that a party disagrees as to whether the mediator shall serve, or in the event that the mediator's conflict of interest might reasonably be viewed as undermining the integrity of the mediation, the mediator shall be replaced.

M–6. Vacancies

If any mediator shall become unwilling or unable to serve, the AAA will appoint another mediator, unless the parties agree otherwise, in accordance with section M–4.

M–7. Duties and Responsibilities of the Mediator

a) The mediator shall conduct the mediation based on the principle of party self-determination. Self-determination is the act of coming to a voluntary, uncoerced decision in which each party makes free and informed choices as to process and outcome.

b) The mediator is authorized to conduct separate or ex parte meetings and other communications with the parties and/or their representatives, before, during, and after any scheduled mediation conference. Such communications may be conducted via telephone, in writing, via email, online, in person or otherwise.

c) The parties are encouraged to exchange all documents pertinent to the relief requested. The mediator may request the exchange of memoranda on issues, including the underlying interests and the history of the parties' negotiations. Information that a party wishes to keep confidential may be sent to the mediator, as necessary, in a separate communication with the mediator.

d) The mediator does not have the authority to impose a settlement on the parties but will attempt to help them reach a satisfactory resolution of their dispute. Subject to the discretion of the mediator, the mediator may make oral or written recommendations for settlement to a party privately or, if the parties agree, to all parties jointly.

e) In the event a complete settlement of all or some issues in dispute is not achieved within the scheduled mediation session(s), the mediator may continue to communicate with the parties, for a period of time, in an ongoing effort to facilitate a complete settlement.

The mediator is not a legal representative of any party and has no fiduciary duty to any party.

M–8. Responsibilities of the Parties

The parties shall ensure that appropriate representatives of each party, having authority to consummate a settlement, attend the mediation conference.

Prior to and during the scheduled mediation conference session(s) the parties and their representatives shall, as appropriate to each party's circumstances, exercise their best efforts to prepare for and engage in a meaningful and productive mediation.

M–9. Privacy

Mediation sessions and related mediation communications are private proceedings. The parties and their representatives may attend mediation sessions. Other persons may attend only with the permission of the parties and with the consent of the mediator.

M–10. Confidentiality

Subject to applicable law or the parties' agreement, confidential information disclosed to a mediator by the parties or by other participants (witnesses) in the course of the mediation shall not be divulged by the mediator. The mediator shall maintain the confidentiality of all information obtained in the mediation, and all records, reports, or other documents received by a mediator while serving in that capacity shall be confidential.

The mediator shall not be compelled to divulge such records or to testify in regard to the mediation in any adversary proceeding or judicial forum.

The parties shall maintain the confidentiality of the mediation and shall not rely on, or introduce as evidence in any arbitral, judicial, or other proceeding the following, unless agreed to by the parties or required by applicable law:

a) Views expressed or suggestions made by a party or other participant with respect to a possible settlement of the dispute;

b) Admissions made by a party or other participant in the course of the mediation proceedings;

c) Proposals made or views expressed by the mediator; or

d) The fact that a party had or had not indicated willingness to accept a proposal for settlement made by the mediator.

M–11. No Stenographic Record

There shall be no stenographic record of the mediation process.

M–12. Termination of Mediation

The mediation shall be terminated:

a) By the execution of a settlement agreement by the parties; or

b) By a written or verbal declaration of the mediator to the effect that further efforts at mediation would not contribute to a resolution of the parties' dispute; or

c) By a written or verbal declaration of all parties to the effect that the mediation proceedings are terminated; or

d) When there has been no communication between the mediator and any party or party's representative for 21 days following the conclusion of the mediation conference.

M–13. Exclusion of Liability

Neither the AAA nor any mediator is a necessary party in judicial proceedings relating to the mediation. Neither the AAA nor any mediator shall be liable to any party for any error, act or omission in connection with any mediation conducted under these procedures.

M–14. Interpretation and Application of Procedures

The mediator shall interpret and apply these procedures insofar as they relate to the mediator's duties and responsibilities. All other procedures shall be interpreted and applied by the AAA.

M–15. Deposits

Unless otherwise directed by the mediator, the AAA will require the parties to deposit in advance of the mediation conference such sums of money as it, in consultation with the mediator, deems necessary to cover the costs and expenses of the mediation and shall render an accounting to the parties and return any unexpended balance at the conclusion of the mediation.

M–16. Expenses

All expenses of the mediation, including required traveling and other expenses or charges of the mediator, shall be borne equally by the parties unless they agree otherwise. The expenses of participants for either side shall be paid by the party requesting the attendance of such participants.

M–17. Cost of the Mediation

There is no filing fee to initiate a mediation or a fee to request the AAA to invite parties to mediate.

The cost of mediation is based on the hourly mediation rate published on the mediator's AAA profile. This rate covers both mediator compensation and an allocated portion for the AAA's services. There is a four-hour minimum charge for a mediation conference. Expenses referenced in Section M–16 may also apply.

If a matter submitted for mediation is withdrawn or cancelled or results in a settlement after the agreement to mediate is filed but prior to the mediation conference the cost is $250 plus any mediator time and charges incurred.

The parties will be billed equally for all costs unless they agree otherwise.

If you have questions about mediation costs or services visit our website at www.adr.org or contact your local AAA office.

Conference Room Rental

The costs described above do not include the use of AAA conference rooms. Conference rooms are available on a rental basis. Please contact your local AAA office for availability and rates.

COMMERCIAL ARBITRATION RULES

R–1. Agreement of Parties*†

(a) The parties shall be deemed to have made these rules a part of their arbitration agreement whenever they have provided for arbitration by the

---

* The AAA applies the *Supplementary Procedures for Consumer–Related Disputes* to arbitration clauses in agreements between individual consumers and businesses where the business has a standardized, systematic application of arbitration clauses with customers and where the terms and conditions of the purchase of standardized, consumable goods or services are nonnegotiable or primarily non-negotiable in most or all of its terms, conditions, features, or choices. The product or service must be for personal or household use. The AAA will have the discretion to apply or not to apply the Supplementary Procedures and the parties will be able to bring any disputes concerning the application or non-application to the attention of the arbitrator. Consumers are not prohibited from seeking relief in a small claims court for disputes or claims within the scope of its jurisdiction, even in consumer arbitration cases filed by the business.

† A dispute arising out of an employer promulgated plan will be administered under the AAA's National Rules for the Resolution of Employment Disputes.

American Arbitration Association (hereinafter AAA) under its Commercial Arbitration Rules or for arbitration by the AAA of a domestic commercial dispute without specifying particular rules. These rules and any amendment of them shall apply in the form in effect at the time the administrative requirements are met for a demand for arbitration or submission agreement received by the AAA. The parties, by written agreement, may vary the procedures set forth in these rules. After appointment of the arbitrator, such modifications may be made only with the consent of the arbitrator.

(b) Unless the parties or the AAA determines otherwise, the Expedited Procedures shall apply in any case in which no disclosed claim or counterclaim exceeds $75,000, exclusive of interest and arbitration fees and costs. Parties may also agree to use these procedures in larger cases. Unless the parties agree otherwise, these procedures will not apply in cases involving more than two parties. The Expedited Procedures shall be applied as described in Sections E–1 through E–10 of these rules, in addition to any other portion of these rules that is not in conflict with the Expedited Procedures.

(c) Unless the parties agree otherwise, the Procedures for Large, Complex Commercial Disputes shall apply to all cases in which the disclosed claim or counterclaim of any party is at least $500,000, exclusive of claimed interest, arbitration fees and costs. Parties may also agree to use the Procedures in cases involving claims or counterclaims under $500,000, or in nonmonetary cases. The Procedures for Large, Complex Commercial Disputes shall be applied as described in Sections L–1 through L–4 of these rules, in addition to any other portion of these rules that is not in conflict with the Procedures for Large, Complex Commercial Disputes.

(d) All other cases shall be administered in accordance with Sections R–1 through R–54 of these rules.

R–2. AAA and Delegation of Duties

When parties agree to arbitrate under these rules, or when they provide for arbitration by the AAA and an arbitration is initiated under these rules, they thereby authorize the AAA to administer the arbitration. The authority and duties of the AAA are prescribed in the agreement of the parties and in these rules, and may be carried out through such of the AAA's representatives as it may direct. The AAA may, in its discretion, assign the administration of an arbitration to any of its offices.

R–3. National Roster of Arbitrators

The AAA shall establish and maintain a National Roster of Commercial Arbitrators ("National Roster") and shall appoint arbitrators as provided in these rules. The term "arbitrator" in these rules refers to the arbitration panel, constituted for a particular case, whether composed of one or more arbitrators, or to an individual arbitrator, as the context requires.

R–4. Initiation under an Arbitration Provision in a Contract

(a) Arbitration under an arbitration provision in a contract shall be initiated in the following manner:

(i) The initiating party (the "claimant") shall, within the time period, if any, specified in the contract(s), give to the other party (the "respondent") written notice of its intention to arbitrate (the "demand"), which demand shall contain a statement setting forth the nature of the dispute, the names and addresses of all other parties, the amount involved, if any, the remedy sought, and the hearing locale requested.

(ii) The claimant shall file at any office of the AAA two copies of the demand and two copies of the arbitration provisions of the contract, together with the appropriate filing fee as provided in the schedule included with these rules.

(iii) The AAA shall confirm notice of such filing to the parties.

(b) A respondent may file an answering statement in duplicate with the AAA within 15 days after confirmation of notice of filing of the demand is sent by the AAA. The respondent shall, at the time of any such filing, send a copy of the answering statement to the claimant. If a counterclaim is asserted, it shall contain a statement setting forth the nature of the counterclaim, the amount involved, if any, and the remedy sought. If a counterclaim is made, the party making the counterclaim shall forward to the AAA with the answering statement the appropriate fee provided in the schedule included with these rules.

(c) If no answering statement is filed within the stated time, respondent will be deemed to deny the claim. Failure to file an answering statement shall not operate to delay the arbitration.

(d) When filing any statement pursuant to this section, the parties are encouraged to provide descriptions of their claims in sufficient detail to make the circumstances of the dispute clear to the arbitrator.

R–5. Initiation under a Submission

Parties to any existing dispute may commence an arbitration under these rules by filing at any office of the AAA two copies of a written submission to arbitrate under these rules, signed by the parties. It shall contain a statement of the nature of the dispute, the names and addresses of all parties, any claims and counterclaims, the amount involved, if any, the remedy sought, and the hearing locale requested, together with the appropriate filing fee as provided in the schedule included with these rules. Unless the parties state otherwise in the submission, all claims and counterclaims will be deemed to be denied by the other party.

R–6. Changes of Claim

After filing of a claim, if either party desires to make any new or different claim or counterclaim, it shall be made in writing and filed with the AAA.

The party asserting such a claim or counterclaim shall provide a copy to the other party, who shall have 15 days from the date of such transmission within which to file an answering statement with the AAA. After the arbitrator is appointed, however, no new or different claim may be submitted except with the arbitrator's consent.

R–7. Jurisdiction

(a) The arbitrator shall have the power to rule on his or her own jurisdiction, including any objections with respect to the existence, scope or validity of the arbitration agreement.

(b) The arbitrator shall have the power to determine the existence or validity of a contract of which an arbitration clause forms a part. Such an arbitration clause shall be treated as an agreement independent of the other terms of the contract. A decision by the arbitrator that the contract is null and void shall not for that reason alone render invalid the arbitration clause.

(c) A party must object to the jurisdiction of the arbitrator or to the arbitrability of a claim or counterclaim no later than the filing of the answering statement to the claim or counterclaim that gives rise to the objection. The arbitrator may rule on such objections as a preliminary matter or as part of the final award.

R–8. Mediation

At any stage of the proceedings, the parties may agree to conduct a mediation conference under the

Commercial Mediation Procedures in order to facilitate settlement. The mediator shall not be an arbitrator appointed to the case. Where the parties to a pending arbitration agree to mediate under the AAA's rules, no additional administrative fee is required to initiate the mediation.

R–9. Administrative Conference

At the request of any party or upon the AAA's own initiative, the AAA may conduct an administrative conference, in person or by telephone, with the parties and/or their representatives. The conference may address such issues as arbitrator selection, potential mediation of the dispute, potential exchange of information, a timetable for hearings and any other administrative matters.

R–10. Fixing of Locale

The parties may mutually agree on the locale where the arbitration is to be held. If any party requests that the hearing be held in a specific locale and the other party files no objection thereto within 15 days after notice of the request has been sent to it by the AAA, the locale shall be the one requested. If a party objects to the locale requested by the other party, the AAA shall have the power to determine the locale, and its decision shall be final and binding.

R–11. Appointment from National Roster

If the parties have not appointed an arbitrator and have not provided any other method of appointment, the arbitrator shall be appointed in the following manner:

(a) Immediately after the filing of the submission or the answering statement or the expiration of the time within which the answering statement is to be filed, the AAA shall send simultaneously to each party to the dispute an identical list of 10 (unless the AAA decides that a different number is appropriate) names of persons chosen from the National Roster. The parties are encouraged to agree to an arbitrator from the submitted list and to advise the AAA of their agreement.

(b) If the parties are unable to agree upon an arbitrator, each party to the dispute shall have 15 days from the transmittal date in which to strike names objected to, number the remaining names in order of preference, and return the list to the AAA. If a party does not return the list within the time specified, all persons named therein shall be deemed acceptable. From among the persons who have been approved on both lists, and in accordance with the designated order of mutual preference, the AAA shall invite the acceptance of an arbitrator to serve. If the parties fail to agree on any of the persons named, or if acceptable arbitrators are unable to act, or if for any other reason the appointment cannot be made from the submitted lists, the AAA shall have the power to make the appointment from among other members of the National Roster without the submission of additional lists.

(c) Unless the parties agree otherwise when there are two or more claimants or two or more respondents, the AAA may appoint all the arbitrators.

R–12.   Direct Appointment by a Party

(a) If the agreement of the parties names an arbitrator or specifies a method of appointing an arbitrator, that designation or method shall be followed. The notice of appointment, with the name and address of the arbitrator, shall be filed with the AAA by the appointing party. Upon the request of any appointing party, the AAA shall submit a list of members of the National Roster from which the party may, if it so desires, make the appointment.

(b) Where the parties have agreed that each party is to name one arbitrator, the arbitrators so named must meet the standards of Section R–17 with respect to impartiality and independence unless the parties have specifically agreed pursuant to Section R–17(a) that the party-appointed arbitrators are to be non-neutral and need not meet those standards.

(c) If the agreement specifies a period of time within which an arbitrator shall be appointed and any party fails to make the appointment within that period, the AAA shall make the appointment.

(d) If no period of time is specified in the agreement, the AAA shall notify the party to make the appointment. If within 15 days after such notice has been sent, an arbitrator has not been appointed by a party, the AAA shall make the appointment.

R–13. Appointment of Chairperson by Party– Appointed Arbitrators or Parties

(a) If, pursuant to Section R–12, either the parties have directly appointed arbitrators, or the arbitrators have been appointed by the AAA, and the parties have authorized them to appoint a chairperson within a specified time and no appointment is made within that time or any agreed extension, the AAA may appoint the chairperson.

(b) If no period of time is specified for appointment of the chairperson and the party-appointed arbitrators or the parties do not make the appointment within 15 days from the date of the appointment of the last party-appointed arbitrator, the AAA may appoint the chairperson.

(c) If the parties have agreed that their party-appointed arbitrators shall appoint the chairperson from the National Roster, the AAA shall furnish to the party-appointed arbitrators, in the manner provided in Section R–11, a list selected from the National Roster, and the appointment of the chairperson shall be made as provided in that Section.

R–14. Nationality of Arbitrator

Where the parties are nationals of different countries, the AAA, at the request of any party or on its own initiative, may appoint as arbitrator a national of a country other than that of any of the parties. The request must be made before the time set for the appointment of the arbitrator as agreed by the parties or set by these rules.

R–15.   Number of Arbitrators

If the arbitration agreement does not specify the number of arbitrators, the dispute shall be heard and determined by one arbitrator, unless the AAA, in its discretion, directs that three arbitrators be appointed. A party may request three arbitrators in the demand or answer, which request the AAA will consider in exercising its discretion regarding the number of arbitrators appointed to the dispute.

R–16.   Disclosure

(a) Any person appointed or to be appointed as an arbitrator shall disclose to the AAA any circumstance likely to give rise to justifiable doubt as to the arbitrator's impartiality or independence, including any bias or any financial or personal interest in the result of the arbitration or any past or present relationship with the parties or their representatives. Such obligation shall remain in effect throughout the arbitration.

(b) Upon receipt of such information from the arbitrator or another source, the AAA shall communicate the information to the parties and, if it deems it appropriate to do so, to the arbitrator and others.

(c) In order to encourage disclosure by arbitrators, disclosure of information pursuant to this Section R–16 is not to be construed as an indication that the arbitrator considers that the disclosed circumstance is likely to affect impartiality or independence.

R–17. Disqualification of Arbitrator

(a) Any arbitrator shall be impartial and independent and shall perform his or her duties with diligence and in good faith, and shall be subject to disqualification for

(i) partiality or lack of independence,

(ii) inability or refusal to perform his or her duties with diligence and in good faith, and

(iii) any grounds for disqualification provided by applicable law. The parties may agree in writing, however, that arbitrators directly appointed by a party pursuant to Section R–12 shall be nonneutral, in which case such arbitrators need not be impartial or independent and shall not be subject to disqualification for partiality or lack of independence.

(b) Upon objection of a party to the continued service of an arbitrator, or on its own initiative, the AAA shall determine whether the arbitrator should be disqualified under the grounds set out above, and shall inform the parties of its decision, which decision shall be conclusive.

R–18. Communication with Arbitrator

(a) No party and no one acting on behalf of any party shall communicate ex parte with an arbitrator or a candidate for arbitrator concerning the arbitration, except that a party, or someone acting on behalf of a party, may communicate ex parte with a candidate for direct appointment pursuant to Section R–12 in order to advise the candidate of the general nature of the controversy and of the anticipated proceedings and to discuss the candidate's qualifications, availability, or independence in relation to the parties or to discuss the suitability of candidates for selection as a third arbitrator where the parties or party-designated arbitrators are to participate in that selection.

(b) Section R–18(a) does not apply to arbitrators directly appointed by the parties who, pursuant to Section R–17(a), the parties have agreed in writing are non-neutral. Where the parties have so agreed under Section R–17(a), the AAA shall as an administrative practice suggest to the parties that they agree further that Section R–18(a) should nonetheless apply prospectively.

R–19. Vacancies

(a) If for any reason an arbitrator is unable to perform the duties of the office, the AAA may, on proof satisfactory to it, declare the office vacant. Vacancies shall be filled in accordance with the applicable provisions of these rules.

(b) In the event of a vacancy in a panel of neutral arbitrators after the hearings have commenced, the remaining arbitrator or arbitrators may continue with the hearing and determination of the controversy, unless the parties agree otherwise.

(c) In the event of the appointment of a substitute arbitrator, the panel of arbitrators shall determine in its sole discretion whether it is necessary to repeat all or part of any prior hearings.

R–20. Preliminary Hearing

(a) At the request of any party or at the discretion of the arbitrator or the AAA, the arbitrator may schedule as soon as practicable a preliminary hearing with the parties and/or their representatives. The preliminary hearing may be conducted by telephone at the arbitrator's discretion.

(b) During the preliminary hearing, the parties and the arbitrator should discuss the future conduct of the case, including clarification of the issues and claims, a schedule for the hearings and any other preliminary matters.

R–21. Exchange of Information

(a) At the request of any party or at the discretion of the arbitrator, consistent with the expedited nature of arbitration, the arbitrator may direct

  i) the production of documents and other information, and

  ii) the identification of any witnesses to be called.

(b) At least five business days prior to the hearing, the parties shall exchange copies of all exhibits they intend to submit at the hearing.

(c) The arbitrator is authorized to resolve any disputes concerning the exchange of information.

R–22. Date, Time, and Place of Hearing

The arbitrator shall set the date, time, and place for each hearing. The parties shall respond to requests for hearing dates in a timely manner, be cooperative in scheduling the earliest practicable date, and adhere to the established hearing schedule. The AAA shall send a notice of hearing to the parties at least 10 days in advance of the hearing date, unless otherwise agreed by the parties.

R–23. Attendance at Hearings

The arbitrator and the AAA shall maintain the privacy of the hearings unless the law provides to the contrary. Any person having a direct interest in the arbitration is entitled to attend hearings. The arbitrator shall otherwise have the power to require the exclusion of any witness, other than a party or other essential person, during the testimony of any other witness. It shall be discretionary with the arbitrator to determine the propriety of the attendance of any other person other than a party and its representatives.

R–24. Representation

Any party may be represented by counsel or other authorized representative. A party intending to be so represented shall notify the other party and the AAA of the name and address of the representative at least three days prior to the date set for the hearing at which that person is first to appear. When such a representative initiates an arbitration or responds for a party, notice is deemed to have been given.

R–25. Oaths

Before proceeding with the first hearing, each arbitrator may take an oath of office and, if required by law, shall do so. The arbitrator may require witnesses to testify under oath administered by any duly qualified person and, if it is required by law or requested by any party, shall do so.

R–26. Stenographic Record

Any party desiring a stenographic record shall make arrangements directly with a stenographer and shall notify the other parties of these arrangements at least three days in advance of the hearing. The requesting party or parties shall pay the cost of the record. If the transcript is agreed by the parties, or determined by the arbitrator to be the official record of the proceeding, it must be provided to the arbitrator and made available to the other parties for inspection, at a date, time, and place determined by the arbitrator.

R–27. Interpreters

Any party wishing an interpreter shall make all arrangements directly with the interpreter and shall assume the costs of the service.

R–28. Postponements

The arbitrator may postpone any hearing upon agreement of the parties, upon request of a party for good cause shown, or upon the arbitrator's own initiative.

R–29. Arbitration in the Absence of a Party or Representative

Unless the law provides to the contrary, the arbitration may proceed in the absence of any party or representative who, after due notice, fails to be present or fails to obtain a postponement. An award shall not be made solely on the default of a party. The arbitrator shall require the party who is present to submit such evidence as the arbitrator may require for the making of an award.

R–30. Conduct of Proceedings

(a) The claimant shall present evidence to support its claim. The respondent shall then present evidence to support its defense. Witnesses for each party shall also submit to questions from the arbitrator and the adverse party. The arbitrator has the discretion to vary this procedure, provided that the parties are treated with equality and that each party has the right to be heard and is given a fair opportunity to present its case.

(b) The arbitrator, exercising his or her discretion, shall conduct the proceedings with a view to expediting the resolution of the dispute and may direct the order of proof, bifurcate proceedings and direct the parties to focus their presentations on issues the decision of which could dispose of all or part of the case.

(c) The parties may agree to waive oral hearings in any case.

R–31. Evidence

(a) The parties may offer such evidence as is relevant and material to the dispute and shall produce such evidence as the arbitrator may deem necessary to an understanding and determination of the dispute. Conformity to legal rules of evidence shall not be necessary. All evidence shall be taken in the presence of all of the arbitrators and all of the parties, except where any of the parties is absent, in default or has waived the right to be present.

(b) The arbitrator shall determine the admissibility, relevance, and materiality of the evidence offered and may exclude evidence deemed by the arbitrator to be cumulative or irrelevant.

(c) The arbitrator shall take into account applicable principles of legal privilege, such as those involving the confidentiality of communications between a lawyer and client.

(d) An arbitrator or other person authorized by law to subpoena witnesses or documents may do so upon the request of any party or independently.

R–32. Evidence by Affidavit and Post-hearing Filing of Documents or Other Evidence

(a) The arbitrator may receive and consider the evidence of witnesses by declaration or affidavit, but shall give it only such weight as the arbitrator deems it entitled to after consideration of any objection made to its admission.

(b) If the parties agree or the arbitrator directs that documents or other evidence be submitted to the arbitrator after the hearing, the documents or other evidence shall be filed with the AAA for transmission to the arbitrator. All parties shall be afforded an opportunity to examine and respond to such documents or other evidence.

R–33.   Inspection or Investigation

An arbitrator finding it necessary to make an inspection or investigation in connection with the arbitration shall direct the AAA to so advise the parties. The arbitrator shall set the date and time and the AAA shall notify the parties. Any party who so desires may be present at such an inspection or investigation. In the event that one or all parties are not present at the inspection or investigation, the arbitrator shall make an oral or written report to the parties and afford them an opportunity to comment.

R–34.   Interim Measures**

(a) The arbitrator may take whatever interim measures he or she deems necessary, including injunctive relief and measures for the protection or conservation of property and disposition of perishable goods.

** The Optional Rules may be found below.

(b) Such interim measures may take the form of an interim award, and the arbitrator may require security for the costs of such measures.

(c) A request for interim measures addressed by a party to a judicial authority shall not be deemed incompatible with the agreement to arbitrate or a waiver of the right to arbitrate.

R–35. Closing of Hearing

The arbitrator shall specifically inquire of all parties whether they have any further proofs to offer or witnesses to be heard. Upon receiving negative replies or if satisfied that the record is complete, the arbitrator shall declare the hearing closed. If briefs are to be filed, the hearing shall b e declared closed as of the final date set by the arbitrator for the receipt of briefs. If documents are to be filed as provided in Section R–32 and the date set for their receipt is later than that set for the receipt of briefs, the later date shall be the closing date of the hearing. The time limit within which the arbitrator is required to make the award shall commence, in the absence of other agreements by the parties, upon the closing of the hearing.

R–36. Reopening of Hearing

The hearing may be reopened on the arbitrator's initiative, or upon application of a party, at any time before the award is made. If reopening the hearing would prevent the making of the award within the specific time agreed on by the parties in the contract(s) out of which the controversy has arisen, the matter may not be reopened unless the parties agree on an extension of time. When no specific date is fixed in the contract, the arbitrator may reopen the hearing and shall have 30 days from the closing of the reopened hearing within which to make an award.

R–37. Waiver of Rules

Any party who proceeds with the arbitration after knowledge that any provision or requirement of these rules has not been complied with and who fails to state an objection in writing shall be deemed to have waived the right to object.

R–38. Extensions of Time

The parties may modify any period of time by mutual agreement. The AAA or the arbitrator may for good cause extend any period of time established by these rules, except the time for making the award. The AAA shall notify the parties of any extension.

R–39. Serving of Notice

(a) Any papers, notices, or process necessary or proper for the initiation or continuation of an arbitration under these rules, for any court action in connection therewith, or for the entry of judgment on any award made under these rules may be served on a party by mail addressed to the party, or its representative at the last known address or by personal service, in or outside the state where the arbitration is to be held, provided that reasonable opportunity to be heard with regard to the dispute is or has been granted to the party.

(b) The AAA, the arbitrator and the parties may also use overnight delivery or electronic facsimile transmission (fax), to give the notices required by these rules. Where all parties and the arbitrator agree, notices may be transmitted by electronic mail (E-mail), or other methods of communication.

(c) Unless otherwise instructed by the AAA or by the arbitrator, any documents submitted by any party to the AAA or to the arbitrator shall simultaneously be provided to the other party or parties to the arbitration.

R–40. Majority Decision

When the panel consists of more than one arbitrator, unless required by law or by the arbitration agreement, a majority of the arbitrators must make all decisions.

R–41. Time of Award

The award shall be made promptly by the arbitrator and, unless otherwise agreed by the parties or specified by law, no later than 30 days from the date of closing the hearing, or, if oral hearings have been waived, from the date of the AAA's transmittal of the final statements and proofs to the arbitrator.

R–42. Form of Award

(a) Any award shall be in writing and signed by a majority of the arbitrators. It shall be executed in the manner required by law.

(b) The arbitrator need not render a reasoned award unless the parties request such an award in writing prior to appointment of the arbitrator or unless the arbitrator determines that a reasoned award is appropriate.

R–43.   Scope of Award

(a) The arbitrator may grant any remedy or relief that the arbitrator deems just and equitable and within the scope of the agreement of the parties, including, but not limited to, specific performance of a contract.

(b) In addition to a final award, the arbitrator may make other decisions, including interim, interlocutory, or partial rulings, orders, and awards. In any interim, interlocutory, or partial award, the arbitrator may assess and apportion the fees, expenses, and compensation related to such award as the arbitrator determines is appropriate.

(c) In the final award, the arbitrator shall assess the fees, expenses, and compensation provided in Sections R–49, R–50, and R–51. The arbitrator may apportion such fees, expenses, and compensation among the parties in such amounts as the arbitrator determines is appropriate.

(d) The award of the arbitrator(s) may include:

(i) interest at such rate and from such date as the arbitrator(s) may deem appropriate; and

(ii) an award of attorneys' fees if all parties have requested such an award or it is authorized by law or their arbitration agreement.

R–44. Award upon Settlement

If the parties settle their dispute during the course of the arbitration and if the parties so request, the arbitrator may set forth the terms of the settlement in a "consent award." A consent award must include an allocation of arbitration costs, including administrative fees and expenses as well as arbitrator fees and expenses.

R–45. Delivery of Award to Parties

Parties shall accept as notice and delivery of the award the placing of the award or a true copy thereof in the mail addressed to the parties or their representatives at the last known addresses, personal or electronic service of the award, or the filing of the award in any other manner that is permitted by law.

R–46. Modification of Award

Within 20 days after the transmittal of an award, any party, upon notice to the other parties, may request the arbitrator, through the AAA, to correct any clerical, typographical, or computational errors in the award. The arbitrator is not empowered to redetermine the merits of any claim already decided. The other parties shall be given 10 days to respond to the request. The arbitrator shall dispose of the request within 20 days after transmittal by the AAA to the arbitrator of the request and any response thereto.

R–47. Release of Documents for Judicial Proceedings

The AAA shall, upon the written request of a party, furnish to the party, at the party's expense, certified copies of any papers in the AAA's possession that may be required in judicial proceedings relating to the arbitration.

R–48. Applications to Court and Exclusion of Liability

(a) No judicial proceeding by a party relating to the subject matter of the arbitration shall be deemed a waiver of the party's right to arbitrate.

(b) Neither the AAA nor any arbitrator in a proceeding under these rules is a necessary or proper party in judicial proceedings relating to the arbitration.

(c) Parties to an arbitration under these rules shall be deemed to have consented that judgment upon the arbitration award may be entered in any federal or state court having jurisdiction thereof.

(d) Parties to an arbitration under these rules shall be deemed to have consented that neither the AAA nor any arbitrator shall be liable to any party in any action for damages or injunctive relief for any act or omission in connection with any arbitration under these rules.

R–49. Administrative Fees

As a not-for-profit organization, the AAA shall prescribe an initial filing fee and a case service fee

to compensate it for the cost of providing administrative services. The fees in effect when the fee or charge is incurred shall be applicable. The filing fee shall be advanced by the party or parties making a claim or counterclaim, subject to final apportionment by the arbitrator in the award. The AAA may, in the event of extreme hardship on the part of any party, defer or reduce the administrative fees.

R–50. Expenses

The expenses of witnesses for either side shall be paid by the party producing such witnesses. All other expenses of the arbitration, including required travel and other expenses of the arbitrator, AAA representatives, and any witness and the cost of any proof produced at the direct request of the arbitrator, shall be borne equally by the parties, unless they agree otherwise or unless the arbitrator in the award assesses such expenses or any part thereof against any specified party or parties.

R–51. Neutral Arbitrator's Compensation

(a) Arbitrators shall be compensated at a rate consistent with the arbitrator's stated rate of compensation.

(b) If there is disagreement concerning the terms of compensation, an appropriate rate shall be established with the arbitrator by the AAA and confirmed to the parties.

(c) Any arrangement for the compensation of a neutral arbitrator shall be made through the AAA

and not directly between the parties and the arbitrator.

R–52. Deposits

The AAA may require the parties to deposit in advance of any hearings such sums of money as it deems necessary to cover the expense of the arbitration, including the arbitrator's fee, if any, and shall render an accounting to the parties and return any unexpended balance at the conclusion of the case.

R–53. Interpretation and Application of Rules

The arbitrator shall interpret and apply these rules insofar as they relate to the arbitrator's powers and duties. When there is more than one arbitrator and a difference arises among them concerning the meaning or application of these rules, it shall be decided by a majority vote. If that is not possible, either an arbitrator or a party may refer the question to the AAA for final decision. All other rules shall be interpreted and applied by the AAA.

R–54. Suspension for Nonpayment

If arbitrator compensation or administrative charges have not been paid in full, the AAA may so inform the parties in order that one of them may advance the required payment. If such payments are not made, the arbitrator may order the suspension or termination of the proceedings. If no arbitrator has yet been appointed, the AAA may suspend the proceedings.

EXPEDITED PROCEDURES

E–1. Limitation on Extensions

Except in extraordinary circumstances, the AAA or the arbitrator may grant a party no more than one seven-day extension of time to respond to the demand for arbitration or counterclaim as provided in Section R–4.

E–2. Changes of Claim or Counterclaim

A claim or counterclaim may be increased in amount, or a new or different claim or counterclaim added, upon the agreement of the other party, or the consent of the arbitrator. After the arbitrator is appointed, however, no new or different claim or counterclaim may be submitted except with the arbitrator's consent. If an increased claim or counterclaim exceeds $75,000, the case will be administered under the regular procedures unless all parties and the arbitrator agree that the case may continue to be processed under the Expedited Procedures.

E–3. Serving of Notices

In addition to notice provided by Section R–39(b), the parties shall also accept notice by telephone. Telephonic notices by the AAA shall subsequently be confirmed in writing to the parties. Should there be a failure to confirm in writing any such oral notice, the proceeding shall nevertheless be valid if notice has, in fact, been given by telephone.

E–4. Appointment and Qualifications of Arbitrator

(a) The AAA shall simultaneously submit to each party an identical list of five proposed arbitrators drawn from its National Roster from which one arbitrator shall be appointed.

(b) The parties are encouraged to agree to an arbitrator from this list and to advise the AAA of their agreement. If the parties are unable to agree upon an arbitrator, each party may strike two names from the list and return it to the AAA within seven days from the date of the AAA's mailing to the parties. If for any reason the appointment of an arbitrator cannot be made from the list, the AAA may make the appointment from other members of the panel without the submission of additional lists.

(c) The parties will be given notice by the AAA of the appointment of the arbitrator, who shall be subject to disqualification for the reasons specified in Section R–17. The parties shall notify the AAA within seven days of any objection to the arbitrator appointed. Any such objection shall be for cause and shall be confirmed in writing to the AAA with a copy to the other party or parties.

E–5. Exchange of Exhibits

At least two business days prior to the hearing, the parties shall exchange copies of all exhibits they intend to submit at the hearing. The arbitrator shall resolve disputes concerning the exchange of exhibits.

E–6. Proceedings on Documents

Where no party's claim exceeds $10,000, exclusive of interest and arbitration costs, and other cases in which the parties agree, the dispute shall be resolved by submission of documents, unless any party requests an oral hearing, or the arbitrator determines that an oral hearing is necessary. The arbitrator shall establish a fair and equitable procedure for the submission of documents.

E–7. Date, Time, and Place of Hearing

In cases in which a hearing is to be held, the arbitrator shall set the date, time, and place of the hearing, to be scheduled to take place within 30 days of confirmation of the arbitrator's appointment. The AAA will notify the parties in advance of the hearing date.

E–8. The Hearing

(a) Generally, the hearing shall not exceed one day. Each party shall have equal opportunity to submit its proofs and complete its case. The arbitrator shall determine the order of the hearing, and may require further submission of documents within two days after the hearing. For good cause shown, the arbitrator may schedule additional hearings within seven business days after the initial day of hearings.

(b) Generally, there will be no stenographic record. Any party desiring a stenographic record may

arrange for one pursuant to the provisions of Section R–26.

E–9. Time of Award

Unless otherwise agreed by the parties, the award shall be rendered not later than 14 days from the date of the closing of the hearing or, if oral hearings have been waived, from the date of the AAA's transmittal of the final statements and proofs to the arbitrator.

E–10. Arbitrator's Compensation

Arbitrators will receive compensation at a rate to be suggested by the AAA regional office.

PROCEDURES FOR LARGE, COMPLEX COMMERCIAL DISPUTES

L–1. Administrative Conference

Prior to the dissemination of a list of potential arbitrators, the AAA shall, unless the parties agree otherwise, conduct an administrative conference with the parties and/or their attorneys or other representatives by conference call. The conference will take place within 14 days after the commencement of the arbitration. In the event the parties are unable to agree on a mutually acceptable time for the conference, the AAA may contact the parties individually to discuss the issues contemplated herein. Such administrative conference shall be conducted for the following purposes and for such additional purposes as the parties or the AAA may deem appropriate:

(a) to obtain additional information about the nature and magnitude of the dispute and the anticipated length of hearing and scheduling;

(b) to discuss the views of the parties about the technical and other qualifications of the arbitrators;

(c) to obtain conflicts statements from the parties; and

(d) to consider, with the parties, whether mediation or other non-adjudicative methods of dispute resolution might be appropriate.

L-2. Arbitrators

(a) Large, Complex Commercial Cases shall be heard and determined by either one or three arbitrators, as may be agreed upon by the parties. If the parties are unable to agree upon the number of arbitrators and a claim or counterclaim involves at least $1,000,000, then three arbitrator(s) shall hear and determine the case. If the parties are unable to agree on the number of arbitrators and each claim and counterclaim is less than $1,000,000, then one arbitrator shall hear and determine the case.

(b) The AAA shall appoint arbitrator(s) as agreed by the parties. If they are unable to agree on a method of appointment, the AAA shall appoint arbitrators from the Large, Complex Commercial Case Panel, in the manner provided in the Regular Commercial Arbitration Rules. Absent agreement of the parties, the arbitrator(s) shall not have served as

the mediator in the mediation phase of the instant proceeding.

L–3. Preliminary Hearing

As promptly as practicable after the selection of the arbitrator(s), a preliminary hearing shall be held among the parties and/or their attorneys or other representatives and the arbitrator(s). Unless the parties agree otherwise, the preliminary hearing will be conducted by telephone conference call rather than in person. At the preliminary hearing the matters to be considered shall include, without limitation:

(a) service of a detailed statement of claims, damages and defenses, a statement of the issues asserted by each party and positions with respect thereto, and any legal authorities the parties may wish to bring to the attention of the arbitrator(s);

(b) stipulations to uncontested facts;

(c) the extent to which discovery shall be conducted;

(d) exchange and premarking of those documents which each party believes may be offered at the hearing;

(e) the identification and availability of witnesses, including experts, and such matters with respect to witnesses including their biographies and expected testimony as may be appropriate;

(f) whether, and the extent to which, any sworn statements and/or depositions may be introduced;

(g) the extent to which hearings will proceed on consecutive days;

(h) whether a stenographic or other official record of the proceedings shall be maintained;

(i) the possibility of utilizing mediation or other non-adjudicative methods of dispute resolution; and

(j) the procedure for the issuance of subpoenas.

By agreement of the parties and/or order of the arbitrator(s), the pre-hearing activities and the hearing procedures that will govern the arbitration will be memorialized in a Scheduling and Procedure Order.

L–4. Management of Proceedings

(a) Arbitrator(s) shall take such steps as they may deem necessary or desirable to avoid delay and to achieve a just, speedy and cost-effective resolution of Large, Complex Commercial Cases.

(b) Parties shall cooperate in the exchange of documents, exhibits and information within such party's control if the arbitrator(s) consider such production to be consistent with the goal of achieving a just, speedy and cost-effective resolution of a Large, Complex Commercial Case.

(c) The parties may conduct such discovery as may be agreed to by all the parties provided, however, that the arbitrator(s) may place such limitations on the conduct of such discovery as the arbitrator(s) shall deem appropriate. If the parties cannot agree

on production of documents and other information, the arbitrator(s), consistent with the expedited nature of arbitration, may establish the extent of the discovery.

(d) At the discretion of the arbitrator(s), upon good cause shown and consistent with the expedited nature of arbitration, the arbitrator(s) may order depositions of, or the propounding of interrogatories to, such persons who may possess information determined by the arbitrator(s) to be necessary to determination of the matter.

(e) The parties shall exchange copies of all exhibits they intend to submit at the hearing 10 business days prior to the hearing unless the arbitrator(s) determine otherwise.

(f) The exchange of information pursuant to this rule, as agreed by the parties and/or directed by the arbitrator(s), shall be included within the Scheduling and Procedure Order.

(g) The arbitrator is authorized to resolve any disputes concerning the exchange of information.

(h) Generally hearings will be scheduled on consecutive days or in blocks of consecutive days in order to maximize efficiency and minimize costs.

OPTIONAL RULES FOR EMERGENCY MEASURES OF PROTECTION

O-1. Applicability

Where parties by special agreement or in their arbitration clause have adopted these rules for

emergency measures of protection, a party in need of emergency relief prior to the constitution of the panel shall notify the AAA and all other parties in writing of the nature of the relief sought and the reasons why such relief is required on an emergency basis. The application shall also set forth the reasons why the party is entitled to such relief. Such notice may be given by facsimile transmission, or other reliable means, but must include a statement certifying that all other parties have been notified or an explanation of the steps taken in good faith to notify other parties.

O–2. Appointment of Emergency Arbitrator

Within one business day of receipt of notice as provided in Section O–1, the AAA shall appoint a single emergency arbitrator from a special AAA panel of emergency arbitrators designated to rule on emergency applications. The emergency arbitrator shall immediately disclose any circumstance likely, on the basis of the facts disclosed in the application, to affect such arbitrator's impartiality or independence. Any challenge to the appointment of the emergency arbitrator must be made within one business day of the communication by the AAA to the parties of the appointment of the emergency arbitrator and the circumstances disclosed.

O–3. Schedule

The emergency arbitrator shall as soon as possible, but in any event within two business days of appointment, establish a schedule for consideration

of the application for emergency relief. Such schedule shall provide a reasonable opportunity to all parties to be heard, but may provide for proceeding by telephone conference or on written submissions as alternatives to a formal hearing.

O–4. Interim Award

If after consideration the emergency arbitrator is satisfied that the party seeking the emergency relief has shown that immediate and irreparable loss or damage will result in the absence of emergency relief, and that such party is entitled to such relief, the emergency arbitrator may enter an interim award granting the relief and stating the reasons therefore.

O–5. Constitution of the Panel

Any application to modify an interim award of emergency relief must be based on changed circumstances and may be made to the emergency arbitrator until the panel is constituted; thereafter such a request shall be addressed to the panel. The emergency arbitrator shall have no further power to act after the panel is constituted unless the parties agree that the emergency arbitrator is named as a member of the panel.

O–6. Security

Any interim award of emergency relief may be conditioned on provision by the party seeking such relief of appropriate security.

O–7. Special Master

A request for interim measures addressed by a party to a judicial authority shall not be deemed incompatible with the agreement to arbitrate or a waiver of the right to arbitrate. If the AAA is directed by a judicial authority to nominate a special master to consider and report on an application for emergency relief, the AAA shall proceed as provided in Section O–1 of this article and the references to the emergency arbitrator shall be read to mean the special master, except that the special master shall issue a report rather than an interim award.

O–8. Costs

The costs associated with applications for emergency relief shall initially be apportioned by the emergency arbitrator or special master, subject to the power of the panel to determine finally the apportionment of such costs.

ADMINISTRATIVE FEES

The administrative fees of the AAA are based on the amount of the claim or counterclaim. Arbitrator compensation is not included in this schedule. Unless the parties agree otherwise, arbitrator compensation and administrative fees are subject to allocation by the arbitrator in the award.

In an effort to make arbitration costs reasonable for consumers, the AAA has a separate fee schedule for consumer-related disputes. Please refer to Section C–8 of the *Supplementary Procedures for Con-*

sumer–Related Disputes when filing a consumer-related claim.

The AAA applies the *Supplementary Procedures for Consumer–Related Disputes* to arbitration clauses in agreements between individual consumers and businesses where the business has a standardized, systematic application of arbitration clauses with customers and where the terms and conditions of the purchase of standardized, consumable goods or services are non-negotiable or primarily non-negotiable in most or all of its terms, conditions, features, or choices. The product or service must be for personal or household use. The AAA will have the discretion to apply or not to apply the Supplementary Procedures and the parties will be able to bring any disputes concerning the application or non-application to the attention of the arbitrator. Consumers are not prohibited from seeking relief in a small claims court for disputes or claims within the scope of its jurisdiction, even in consumer arbitration cases filed by the business.

Fees

An initial filing fee is payable in full by a filing party when a claim, counterclaim or additional claim is filed. A case service fee will be incurred for all cases that proceed to their first hearing. This fee will be payable in advance at the time that the first hearing is scheduled. This fee will be refunded at the conclusion of the case if no hearings have occurred. However, if the Association is not notified at least 24 hours before the time of the scheduled hearing, the case service fee will remain due and will not be refunded.

These fees will be billed in accordance with the following schedule:

Amount of Claim	Initial Filing Fee	Case Service Fee
Above $0 to $10,000	$ 750	$ 200
Above $10,000 to $75,000	$ 950	$ 300
Above $75,000 to $150,000	$ 1,800	$ 750
Above $150,000 to $300,000	$ 2,750	$1,250
Above $300,000 to $500,000	$ 4,250	$1,750
Above $500,000 to $1,000,000	$ 6,000	$2,500
Above $1,000,000 to $5,000,000	$ 8,000	$3,250
Above $5,000,000 to $10,000,000	$10,000	$4,000
Above $10,000,000	*	*
Nonmonetary Claims**	$ 3,250	$1,250

** This fee is applicable only when a claim or counterclaim is not for a monetary amount. Where a monetary claim amount is not known, parties will be required to state a range of claims or be subject to the highest possible filing fee.

Fee Schedule for Claims in Excess of $10 Million

The following is the fee schedule for use in disputes involving claims in excess of $10 million. If you have any questions, please consult your local AAA office or case management center.

Claim Size	Fee	Case Service Fee
$10 million and above	Base fee of $12,500 plus .01% of the amount of claim above $10 million.	$6,000
	Filing fees capped at $65,000	

Fees are subject to increase if the amount of a claim or counterclaim is modified after the initial filing date. Fees are subject to decrease if the amount of a claim or counterclaim is modified before the first hearing.

The minimum fees for any case having three or more arbitrators are $2,750 for the filing fee, plus a $1,250 case service fee. Expedited Procedures are applied in any case where no disclosed claim or counterclaim exceeds $75,000, exclusive of interest and arbitration costs.

Parties on cases held in abeyance for one year by agreement, will be assessed an annual abeyance fee of $300. If a party refuses to pay the assessed fee, the other party or parties may pay the entire fee on behalf of all parties, otherwise the matter will be closed.

Refund Schedule

The AAA offers a refund schedule on filing fees. For cases with claims up to $75,000, a minimum filing fee of $300 will not be refunded. For all other cases, a minimum fee of $500 will not be refunded. Subject to the minimum fee requirements, refunds will be calculated as follows:

- 100% of the filing fee, above the minimum fee, will be refunded if the case is settled or withdrawn within five calendar days of filing.

- 50% of the filing fee will be refunded if the case is settled or withdrawn between six and 30 calendar days of filing.

- 25% of the filing fee will be refunded if the case is settled or withdrawn between 31 and 60 calendar days of filing.

No refund will be made once an arbitrator has been appointed (this includes one arbitrator on a three-arbitrator panel). No refunds will be granted on awarded cases.

Note: the date of receipt of the demand for arbitration with the AAA will be used to calculate refunds of filing fees for both claims and counter-claims.

Hearing Room Rental

The fees described above do not cover the rental of hearing rooms, which are available on a rental basis. Check with the AAA for availability and rates.

APPENDIX G

MANDATED PARTICIPATION AND SETTLEMENT COERCION: DISPUTE RESOLUTION AS IT RELATES TO THE COURTS

Note: *This material was originally published in 1991 by the Society of Professionals in Dispute Resolution (SPIDR). Reproduced with permission from the Association for Conflict Resolution (ACR), a merged organization of AFM, CREnet, and SPIDR. www.ACRnet.org.*

Report #1 of the Law and Public Policy Committee of the Society of Professionals in Dispute Resolution

Approved by the Board of Directors of the Society of Professionals in Dispute Resolution on January 5, 1991

EXECUTIVE SUMMARY

Some jurisdictions by statute, rule of procedure, or court rule have required participation in dispute resolution processes such as mediation, summary jury trials, and court-annexed arbitration. The imposition of compulsory participation reflects views by legislatures or courts that benefits accrue to the courts, parties, and/or public when the use of dispute resolution procedures is not restricted to cases in which all parties agree to participate. As the use of mandatory dispute resolution has expanded, a variety of public policy issues have emerged.

The Society of Professionals in Dispute Resolution (SPIDR) and others in the field have a valuable role to play in helping to promote thoughtful and consistent public policies on these important issues. The purpose of this report is to examine the benefits and possible disadvantages of mandated participation and settlement coercion[1] and to make recommendations to policymakers. This Executive Summary of the recommendations is followed by a more extensive explanation.

Mandating participation in non-binding dispute resolution processes often is appropriate. However, compulsory programs should be carefully designed to reflect a variety of important concerns. These concerns include the monetary and emotional costs for the parties, as well as the interests of the parties in achieving results that suit their needs and that will last; the justice system's ability to deliver results that do not harm the interests of those groups that have historically operated at a disadvantage in this society; the need to have courts that function efficiently and effectively; the importance of the public's trust in the justice system; the interests of

1. The Committee uses the term settlement ''coercion'' to refer to the requirements added to compulsory dispute resolution processes (as distinguished from the settlement pressure normally exerted during litigation even when dispute resolution is not mandatory by the cost of litigation, the desire to avoid publicity, and other forces.) (See p. 6.)

non-parties whose lives are affected and sometimes disrupted by litigation;[2] the importance of the courts' development of legal precedent; and the general interest in maximizing party choice. In weighing these valid and sometimes competing concerns, policymakers should be cautious not to give undue emphasis to the desire to facilitate the efficient administration of court business and thereby subordinate other important interests. Participation should be mandated only when the compulsory program is more likely to serve these broad interests of parties, the justice system, and the public, than would procedures that would be used absent mandatory dispute resolution. (See Recommendation 1.)

Mandatory dispute resolution raises different issues than dispute resolution chosen by the parties and should be imposed only when the following criteria are met:

1. The funding for mandatory dispute resolution programs is provided on a basis comparable to funding for trials. (See Recommendation 2.)

2. Coercion to settle in the form of reports to the trier of fact and of financial disincentives to trial is not used in connection with mandated mediation. In connection with court-annexed arbitration, the financial disincentives, if any, are clear, commensurate with the interests at stake, and used only when the

2. For example, some might argue that the public interest in decreasing disruption in the lives of children may be served by mandating mediation of child custody disputes, even if the divorcing parents would prefer to prolong the litigation and the court would not realize savings.

parties can afford to risk their imposition and proceed to trial. (See Recommendation 3.)

3. Mandatory participation is used only when a high quality program (i) is readily accessible, (ii) permits party participation, (iii) permits lawyer participation when the parties wish it, and (iv) provides clarity about the precise procedures that are being required. (See Recommendation 4.)

In addition, the following practices should be used in connection with mandatory programs:

1. Plans for mandated dispute resolution programs should be formed in consultation with judges, other court officials, lawyers, and other dispute resolution professionals, as well as representatives of the public. Mandatory programs should be monitored to insure that they constitute an improvement over existing procedures, using criteria listed in Recommendation 1. The programs should be altered or discontinued when appropriate. (See Recommendation 5.)

2. Procedures for compulsory referrals should include, to the extent feasible, case assessment by a person knowledgeable about dispute resolution procedures and should provide for timely consideration of motions for exclusion. (See Recommendation 6.)

3. Requirements for participation and sanctions for noncompliance should be clearly defined. (See Recommendation 7.)

APPENDIX H

ETHICAL STANDARDS OF PROFESSIONAL RESPONSIBILTY FOR THE SOCIETY OF PROFESSIONALS IN DISPUTE RESOLUTION

Note: *This material was originally published in 1986 by the Society of Professionals in Dispute Resolution (SPIDR). Reproduced with permission from the Association for Conflict Resolution (ACR), a merged organization of AFM, CREnet, and SPIDR. www.ACRnet.org.*

(Adopted by the Board of Directors, June 2, 1986)

INTRODUCTION

The Society for Professionals in Dispute Resolution was established in 1973 to promote the peaceful resolution of disputes. Members of the society believe that resolving disputes through negotiation, mediation, arbitration and other neutral interventions can be of great benefit to disputing parties and to society. In 1983 the SPIDR Board charged the Ethics Committee with the task of developing ethical standards of professional responsibility. The Committee membership represented all the various sectors and disciplines within SPIDR. This document, adopted by the Board on June 2, 1986 is the result of that charge.

The purpose of this document is to promote among SPIDR members and associates ethical conduct and a high level of competency among SPIDR members, including honesty, integrity, impartiality, and the exercise of good judgment in their dispute resolution efforts. It is hoped that this document also will help to (1) define the profession of dispute resolution, (2) educate the public and (3) inform users of dispute resolution services.

Application of Standards

Adherence to these ethical standards by SPIDR members and associates is basic to professional responsibility. SPIDR members and associates commit themselves to be guided in their professional conduct by these standards. The SPIDR Board of Directors or its designee is available to advise members and associates about interpretation of these standards. Other neutral practitioners and organizations are welcome to follow these standards.

Scope

It is recognized that SPIDR members and associates resolve disputes in various sectors within the disciplines of dispute resolution and have their own codes of professional conduct. These standards have been developed as general guidelines of practice for neutral disciplines represented in the SPIDR membership. Ethical considerations relevant to some, but not to all, of these disciplines are not covered by these standards.

ETHICAL STANDARDS OF PROFESSIONAL RESPONSIBILITY FOR THE SOCIETY OF PROFESSIONALS IN DISPUTE RESOLUTION

General Responsibilities

Neutrals have a duty to the parties, to the profession, and to themselves. They should be honest and unbiased, act in good faith, be diligent, and not seek to advance their own interests at the expense of the parties.

Neutrals must act fairly in dealing with the parties, have no personal interest in the terms of the settlement, show no bias toward individuals and institutions involved in the dispute, be reasonably available as requested by the parties, and be certain that the parties are informed of the process in which they are involved.

Responsibilities to the Parties

1. *Impartiality.* The neutral must maintain impartiality toward all parties. Impartiality means freedom from favoritism or bias either by word or by action, and a commitment to serve all parties as opposed to a single party.

2. *Informed Consent.* The neutral has an obligation to assure that all parties understand the nature of the process, the procedures, the particular role of the neutral, and the parties' relationship to the neutral.

3. *Confidentiality.* Maintaining confidentiality is critical to the dispute resolution process. Confiden-

tiality encourages candor, a full exploration of the issues and a neutral's acceptability. There may be some types of cases, however, in which confidentiality is not protected. In such cases, the neutral must advise the parties, when appropriate in the dispute resolution process, that the confidentiality of the proceedings cannot necessarily be maintained. Except in such instances, the neutral must resist all attempts to cause him or her to reveal any information outside the process. A commitment by the neutral to hold information in confidence within the process also must be honored.

4. *Conflict of Interest.* The neutral must refrain from entering or continuing in any dispute if he or she believes or perceives that participation as a neutral would be a clear conflict of interest. The neutral also must disclose any circumstance that may create or give the appearance of a conflict of interest and any circumstance that may reasonably raise a question as to the neutral's impartiality.

The duty to disclose is a continuing obligation throughout the process.

5. *Promptness.* The neutral shall exert every effort to expedite the process.

6. *The Settlement and Its Consequences.* The dispute resolution process belongs to the parties. The neutral has no vested interest in the terms of a settlement, but must be satisfied that agreements in which he or she has participated will not impugn the integrity of the process. The neutral has a responsibility to see that the parties consider the

terms of a settlement. If the neutral is concerned about the possible consequences of a proposed agreement, and the needs of the parties dictate, the neutral must inform the parties of that concern. In adhering to this standard the neutral may find it advisable to educate the parties, to refer one or more parties for specialized advice, or to withdraw from the case. In no case, however, shall the neutral violate section 3 above, Confidentiality, of these standards.

Unrepresented Interests

The neutral must consider circumstances where interests are not represented in the process. The neutral has an obligation, where in his or her judgment the needs of the parties dictate, to assure that such interests have been considered by the principal parties.

Use of Multiple Procedures

The use of more than one dispute resolution procedure by the same neutral involves additional responsibilities. Where the use of more than one procedure is initially contemplated, the neutral must take care at the outset to advise the parties of the nature of the procedures and the consequences of revealing information during any one procedure which the neutral may later use for decision making or may share with another decision maker. Where the use of more than one procedure is contemplated after the initiation of the dispute resolution process, the neutral must explain the consequences and afford the parties an opportunity to select another neutral for the subsequent procedures. It is also incumbent upon the neutral to advise the parties of the transition from one dispute resolution process to another.

Background and Qualification

A neutral should accept responsibility only in cases where the neutral has sufficient knowledge regarding the appropriate process and subject matter to be effective. A neutral has a responsibility to maintain and improve his or her professional skills.

Disclosure of Fees

It is the duty of the neutral to explain to the parties at the outset of the process, the bases of compensation, fees and charges, if any.

Support of the Profession

The experienced neutral should participate in the development of new practitioners in the field and engage in efforts to educate the public about the value and use of neutral dispute resolution procedures. The neutral should provide *pro bono* services, as appropriate.

Responsibilities of Neutrals Working on the Same Case

In the event that more than one neutral is involved in the resolution of a dispute, each has an obligation to inform the others regarding his or her entry in the case. Neutrals working with the same parties should maintain an open and professional relationship with each other.

Advertising & Solicitation

A neutral must be aware that some forms of advertising and solicitation are inappropriate and in some conflict resolution disciplines, such as labor arbitration, are impermissible. All advertising must honestly represent the services to be rendered. No claims of specific results or promises which imply favor of one side over another for the purpose of obtaining business should be made. No commissions, rebates or other similar forms of remuneration should be given or received by a neutral for the referral of clients.

APPENDIX I

THE UNIFORM ARBITRATION ACT

[ACT RELATING TO ARBITRATION AND TO MAKE UNIFORM THE LAW WITH REFERENCE THERETO]

Section 1. (*Validity of Arbitration Agreement.*)

A written agreement to submit any existing controversy to arbitration or a provision in a written contract to submit to arbitration any controversy thereafter arising between the parties is valid, enforceable and irrevocable, save upon such grounds as exist at law or in equity for the revocation of any contract. This act also applies to arbitration agreements between employers and employees or between their respective representatives (unless otherwise provided in the agreement).

Section 2. (*Proceedings to Compel or Stay Arbitration.*)

(a) On application of a party showing an agreement described in Section 1, and the opposing party's refusal to arbitrate, the Court shall order the parties to proceed with arbitration, but if the opposing party denies the existence of the agreement to arbitrate, the Court shall proceed summarily to the determination of the issue raised and shall order arbitration if found for the moving party, otherwise, the application shall be denied.

(b) On application, the court may stay an arbitration proceeding commenced or threatened on a showing that there is no agreement to arbitrate. Such an issue, when in substantial and bona fide dispute, shall be forthwith and summarily tried and the stay ordered if found for the moving party. If found for the opposing party, the court shall order the parties to proceed to arbitration.

(c) If an issue referable to arbitration under the alleged agreement is involved in an action or proceeding pending in a court having jurisdiction to hear applications under subdivision (a) of this Section, the application shall be made therein. Otherwise and subject to Section 18, the application may be made in any court of competent jurisdiction.

(d) Any action or proceeding involving an issue subject to arbitration shall be stayed if an order for arbitration or an application therefor has been made under this section or, if the issue is severable, the stay may be with respect thereto only. When the application is made in such action or proceeding, the order for arbitration shall include such stay.

(e) An order for arbitration shall not be refused on the ground that the claim in issue lacks merit or bona fides or because any fault or grounds for the claim sought to be arbitrated have not been shown.

Section 3. (*Appointment of Arbitrators by Court.*)

If the arbitration agreement provides a method of appointment of arbitrators, this method shall be followed. In the absence thereof, or if the agreed method fails or for any reason cannot be followed, or when an arbitrator appointed fails or is unable to act and his successor has not been duly appointed, the court on application of a party shall appoint one or more arbitrators. An arbitrator so appointed has all the powers of one specifically named in the agreement.

Section 4. (*Majority Action by Arbitrators.*)

The powers of the arbitrators may be exercised by a majority unless otherwise provided by the agreement or by this act.

Section 5. (*Hearing.*)

Unless otherwise provided by the agreement:

(a) The arbitrators shall appoint a time and place for the hearing and cause notification to the parties to be served personally or by registered mail not less than five days before the hearing. Appearance at the hearing waives such notice. The arbitrators may adjourn the hearing from time to time as necessary and, on request of a party and for good cause, or upon their own motion may postpone the hearing to a time not later than the date fixed by the agreement for making the award unless the parties consent to a later date. The arbitrators may hear and determine the controversy upon the evidence produced notwithstanding the failure of a party duly notified to appear. The court on application may direct the arbitrators to proceed promptly with the hearing and determination of the controversy.

(b) The parties are entitled to be heard, to present evidence material to the controversy and to cross-examine witnesses appearing at the hearing.

(c) The hearing shall be conducted by all the arbitrators but a majority may determine any question and render a final award. If, during the course of the hearing, an arbitrator for any reason ceases to act, the remaining arbitrator or arbitrators appointed to act as neutrals may continue with the hearing and determination of the controversy.

Section 6. (*Representation by Attorney.*)

A party has the right to be represented by an attorney at any proceeding or hearing under this act. A waiver thereof prior to the proceeding or hearing is ineffective.

Section 7. (*Witnesses, Subpoenas, Depositions.*)

(a) The arbitrators may issue (cause to be issued) subpoenas for the attendance of witnesses and for the production of books, records, documents and other evidence, and shall have the power to administer oaths. Subpoenas so issued shall be served, and upon application to the Court by a party or the arbitrators, enforced, in the manner provided by law for the service and enforcement of subpoenas in a civil action.

(b) On application of a party and for use as evidence, the arbitrators may permit a deposition to be taken, in the manner and upon the terms designated by the arbitrators, of a witness who cannot be subpoenaed or is unable to attend the hearing.

(c) All provisions of law compelling a person under subpoena to testify are applicable.

(d) Fees for attendance as a witness shall be the same as for a witness in the _____ Court.

Section 8. (*Award.*)

(a) The award shall be in writing and signed by the arbitrators joining in the award. The arbitrators shall deliver a copy to each party personally or by registered mail, or as provided in the agreement.

(b) An award shall be made within the time fixed therefor by the agreement or, if not so fixed, within such time as the court orders on application of a party. The parties may extend the time in writing either before or after the expiration thereof. A party waives the objection that an award was not made within the time required unless he notifies the arbitrators of his objection prior to the delivery of the award to him.

Section 9. (*Change of Award by Arbitrators.*)

On application of a party or, if an application to the court is pending under Sections 11, 12 or 13, on submission to the arbitrators by the court under such conditions as the court may order, the arbitrators may modify or correct the award upon the grounds stated in paragraphs (1) and (3) of subdivision (a) of Section 13, or for the purpose of clarifying the award. The application shall be made within twenty days after delivery of the award to the applicant. Written notice thereof shall be given forthwith to the opposing party, stating he must serve his objections thereto, if any, within ten days from the notice. The award so modified or corrected is subject to the provisions of Sections 11, 12 and 13.

Section 10. (*Fees and Expenses of Arbitration.*)

Unless otherwise provided in the agreement to arbitrate, the arbitrators' expenses and fees, together with other expenses, not including counsel fees, incurred in the conduct of the arbitration, shall be paid as provided in the award.

Section 11. (*Confirmation of an Award.*)

Upon application of a party, the Court shall confirm an award, unless within the time limits hereinafter imposed grounds are urged for vacating or modifying or correcting the award, in which case the court shall proceed as provided in Sections 12 and 13.

Section 12. (*Vacating an Award.*)

(a) Upon application of a party, the court shall vacate an award where:

(1) The award was procured by corruption, fraud or other undue means;

(2) There was evident partiality by an arbitrator appointed as a neutral or corruption in any of the arbitrators or misconduct prejudicing the rights of any party;

(3) The arbitrators exceeded their powers;

(4) The arbitrators refused to postpone the hearing upon sufficient cause being shown therefor or refused to hear evidence material to the controversy or otherwise so conducted the hearing, contrary to the provisions of Section 5, as to prejudice substantially the rights of a party; or

(5) There was no arbitration agreement and the issue was not adversely determined in proceedings under Section 2 and the party did not participate in the arbitration hearing without raising the objection;

But the fact that the relief was such that it could not or would not be granted by a court of law or equity is not ground for vacating or refusing to confirm the award.

(b) An application under this Section shall be made within ninety days after delivery of a copy of the award to the applicant, except that, if predicated upon corruption, fraud or other undue means, it shall be made within ninety days after such grounds are known or should have been known.

(c) In vacating the award on grounds other than stated in clause (5) of Subsection (a) the court may order a rehearing before new arbitrators chosen as provided in the agreement, or in the absence thereof, by the court in accordance with Section 3, or, if the award is vacated on grounds set forth in clauses (3), and (4) of Subsection (a) the court may order a rehearing before the arbitrators who made the award or their successors appointed in accordance with Section 3. The time within which the agreement requires the award to be made is applicable to the rehearing and commences from the date of the order.

(d) If the application to vacate is denied and no motion to modify or correct the award is pending, the court shall confirm the award.

Section 13. (*Modification or Correction of Award.*)

(a) Upon application made within ninety days after delivery of a copy of the award to the applicant, the court shall modify or correct the award where:

(1) There was an evident miscalculation of figures or an evident mistake in the description of any person, thing or property referred to in the award;

(2) The arbitrators have awarded upon a matter not submitted to them and the award may be corrected without affecting the merits of the decision upon the issues submitted; or

(3) The award is imperfect in a matter of form, not affecting the merits of the controversy.

(b) If the application is granted, the court shall modify and correct the award so as to effect its intent and shall confirm the award as so modified and corrected. Otherwise, the court shall confirm the award as made.

(c) An application to modify or correct an award may be joined in the alternative with an application to vacate the award.

Section 14. (*Judgment or Decree on Award.*)

Upon the granting of an order confirming, modifying or correcting an award, judgment or decree shall be entered in conformity therewith and be enforced as any other judgment or decree. Costs of the application and of the proceedings subsequent thereto, and disbursements may be awarded by the court.

* [Section 15. (*Judgment Roll, Docketing.*)

(a) On entry of judgment or decree, the clerk shall prepare the judgment roll consisting, to the extent filed, of the following:

(1) The agreement and each written extension of the time within which to make the award;

(2) The award;

(3) A copy of the order confirming, modifying or correcting the award; and

(4) A copy of the judgment or decree.

(b) The judgment or decree may be docketed as if rendered in an action.]

* Brackets and parentheses enclose language which the Commissioners suggest may be used by those States desiring to do so.

Section 16. (*Applications to Court.*)

Except as otherwise provided, an application to the court under this act shall be by motion and shall be heard in the manner and upon the notice provided by law or rule of court for the making and hearing of motions. Unless the parties have agreed otherwise, notice of an initial application for an order shall be served in the manner provided by law for the service of a summons in an action.

Section 17. (*Court, Jurisdiction.*)

The term "court" means any court of competent jurisdiction of this State. The making of an agreement described in Section 1 providing for arbitration in this State confers jurisdiction on the court to enforce the agreement under this Act and to enter judgment on an award thereunder.

Section 18. (*Venue.*)

An initial application shall be made to the court of the (county) in which the agreement provides the arbitration hearing shall be held or, if the hearing has been held, in the county in which it was held. Otherwise the application shall be made in the (county) where the adverse party resides or has a place of business or, if he has no residence or place of business in this State, to the court of any (county). All subsequent applications shall be made to the court hearing the initial application unless the court otherwise directs.

Section 19. (*Appeals.*)

(a) An appeal may be taken from:

(1) An order denying an application to compel arbitration made under Section 2;

(2) An order granting an application to stay arbitration made under Section 2(b);

(3) An order confirming or denying confirmation of an award;

(4) An order modifying or correcting an award;

(5) An order vacating an award without directing a rehearing; or

(6) A judgment or decree entered pursuant to the provisions of this act.

(b) The appeal shall be taken in the manner and to the same extent as from orders or judgments in a civil action.

Section 20. (*Act Not Retroactive.*)

This act applies only to agreements made subsequent to the taking effect of this act.

Section 21. (*Uniformity of Interpretation.*)

This act shall be so construed as to effectuate its general purpose to make uniform the law of those states which enact it.

Section 22. (*Constitutionality.*)

If any provision of this act or the application thereof to any person or circumstance is held invalid, the invalidity shall not affect other provisions or applications of the act which can be given without the invalid provision or application, and to this end the provisions of this act are severable.

Section 23. (*Short title.*)

This act may be cited as the Uniform Arbitration Act.

Section 24. (*Repeal.*)

All acts or parts of acts which are inconsistent with the provisions of this act are hereby repealed.

Section 25. (*Time of Taking Effect.*)

This act shall take effect _____.

APPENDIX J

FEDERAL ARBITRATION ACT

(FORMERLY UNITED STATES ARBITRATION ACT)

9 U.S.C. § 1 (1925)

Arbitration

CHAPTER 1. GENERAL PROVISIONS

Sec.
1. "Maritime Transactions," and "Commerce" Defined; Exceptions to Operation of Title.
2. Validity, Irrevocability, and Enforcement of Agreements to Arbitrate.
3. Stay of Proceedings Where Issue Therein Referable to Arbitration.
4. Failure to Arbitrate Under Agreement; Petition to United States Court Having Jurisdiction for Order to Compel Arbitration; Notice and Service Thereof; Hearing and Determination.
5. Appointment of Arbitrators or Umpire.
6. Application Heard as Motion.
7. Witnesses Before Arbitrators; Fees; Compelling Attendance.
8. Proceedings Begun by Libel in Admiralty and Seizure of Vessel or Property.
9. Award of Arbitrators; Confirmation; Jurisdiction; Procedure.
10. Same; Vacation; Grounds; Rehearing.
11. Same; Modification or Correction; Grounds; Order.

Sec.

12. Notice of Motions to Vacate or Modify; Service; Stay of Proceedings.
13. Papers Filed With Order on Motions; Judgment; Docketing; Force and Effect; Enforcement.
14. Contracts Not Affected.
15. Inapplicability of the Act of State Doctrine.
16. Appeals.

CHAPTER 2. CONVENTION ON THE RECOGNITION AND ENFORCEMENT OF FOREIGN ARBITRAL AWARDS

201. Enforcement of Convention.
202. Agreement or Award Falling Under the Convention.
203. Jurisdiction; Amount in Controversy.
204. Venue.
205. Removal of Cases From State Courts.
206. Order to Compel Arbitration; Appointment of Arbitrators.
207. Award of Arbitrators; Confirmation; Jurisdiction; Proceeding.
208. Chapter 1; Residual Application.

CHAPTER 1. GENERAL PROVISIONS

§ 1. "Maritime Transactions," and "Commerce" Defined; Exceptions to Operation of Title

"Maritime transactions", as herein defined, means charter parties, bills of lading of water carriers, agreements relating to wharfage, supplies furnished vessels or repairs to vessels, collisions, or any other matters in foreign commerce which, if the subject of controversy, would be embraced within admiralty jurisdiction; "commerce", as herein defined, means commerce among the several States or with foreign nations, or in any Territory of the United States or in the District of Columbia, or between any such Territory and another, or between any such Territory and any State or foreign nation, or between the District of Columbia and any State or Territory or foreign nation, but nothing herein contained shall apply to contracts of employment of seamen, railroad employees, or any other class of workers engaged in foreign or interstate commerce.

§ 2. Validity, Irrevocability, and Enforcement of Agreements to Arbitrate

A written provision in any maritime transaction or a contract evidencing a transaction involving commerce to settle by arbitration a controversy thereafter arising out of such contract or transaction, or the refusal to perform the whole or any part thereof, or an agreement in writing to submit to arbitration an existing controversy arising out of such a contract, transaction, or refusal, shall be valid, irrevocable, and enforceable, save upon such grounds as exist at law or in equity for the revocation of any contract.

§ 3. Stay of Proceedings Where Issue Therein Referable to Arbitration

If any suit or proceeding be brought in any of the courts of the United States upon any issue referable to arbitration under an agreement in writing for such arbitration, the court in which such suit is pending, upon being satisfied that the issue involved in such suit or proceeding is referable to arbitration under such an agreement, shall on application of one of the parties stay the trial of the action until such arbitration has been had in accordance with the terms of the agreement, providing the applicant for the stay is not in default in proceeding with such arbitration.

§ 4. Failure to Arbitrate Under Agreement; Petition to United States Court Having Jurisdiction for Order to Compel Arbitration; Notice and Service Thereof; Hearing and Determination

A party aggrieved by the alleged failure, neglect, or refusal of another to arbitrate under a written agreement for arbitration may petition any United States district court which, save for such agreement, would have jurisdiction under Title 28, in a civil action or in admiralty of the subject matter of a suit arising out of the controversy between the parties, for an order directing that such arbitration proceed in the manner provided for in such agreement. Five days' notice in writing of such application shall be served upon the party in default. Service thereof shall be made in the manner provided by the Federal Rules of Civil Procedure. The court shall hear the parties, and upon being satisfied that the making of the agreement for arbitration or the failure to comply therewith is not in issue, the court shall make an order directing the parties to proceed to arbitration in accordance with the terms of the agreement. The hearing and proceedings, under such agreement, shall be within the district in which the petition for an order directing such arbitration is filed. If the making of the arbitration agreement or the failure, neglect, or refusal to perform the same be in issue, the court shall proceed summarily to the trial thereof. If no jury trial be demanded by the party alleged to be in default, or if the matter in dispute is within admiralty jurisdiction, the court shall hear and determine such issue. Where such an issue is raised, the party alleged to be in default may, except in cases of admiralty, on or before the return day of the notice of application, demand a jury trial of such issue, and upon such demand the court shall make an order referring the issue or issues to a jury in the manner provided by the Federal Rules of Civil Procedure, or may specially call a jury for that purpose. If the jury find that no agreement in writing for arbitration was made or that there is no default in proceeding thereunder, the proceeding shall be dismissed. If the jury find that an agreement for arbitration was made in writing and that there is a default in proceeding thereunder, the court shall make an order summarily directing the parties to proceed with the arbitration in accordance with the terms thereof.

§ 5. Appointment of Arbitrators or Umpire

If in the agreement provision be made for a method of naming or appointing an arbitrator or arbitrators or an umpire, such method shall be followed; but if no method be provided therein, or if a method be provided and any party thereto shall fail to avail himself of such method, or if for any other reason there shall be a lapse in the naming of an arbitrator or arbitrators or umpire, or in filling a vacancy, then upon the application of either party to the controversy the court shall designate and appoint an arbitrator or arbitrators or umpire, as the case may require, who shall act under the said agreement with the same force and effect as if he or they had been specifically named therein; and unless otherwise provided in the agreement the arbitration shall be by a single arbitrator.

§ 6. Application Heard as Motion

Any application to the court hereunder shall be made and heard in the manner provided by law for the making and hearing of motions, except as otherwise herein expressly provided.

§ 7. Witnesses Before Arbitrators; Fees; Compelling Attendance

The arbitrators selected either as prescribed in this title or otherwise, or a majority of them, may summon in writing any person to attend before them or any of them as a witness and in a proper case to bring with him or them any book, record, document, or paper which may be deemed material as evidence in the case. The fees for such attendance shall be the same as the fees of witnesses before masters of the United States courts. Said summons shall issue in the name of the arbitrator or arbitrators, or a majority of them, and shall be signed by the arbitrators, or a majority of them, and shall be directed to the said person and shall be served in the same manner as subpoenas to appear and testify before the court; if any person or persons so summoned to testify shall refuse or neglect to obey said summons, upon petition the United States district court for the district in which such arbitrators, or a majority of them, are sitting may compel the attendance of such person or persons before said arbitrator or arbitrators, or punish said person or persons for contempt in the same manner provided by law for securing the attendance of witnesses or their punishment for neglect or refusal to attend in the courts of the United States.

§ 8. Proceedings Begun by Libel in Admiralty and Seizure of Vessel or Property

If the basis of jurisdiction be a cause of action otherwise justiciable in admiralty, then, notwithstanding anything herein to the contrary, the party claiming to be aggrieved may begin his proceeding hereunder by libel and seizure of the vessel or other property of the other party according to the usual course of admiralty proceedings, and the court shall then have jurisdiction to direct the parties to proceed with the arbitration and shall retain jurisdiction to enter its decree upon the award.

§ 9. Award of Arbitrators; Confirmation; Jurisdiction; Procedure

If the parties in their agreement have agreed that a judgment of the court shall be entered upon the award made pursuant to the arbitration, and shall specify the court, then at any time within one year after the award is made any party to the arbitration may apply to the court so specified for an order confirming the award, and thereupon the court must grant such an order unless the award is vacated, modified, or corrected as prescribed in sections 10 and 11 of this title. If no court is specified in the agreement of the parties, then such application may be made to the United States court in and for the district within which such award was made. Notice of the application shall be served upon the adverse party, and thereupon the court shall have jurisdiction of such party as though he had appeared generally in the proceeding. If the adverse party is a resident of the district within which the award was made, such service shall be made upon the adverse party or his attorney as prescribed by law for service of notice of motion in an action in the same court. If the adverse party shall be a nonresident, then the notice of the application shall be served by the marshal of any district within which the adverse party may be found in like manner as other process of the court.

§ 10.   Same; Vacation; Grounds; Rehearing

(a) In any of the following cases the United States court in and for the district wherein the award was made may make an order vacating the award upon the application of any party to the arbitration—

(1) where the award was procured by corruption, fraud, or undue means.

(2) where there was evident partiality or corruption in the arbitrators, or either of them.

(3) where the arbitrators were guilty of misconduct in refusing to postpone the hearing, upon sufficient cause shown, or in refusing to hear evidence pertinent and material to the controversy; or of any other misbehavior by which the rights of any party have been prejudiced.

(4) where the arbitrators exceeded their powers, or so imperfectly executed them that a mutual, final, and definite award upon the subject matter submitted was not made.

(b) If an award is vacated and the time within which the agreement required the award to be made has not expired the court may, in its discretion, direct a rehearing by the arbitrators.

(c) The United States district court for the district wherein an award was made that was issued pursuant to section 580 of title 5 may make an order vacating the award upon the application of a person, other than a party to the arbitration, who is adversely affected or aggrieved by the award, if the use of arbitration or the award is clearly inconsistent with the factors set forth in section 572 of title 5.

§ 11. Same; Modification or Correction; Grounds; Order

In either of the following cases the United States court in and for the district wherein the award was made may make an order modifying or correcting the award upon the application of any party to the arbitration—

(a) Where there was an evident material miscalculation of figures or an evident material mistake in the description of any person, thing, or property referred to in the award.

(b) Where the arbitrators have awarded upon a matter not submitted to them, unless it is a matter not affecting the merits of the decision upon the matter submitted.

(c) Where the award is imperfect in matter of form not affecting the merits of the controversy.

The order may modify and correct the award, so as to effect the intent thereof and promote justice between the parties.

§ 12. Notice of Motions to Vacate or Modify; Service; Stay of Proceedings

Notice of a motion to vacate, modify, or correct an award must be served upon the adverse party or his attorney within three months after the award is filed or delivered. If the adverse party is a resident of the district within which the award was made, such service shall be made upon the adverse party or his attorney as prescribed by law for service of notice of motion in an action in the same court. If the adverse party shall be a nonresident then the notice of the application shall be served by the marshal of any district within which the adverse party may be found in like manner as other process of the court. For the purposes of the motion any judge who might make an order to stay the proceedings in an action brought in the same court may make an order, to be served with the notice of motion, staying the proceedings of the adverse party to enforce the award.

§ 13. Papers Filed With Order on Motions; Judgment; Docketing; Force and Effect; Enforcement

The party moving for an order confirming, modifying, or correcting an award shall, at the time such order is filed with the clerk for the entry of judgment thereon, also file the following papers with the clerk:

(a) The agreement; the selection or appointment, if any, of an additional arbitrator or umpire; and each written extension of the time, if any, within which to make the award.

(b) The award.

(c) Each notice, affidavit, or other paper used upon an application to confirm, modify, or correct the award, and a copy of each order of the court upon such an application.

The judgment shall be docketed as if it was rendered in an action.

The judgment so entered shall have the same force and effect, in all respects, as, and be subject to all the provisions of law relating to, a judgment in an action; and it may be enforced as if it had been rendered in an action in the court in which it is entered.

§ 14. Contracts Not Affected

This title shall not apply to contracts made prior to January 1, 1926.

§ 15. Inapplicability of the Act of State Doctrine

Enforcement of arbitral agreements, confirmation of arbitral awards, and execution upon judgments based on orders confirming such awards shall not be refused on the basis of the Act of State doctrine.

§ 16. Appeals

(a) An appeal may be taken from—

(1) an order—

(A) refusing a stay of any action under section 3 of this title,

(B) denying a petition under section 4 of this title to order arbitration to proceed,

(C) denying an application under section 206 of this title to compel arbitration,

(D) confirming or denying confirmation of an award or partial award, or

(E) modifying, correcting, or vacating an award;

(2) an interlocutory order granting, continuing, or modifying an injunction against an arbitration that is subject to this title; or

(3) a final decision with respect to an arbitration that is subject to this title.

(b) Except as otherwise provided in section 1292(b) of title 28, an appeal may not be taken from an interlocutory order—

(1) granting a stay of any action under section 3 of this title;

(2) directing arbitration to proceed under section 4 of this title;

(3) compelling arbitration under section 206 of this title; or

(4) refusing to enjoin an arbitration that is subject to this title.

CHAPTER 2. CONVENTION ON THE RECOGNITION AND ENFORCEMENT OF FOREIGN ARBITRAL AWARDS

§ 201. Enforcement of Convention

The Convention on the Recognition and Enforcement of Foreign Arbitral Awards of June 10, 1958, shall be enforced in United States courts in accordance with this chapter.

§ 202. Agreement or Award Falling Under the Convention

An arbitration agreement or arbitral award arising out of a legal relationship, whether contractual or not, which is considered as commercial, including a transaction, contract, or agreement described in section 2 of this title, falls under the Convention. An agreement or award arising out of such a relationship which is entirely between citizens of the United States shall be deemed not to fall under the Convention unless that relationship involves property located abroad, envisages performance or enforcement abroad, or has some other reasonable relation with one or more foreign states. For the purpose of this section a corporation is a citizen of the United States if it is incorporated or has its principal place of business in the United States.

§ 203. Jurisdiction; Amount in Controversy

An action or proceeding falling under the Convention shall be deemed to arise under the laws and treaties of the United States. The district courts of the United States (including the courts enumerated in section 460 of title 28) shall have original jurisdiction over such an action or proceeding, regardless of the amount in controversy.

§ 204. Venue

An action or proceeding over which the district courts have jurisdiction pursuant to section 203 of this title may be brought in any such court in which save for the arbitration agreement an action or proceeding with respect to the controversy between the parties could be brought, or in such court for the district and division which embraces the place designated in the agreement as the place of arbitration if such place is within the United States.

§ 205. Removal of Cases From State Courts

Where the subject matter of an action or proceeding pending in a State court relates to an arbitration agreement or award falling under the Convention, the defendant or the defendants may, at any time before the trial thereof, remove such action or proceeding to the district court of the United States for the district and division embracing the place where the action or proceeding is pending. The procedure for removal of causes otherwise provided by law shall apply, except that the ground for removal provided in this section need not appear on the face of the complaint but may be shown in the petition for removal. For the purposes of Chapter 1 of this title any action or proceeding removed under this section shall be deemed to have been brought in the district court to which it is removed.

§ 206. Order to Compel Arbitration; Appointment of Arbitrators

A court having jurisdiction under this chapter may direct that arbitration be held in accordance with the agreement at any place therein provided for, whether that place is within or without the United States. Such court may also appoint arbitrators in accordance with the provisions of the agreement.

§ 207. Award of Arbitrators; Confirmation; Jurisdiction; Proceeding

Within three years after an arbitral award falling under the Convention is made, any party to the arbitration may apply to any court having jurisdiction under this chapter for an order confirming the award as against any other party to the arbitration.

The court shall confirm the award unless it finds one of the grounds for refusal or deferral of recognition or enforcement of the award specified in the said Convention.

§ 208. Chapter 1; Residual Application

Chapter 1 applies to actions and proceedings brought under this chapter to the extent that chapter is not in conflict with this chapter or the Convention as ratified by the United States.

APPENDIX K

REVISED UNIFORM ARBITRATION ACT (2000)*

DRAFTED BY THE NATIONAL CONFERENCE
OF COMMISSIONERS ON UNIFORM
STATE LAWS AND BY IT APPROVED
AND RECOMMENDED FOR ENACTMENT IN
ALL THE STATES

UNIFORM ARBITRATION ACT (2000)

SECTION 1. DEFINITIONS.

In this [Act]:

(1) "Arbitration organization" means an association, agency, board, commission, or other entity that is neutral and initiates, sponsors, or administers an arbitration proceeding or is involved in the appointment of an arbitrator.

(2) "Arbitrator" means an individual appointed to render an award, alone or with others, in a controversy that is subject to an agreement to arbitrate.

(3) "Court" means [a court of competent jurisdiction in this State].

* Copyright © 2000.

406

(4) "Knowledge" means actual knowledge.

(5) "Person" means an individual, corporation, business trust, estate, trust, partnership, limited liability company, association, joint venture, government; governmental subdivision, agency, or instrumentality; public corporation; or any other legal or commercial entity.

(6) "Record" means information that is inscribed on a tangible medium or that is stored in an electronic or other medium and is retrievable in perceivable form.

SECTION 2. NOTICE.

(a) Except as otherwise provided in this [Act], a person gives notice to another person by taking action that is reasonably necessary to inform the other person in ordinary course, whether or not the other person acquires knowledge of the notice.

(b) A person has notice if the person has knowledge of the notice or has received notice.

(c) A person receives notice when it comes to the person's attention or the notice is delivered at the person's place of residence or place of business, or at another location held out by the person as a place of delivery of such communications.

SECTION 3. WHEN [ACT] APPLIES.

(a) This [Act] governs an agreement to arbitrate made on or after [the effective date of this [Act]].

(b) This [Act] governs an agreement to arbitrate made before [the effective date of this [Act]] if all the parties to the agreement or to the arbitration proceeding so agree in a record.

(c) On or after [a delayed date], this [Act] governs an agreement to arbitrate whenever made.

SECTION 4. EFFECT OF AGREEMENT TO ARBITRATE; NONWAIVABLE PROVISIONS.

(a) Except as otherwise provided in subsections (b) and (c), a party to an agreement to arbitrate or to an arbitration proceeding may waive or, the parties may vary the effect of, the requirements of this [Act] to the extent permitted by law.

(b) Before a controversy arises that is subject to an agreement to arbitrate, a party to the agreement may not:

(1) waive or agree to vary the effect of the requirements of Section 5(a), 6(a), 8, 17(a), 17(b), 26, or 28;

(2) agree to unreasonably restrict the right under Section 9 to notice of the initiation of an arbitration proceeding;

(3) agree to unreasonably restrict the right under Section 12 to disclosure of any facts by a neutral arbitrator; or

(4) waive the right under Section 16 of a party to an agreement to arbitrate to be represented by a lawyer at any proceeding or hearing under this [Act], but an employer and a labor organization

may waive the right to representation by a lawyer in a labor arbitration.

(c) A party to an agreement to arbitrate or arbitration proceeding may not waive, or the parties may not vary the effect of, the requirements of this section or Section 3(a) or (c), 7, 14, 18, 20(d) or (e), 22, 23, 24, 25(a) or (b), 29, 30, 31, or 32.

SECTION 5. [APPLICATION] FOR JUDICIAL RELIEF.

(a) Except as otherwise provided in Section 28, an [application] for judicial relief under this [Act] must be made by [motion] to the court and heard in the manner provided by law or rule of court for making and hearing [motions].

(b) Unless a civil action involving the agreement to arbitrate is pending, notice of an initial [motion] to the court under this [Act] must be served in the manner provided by law for the service of a summons in a civil action. Otherwise, notice of the motion must be given in the manner provided by law or rule of court for serving [motions] in pending cases.

SECTION 6. VALIDITY OF AGREEMENT TO ARBITRATE.

(a) An agreement contained in a record to submit to arbitration any existing or subsequent controversy arising between the parties to the agreement is valid, enforceable, and irrevocable except upon a ground that exists at law or in equity for the revocation of a contract.

(b) The court shall decide whether an agreement to arbitrate exists or a controversy is subject to an agreement to arbitrate.

(c) An arbitrator shall decide whether a condition precedent to arbitrability has been fulfilled and whether a contract containing a valid agreement to arbitrate is enforceable.

(d) If a party to a judicial proceeding challenges the existence of, or claims that a controversy is not subject to, an agreement to arbitrate, the arbitration proceeding may continue pending final resolution of the issue by the court, unless the court otherwise orders.

SECTION 7. [MOTION] TO COMPEL OR STAY ARBITRATION.

(a) On [motion] of a person showing an agreement to arbitrate and alleging another person's refusal to arbitrate pursuant to the agreement:

(1) if the refusing party does not appear or does not oppose the [motion], the court shall order the parties to arbitrate; and

(2) if the refusing party opposes the [motion], the court shall proceed summarily to decide the issue and order the parties to arbitrate unless it finds that there is no enforceable agreement to arbitrate.

(b) On [motion] of a person alleging that an arbitration proceeding has been initiated or threatened but that there is no agreement to arbitrate, the court shall proceed summarily to decide the issue. If the court finds that there is an enforceable agreement to arbitrate, it shall order the parties to arbitrate.

(c) If the court finds that there is no enforceable agreement, it may not pursuant to subsection (a) or (b) order the parties to arbitrate.

(d) The court may not refuse to order arbitration because the claim subject to arbitration lacks merit or grounds for the claim have not been established.

(e) If a proceeding involving a claim referable to arbitration under an alleged agreement to arbitrate is pending in court, a [motion] under this section must be made in that court. Otherwise a [motion] under this section may be made in any court as provided in Section 27.

(f) If a party makes a [motion] to the court to order arbitration, the court on just terms shall stay any judicial proceeding that involves a claim alleged to be subject to the arbitration until the court renders a final decision under this section.

(g) If the court orders arbitration, the court shall on just terms stay any judicial proceeding that involves a claim subject to the arbitration. If a claim subject to the arbitration is severable, the court may limit the stay to that claim.

SECTION 8. PROVISIONAL REMEDIES.

(a) Before an arbitrator is appointed and is authorized and able to act, the court, upon [motion] of a party to an arbitration proceeding and for good cause shown, may enter an order for provisional remedies to protect the effectiveness of the arbitration proceeding to the same extent and under the same conditions as if the controversy were the subject of a civil action.

(b) After an arbitrator is appointed and is authorized and able to act:

(1) the arbitrator may issue such orders for provisional remedies, including interim awards, as the arbitrator finds necessary to protect the effectiveness of the arbitration proceeding and to promote the fair and expeditious resolution of the controversy, to the same extent and under the same conditions as if the controversy were the subject of a civil action and

(2) a party to an arbitration proceeding may move the court for a provisional remedy only if the matter is urgent and the arbitrator is not able to act timely or the arbitrator cannot provide an adequate remedy.

(c) A party does not waive a right of arbitration by making a [motion] under subsection (a) or (b).

SECTION 9. INITIATION OF ARBITRATION.

(a) A person initiates an arbitration proceeding by giving notice in a record to the other parties to the agreement to arbitrate in the agreed manner between the parties or, in the absence of agreement, by certified or registered mail, return receipt requested and obtained, or by service as authorized for the commencement of a civil action. The notice must describe the nature of the controversy and the remedy sought.

(b) Unless a person objects for lack or insufficiency of notice under Section 15(c) not later than the beginning of the arbitration hearing, the person by appearing at the hearing waives any objection to lack of or insufficiency of notice.

SECTION 10. CONSOLIDATION OF SEPARATE ARBITRATION PROCEEDINGS.

(a) Except as otherwise provided in subsection (c), upon [motion] of a party to an agreement to arbitrate or to an arbitration proceeding, the court may order consolidation of separate arbitration proceedings as to all or some of the claims if:

(1) there are separate agreements to arbitrate or separate arbitration proceedings between the same persons or one of them is a party to a separate agreement to arbitrate or a separate arbitration proceeding with a third person;

(2) the claims subject to the agreements to arbitrate arise in substantial part from the same transaction or series of related transactions;

(3) the existence of a common issue of law or fact creates the possibility of conflicting decisions in the separate arbitration proceedings; and

(4) prejudice resulting from a failure to consolidate is not outweighed by the risk of undue delay or prejudice to the rights of or hardship to parties opposing consolidation.

(b) The court may order consolidation of separate arbitration proceedings as to some claims and allow other claims to be resolved in separate arbitration proceedings.

(c) The court may not order consolidation of the claims of a party to an agreement to arbitrate if the agreement prohibits consolidation.

SECTION 11. APPOINTMENT OF ARBITRATOR; SERVICE AS A NEUTRAL ARBITRATOR.

(a) If the parties to an agreement to arbitrate agree on a method for appointing an arbitrator, that method must be followed, unless the method fails. If the parties have not agreed on a method, the agreed method fails, or an arbitrator appointed fails or is unable to act and a successor has not been appointed, the court, on [motion] of a party to the arbitration proceeding, shall appoint the arbitrator. An arbitrator so appointed has all the powers of an arbitrator designated in the agreement to arbitrate or appointed pursuant to the agreed method.

(b) An individual who has a known, direct, and material interest in the outcome of the arbitration proceeding or a known, existing, and substantial relationship with a party may not serve as an arbitrator required by an agreement to be neutral.

SECTION 12. DISCLOSURE BY ARBITRATOR.

(a) Before accepting appointment, an individual who is requested to serve as an arbitrator, after making a reasonable inquiry, shall disclose to all parties to the agreement to arbitrate and arbitration proceeding and to any other arbitrators any known facts that a reasonable person would consider likely to affect the impartiality of the arbitrator in the arbitration proceeding, including:

(1) a financial or personal interest in the outcome of the arbitration proceeding; and

(2) an existing or past relationship with any of the parties to the agreement to arbitrate or the arbitration proceeding, their counsel or representatives, a witness, or another arbitrator.

(b) An arbitrator has a continuing obligation to disclose to all parties to the agreement to arbitrate and arbitration proceeding and to any other arbitrators any facts that the arbitrator learns after accepting appointment which a reasonable person would consider likely to affect the impartiality of the arbitrator.

(c) If an arbitrator discloses a fact required by subsection (a) or (b) to be disclosed and a party timely objects to the appointment or continued service of the arbitrator based upon the fact disclosed, the objection may be a ground under Section 23(a)(2) for vacating an award made by the arbitrator.

(d) If the arbitrator did not disclose a fact as required by subsection (a) or (b), upon timely objection by a party, the court under Section 23(a)(2) may vacate an award.

(e) An arbitrator appointed as a neutral arbitrator who does not disclose a known, direct, and material interest in the outcome of the arbitration proceeding or a known, existing, and substantial relationship with a party is presumed to act with evident partiality under Section 23(a)(2).

(f) If the parties to an arbitration proceeding agree to the procedures of an arbitration organization or any other procedures for challenges to arbitrators before an award is made, substantial compliance with those procedures is a condition precedent to a [motion] to vacate an award on that ground under Section 23(a)(2).

SECTION 13. ACTION BY MAJORITY.

If there is more than one arbitrator, the powers of an arbitrator must be exercised by a majority of the arbitrators, but all of them shall conduct the hearing under Section 15(c).

SECTION 14. IMMUNITY OF ARBITRATOR; COMPETENCY TO TESTIFY; ATTORNEY'S FEES AND COSTS.

(a) An arbitrator or an arbitration organization acting in that capacity is immune from civil liability to the same extent as a judge of a court of this State acting in a judicial capacity.

(b) The immunity afforded by this section supplements any immunity under other law.

(c) The failure of an arbitrator to make a disclosure required by Section 12 does not cause any loss of immunity under this section.

(d) In a judicial, administrative, or similar proceeding, an arbitrator or representative of an arbitration organization is not competent to testify, and may not be required to produce records as to any statement, conduct, decision, or ruling occurring during the arbitration proceeding, to the same extent as a judge of a court of this State acting in a judicial capacity. This subsection does not apply:

(1) to the extent necessary to determine the claim of an arbitrator, arbitration organization, or representative of the arbitration organization against a party to the arbitration proceeding; or

(2) to a hearing on a [motion] to vacate an award under Section 23(a)(1) or (2) if the [movant] establishes prima facie that a ground for vacating the award exists.

(e) If a person commences a civil action against an arbitrator, arbitration organization, or representative of an arbitration organization arising from the services of the arbitrator, organization, or representative or if a person seeks to compel an arbitrator or a representative of an arbitration organization to testify or produce records in violation of subsection (d), and the court decides that the arbitrator, arbitration organization, or representative of an arbitration organization is immune from civil liability or that the arbitrator or representative of the organization is not competent to testify, the court shall award to the arbitrator, organization, or representative reasonable attorney's fees and other reasonable expenses of litigation.

SECTION 15. ARBITRATION PROCESS.

(a) An arbitrator may conduct an arbitration in such manner as the arbitrator considers appropriate for a fair and expeditious disposition of the proceeding. The authority conferred upon the arbitrator includes the power to hold conferences with the parties to the arbitration proceeding before the hearing and, among other matters, determine the admissibility, relevance, materiality and weight of any evidence.

(b) An arbitrator may decide a request for summary disposition of a claim or particular issue:

(1) if all interested parties agree; or

(2) upon request of one party to the arbitration proceeding if that party gives notice to all other parties to the proceeding, and the other parties have a reasonable opportunity to respond.

(c) If an arbitrator orders a hearing, the arbitrator shall set a time and place and give notice of the hearing not less than five days before the hearing begins. Unless a party to the arbitration proceeding makes an objection to lack or insufficiency of notice not later than the beginning of the hearing, the party's appearance at the hearing waives the objection. Upon request of a party to the arbitration proceeding and for good cause shown, or upon the arbitrator's own initiative, the arbitrator may adjourn the hearing from time to time as necessary but may not postpone the hearing to a time later than that fixed by the agreement to arbitrate for making the award unless the parties to the arbitration proceeding consent to a later date. The arbitrator may hear and decide the controversy upon the evidence produced although a party who was duly notified of the arbitration proceeding did not appear. The court, on request, may direct the arbitrator to conduct the hearing promptly and render a timely decision.

(d) At a hearing under subsection (c), a party to the arbitration proceeding has a right to be heard, to present evidence material to the controversy, and to cross-examine witnesses appearing at the hearing.

(e) If an arbitrator ceases or is unable to act during the arbitration proceeding, a replacement arbitrator must be appointed in accordance with Section 11 to continue the proceeding and to resolve the controversy.

SECTION 16. REPRESENTATION BY LAWYER.

A party to an arbitration proceeding may be represented by a lawyer.

SECTION 17. WITNESSES; SUBPOENAS; DEPOSITIONS; DISCOVERY.

(a) An arbitrator may issue a subpoena for the attendance of a witness and for the production of records and other evidence at any hearing and may administer oaths. A subpoena must be served in the manner for service of subpoenas in a civil action and, upon [motion] to the court by a party to the arbitration proceeding or the arbitrator, enforced in the manner for enforcement of subpoenas in a civil action.

(b) In order to make the proceedings fair, expeditious, and cost effective, upon request of a party to or a witness in an arbitration proceeding, an arbitrator may permit a deposition of any witness to be taken for use as evidence at the hearing, including a witness who cannot be subpoenaed for or is unable to attend a hearing. The arbitrator shall determine the conditions under which the deposition is taken.

(c) An arbitrator may permit such discovery as the arbitrator decides is appropriate in the circumstances, taking into account the needs of the parties to the arbitration proceeding and other affected persons and the desirability of making the proceeding fair, expeditious, and cost effective.

(d) If an arbitrator permits discovery under subsection (c), the arbitrator may order a party to the arbitration proceeding to comply with the arbitrator's discovery-related orders, issuing subpoenas for the attendance of a witness and for the production of records and other evidence at a discovery proceeding, and take action against a noncomplying party to the extent a court could if the controversy were the subject of a civil action in this State.

(e) An arbitrator may issue a protective order to prevent the disclosure of privileged information, confidential information, trade secrets, and other information protected from disclosure to the extent a court could if the controversy were the subject of a civil action in this State.

(f) All laws compelling a person under subpoena to testify and all fees for attending a judicial proceeding, a deposition, or a discovery proceeding as a witness apply to an arbitration proceeding as if the controversy were the subject of a civil action in this State.

(g) The court may enforce a subpoena or discovery-related order for the attendance of a witness within this State and for the production of records and other evidence issued by an arbitrator in connection with an arbitration proceeding in another State upon conditions determined by the court so as to make the arbitration proceeding fair, expeditious, and cost effective. A subpoena or discovery-related order issued by an arbitrator in another state must be served in the manner provided by law for service of subpoenas in a civil action in this State and, upon [motion] to the court by a party to the arbitration proceeding or the arbitrator, enforced in the manner provided by law for enforcement of subpoenas in a civil action in this State.

SECTION 18. JUDICIAL ENFORCEMENT OF PREAWARD RULING BY ARBITRATOR.

If an arbitrator makes a preaward ruling in favor of a party to the arbitration proceeding, the party may request the arbitrator to incorporate the ruling into an award under Section 19. A prevailing party may make a [motion] to the court for an expedited order to confirm the award under Section 22, in which case the court shall summarily decide the [motion]. The court shall issue an order to confirm the award unless the court vacates, modifies, or corrects the award under Section 23 or 24.

SECTION 19. AWARD.

(a) An arbitrator shall make a record of an award. The record must be signed or otherwise authenticated by any arbitrator who concurs with the award. The arbitrator or the arbitration organization shall give notice of the award, including a copy of the award, to each party to the arbitration proceeding.

(b) An award must be made within the time specified by the agreement to arbitrate or, if not specified therein, within the time ordered by the court. The court may extend or the parties to the arbitration proceeding may agree in a record to extend the time. The court or the parties may do so within or after the time specified or ordered. A party waives any objection that an award was not timely made unless the party gives notice of the objection to the arbitrator before receiving notice of the award.

SECTION 20. CHANGE OF AWARD BY ARBITRATOR.

(a) On [motion] to an arbitrator by a party to the arbitration proceeding, the arbitrator may modify or correct an award:

(1) upon the grounds stated in Section 24(a)(1) or (3);

(2) because the arbitrator has not made a final and definite award upon a claim submitted by the parties to the arbitration proceeding; or

(3) to clarify the award.

(b) A [motion] under subsection (a) must be made and notice given to all parties within 20 days after the movant receives notice of the award.

(c) A party to the arbitration proceeding must give notice of any objection to the [motion] within 10 days after receipt of the notice.

(d) If a [motion] to the court is pending under Section 22, 23, or 24, the court may submit the claim to the arbitrator to consider whether to modify or correct the award:

(1) upon a ground stated in Section 24(a)(1) or (3);

(2) because the arbitrator has not made a final and definite award upon a claim submitted by the parties to the arbitration proceeding; or

(3) to clarify the award.

(e) An award modified or corrected pursuant to this section is subject to Sections 19(a), 22, 23, and 24.

SECTION 21. REMEDIES; FEES AND EXPENSES OF ARBITRATION PROCEEDING.

(a) An arbitrator may award punitive damages or other exemplary relief if such an award is authorized by law in a civil action involving the same claim and the evidence produced at the hearing justifies the award under the legal standards otherwise applicable to the claim.

(b) An arbitrator may award reasonable attorney's fees and other reasonable expenses of arbitration if such an award is authorized by law in a civil action involving the same claim or by the agreement of the parties to the arbitration proceeding.

(c) As to all remedies other than those authorized by subsections (a) and (b), an arbitrator may order such remedies as the arbitrator considers just and appropriate under the circumstances of the arbitration proceeding. The fact that such a remedy could not or would not be granted by the court is not a ground for refusing to confirm an award under Section 22 or for vacating an award under Section 23.

(d) An arbitrator's expenses and fees, together with other expenses, must be paid as provided in the award.

(e) If an arbitrator awards punitive damages or other exemplary relief under subsection (a), the arbitrator shall specify in the award the basis in fact justifying and the basis in law authorizing the award and state separately the amount of the punitive damages or other exemplary relief.

SECTION 22. CONFIRMATION OF AWARD.

After a party to an arbitration proceeding receives notice of an award, the party may make a [motion] to the court for an order confirming the award, at which time the court shall issue a confirming order unless the award is modified or corrected pursuant to Section 20 or 24 or is vacated pursuant to Section 23.

SECTION 23. VACATING AWARD.

(a) Upon [motion] to the court by a party to an arbitration proceeding, the court shall vacate an award made in the arbitration proceeding if:

(1) the award was procured by corruption, fraud, or other undue means;

(2) there was:

(A) evident partiality by an arbitrator appointed as a neutral arbitrator;

(B) corruption by an arbitrator; or

(C) misconduct by an arbitrator prejudicing the rights of a party to the arbitration proceeding;

(3) an arbitrator refused to postpone the hearing upon showing of sufficient cause for postponement, refused to consider evidence material to the controversy, or otherwise conducted the hearing contrary to Section 15, so as to prejudice substantially the rights of a party to the arbitration proceeding;

(4) an arbitrator exceeded the arbitrator's powers;

(5) there was no agreement to arbitrate, unless the person participated in the arbitration proceeding without raising the objection under Sec-

tion 15(c) not later than the beginning of the arbitration hearing; or

(6) the arbitration was conducted without proper notice of the initiation of an arbitration as required in Section 9 so as to prejudice substantially the rights of a party to the arbitration proceeding.

(b) A [motion] under this section must be filed within 90 days after the [movant] receives notice of the award pursuant to Section 19 or within 90 days after the [movant] receives notice of a modified or corrected award pursuant to Section 20, unless the [movant] alleges that the award was procured by corruption, fraud, or other undue means, in which case the [motion] must be made within 90 days after the ground is known or by the exercise of reasonable care would have been known by the [movant].

(c) If the court vacates an award on a ground other than that set forth in subsection (a)(5),it may order a rehearing. If the award is vacated on a ground stated in subsection (a)(1) or (2), the rehearing must be before a new arbitrator. If the award is vacated on a ground stated in subsection (a)(3), (4), or (6), the rehearing may be before the arbitrator who made the award or the arbitrator's successor. The arbitrator must render the decision in the rehearing within the same time as that provided in Section 19(b) for an award.

(d) If the court denies a [motion] to vacate an award, it shall confirm the award unless a [motion] to modify or correct the award is pending.

SECTION 24. MODIFICATION OR CORRECTION OF AWARD.

(a) Upon [motion] made within 90 days after the [movant] receives notice of the award pursuant to Section 19 or within 90 days after the [movant] receives notice of a modified or corrected award pursuant to Section 20, the court shall modify or correct the award if:

(1) there was an evident mathematical miscalculation or an evident mistake in the description of a person, thing, or property referred to in the award;

(2) the arbitrator has made an award on a claim not submitted to the arbitrator and the award may be corrected without affecting the merits of the decision upon the claims submitted; or

(3) the award is imperfect in a matter of form not affecting the merits of the decision on the claims submitted.

(b) If a [motion] made under subsection (a) is granted, the court shall modify or correct and confirm the award as modified or corrected. Otherwise, unless a motion to vacate is pending, the court shall confirm the award.

(c) A [motion] to modify or correct an award pursuant to this section may be joined with a [motion] to vacate the award.

SECTION 25. JUDGMENT ON AWARD; ATTORNEY'S FEES AND LITIGATION EXPENSES.

(a) Upon granting an order confirming, vacating without directing a rehearing, modifying, or correcting an award, the court shall enter a judgment in conformity therewith. The judgment may be recorded, docketed, and enforced as any other judgment in a civil action.

(b) A court may allow reasonable costs of the [motion] and subsequent judicial proceedings.

(c) On [application] of a prevailing party to a contested judicial proceeding under Section 22, 23, or 24, the court may add reasonable attorney's fees and other reasonable expenses of litigation incurred in a judicial proceeding after the award is made to a judgment confirming, vacating without directing a rehearing, modifying, or correcting an award.

SECTION 26. JURISDICTION.

(a) A court of this State having jurisdiction over the controversy and the parties may enforce an agreement to arbitrate.

(b) An agreement to arbitrate providing for arbitration in this State confers exclusive jurisdiction on the court to enter judgment on an award under this [Act].

SECTION 27. VENUE.

A [motion] pursuant to Section 5 must be made in the court of the [county] in which the agreement to arbitrate specifies the arbitration hearing is to be held or, if the hearing has been held, in the court of the [county] in which it was held. Otherwise, the [motion] may be made in the court of any [county] in which an adverse party resides or has a place of business or, if no adverse party has a residence or place of business in this State, in the court of any [county] in this State. All subsequent [motions] must be made in the court hearing the initial [motion] unless the court otherwise directs.

SECTION 28. APPEALS.

(a) An appeal may be taken from:

(1) an order denying a [motion] to compel arbitration;

(2) an order granting a [motion] to stay arbitration;

(3) an order confirming or denying confirmation of an award;

(4) an order modifying or correcting an award;

(5) an order vacating an award without directing a rehearing; or

(6) a final judgment entered pursuant to this [Act].

(b) An appeal under this section must be taken as from an order or a judgment in a civil action.

SECTION 29. UNIFORMITY OF APPLICATION AND CONSTRUCTION.

In applying and construing this Uniform Act, consideration must be given to the need to promote uniformity of the law with respect to its subject matter among States that enact it.

SECTION 30. RELATIONSHIP TO ELECTRONIC SIGNATURES IN GLOBAL AND NATIONAL COMMERCE ACT.

The provisions of this Act governing the legal effect, validity, and enforceability of electronic records or electronic signatures, and of contracts performed with the use of such records or signatures conform to the requirements of Section 102 of the Electronic Signatures in Global and National Commerce Act.

SECTION 31. EFFECTIVE DATE.

This [Act] takes effect on [effective date].

SECTION 32. REPEAL.

Effective on [delayed date should be the same as that in Section 3(c)], the [Uniform Arbitration Act] is repealed.

SECTION 33. SAVINGS CLAUSE.

This [Act] does not affect an action or proceeding commenced or right accrued before this [Act] takes effect. Subject to Section 3 of this [Act], an arbitration agreement made before the effective date of this [Act] is governed by the [Uniform Arbitration Act].

APPENDIX L

DEMAND FOR ARBITRATION

<u>   </u>ARBITRATION RULES
(ENTER THE NAME OF THE APPLICABLE RULES)
Demand for Arbitration

MEDIATION: *If you would like the AAA to contact the other parties and attempt to arrange mediation, please check this box.* ☐ *There is no additional administrative fee for this service.*	
Name of Respondent	Name of Representative (if known)
Address:	Name of Firm (if applicable):
	Representative's Address
City State Zip Code	City State Zip Code
Phone No. Fax No.	Phone No. Fax No.
Email Address:	Email Address:

The named claimant, a party to an arbitration agreement dated _____, which provides for arbitration under the _____Arbitration Rules of the American Arbitration Association, hereby demands arbitration.		
THE NATURE OF THE DISPUTE:		
Dollar Amount of Claim $	Other Relief Sought: ☐ Attorneys Fees ☐ Interest	
	☐ Arbitration Costs ☐ Punitive/ Exemplary ☐ Other ____	
AMOUNT OF FILING FEE ENCLOSED WITH THIS DEMAND (please refer to the fee schedule in the rules for the appropriate fee) $		
PLEASE DESCRIBE APPROPRIATE QUALIFICATIONS FOR ARBITRATOR(S) TO BE APPOINTED TO HEAR THIS DISPUTED:		
Hearing locale_____ (check one) ☐ Requested by Claimant ☐ Locale provision included in the contract		
Estimated time needed for hearings overall:	Type of Business: Claimant _____	
_____hours or _____days	Respondent_____	

Is this a dispute between a business and a consumer?	☐ Yes ☐ No
Does this dispute arise out of an employment relationship?	☐ Yes ☐ No

If this dispute arises out of an employment relationship, what was/is the employee's annual wage range? Note: This question is required by California law. ☐ Less than $100,000 ☐ $100,000—$250,000 ☐ Over $250,000

You are hereby notified that copies of our arbitration agreement and this demand are being filed with the American Arbitration Association's Case Management Center, located in (check one) ☐ Atlanta, GA ☐ Dallas, TX ☐ East Providence, RI ☐ Fresno, CA ☐ International Centre, NY, with a request that it commence administration of the arbitration. Under the rules, you may file an answering statement within the timeframe specified in the rules, after notice from the AAA.

Signature (may be signed by a representative) Date:	Name of Representative
Name of Claimant	Name of Firm (if applicable)
Address (to be used in connection with this case):	Representative's Address:
City State Zip Code	City State Zip Code
Phone No. Fax No.	Phone No. Fax No.
Email Address:	Email Address:

To begin proceedings, please send two copies of this Demand and the Arbitration Agreement, along with the filing fee as provided for in the Rules, to the AAA. Send the original Demand to the Respondent.

Please visit our website at www.adr.org if you would like to file this case online. AAA Customer Service can be reached at 800–778–7879

APPENDIX M

TASK FORCE ON ALTERNATIVE DISPUTE RESOLUTION IN EMPLOYMENT, DUE PROCESS PROTOCOL

(1995)*

A DUE PROCESS PROTOCOL FOR MEDIATION AND ARBITRATION OF STATUTORY DISPUTES ARISING OUT OF THE EMPLOYMENT RELATIONSHIP

A. PRE-OR POST-DISPUTE ARBITRATION

The Task Force takes no position on the timing of agreements to mediate and/or arbitrate statutory employment disputes, though it agrees that such agreements be knowingly made. The focus of this Protocol is on standards of exemplary due process.

B. RIGHT OF REPRESENTATION

1. *Choice of Representative*

Employees considering the use of or, in fact, utilizing mediation and/or arbitration procedures

* The Task Force on Alternative Dispute Resolution in Employment was composed of representatives of the American Arbitration Association, American Bar Association, American Civil Liberties Union, Federal Mediation and Conciliation Service, National Academy of Arbitrators, National Employment Lawyers Association, and the Society of Professionals in Dispute Resolution.

433

should have the right to be represented by a spokesperson of their own choosing. The mediation and arbitration procedure should so specify and should include reference to institutions which might offer assistance, such as bar associations, legal service associations, civil rights organizations, civil rights organizations, trade unions, etc.

2. *Fees for Representation*

The amount and method of payment for representation should be determined between the claimant and the representative. We recommend, however, a number of existing systems which provide employer reimbursement of at least a portion of the employee's attorney fees, especially for lower-paid employees. The arbitrator should have the authority to provide for fee reimbursement, in whole or in part, as part of the remedy in accordance with applicable law in the interests of justice.

3. *Access to Information*

One of the advantages of arbitration is that there is usually less time and money spent in pre-trial discovery. Adequate but limited pre-trial discovery is to be encouraged and employees should have access to all information reasonably relevant to mediation and/or arbitration of their claims. The employees' representative should also have reasonable pre-hearing and hearing access to all such information and documentation.

Necessary pre-hearing depositions consistent with the expedited nature of arbitration should be available.

We also recommend that prior to selection of an arbitrator, each side should be provided with the names, addresses and phone numbers of the representatives of the parties in that arbitrator's six most recent cases to aid them in selection.

C. MEDIATOR AND ARBITRATOR QUALIFICATION

1. *Roster Membership*

Mediators and arbitrators selected for such cases should have skill in the conduct of hearings, knowledge of the statutory issues at stake in the dispute, and familiarity with the workplace and employment environment. The roster of available mediators and arbitrators should be established on a non-discriminatory basis, diverse by gender, ethnicity, background, experience, etc., to satisfy the parties that their interests and objectives will be respected and fully considered.

2. *Training*

The creation of a roster containing the foregoing qualifications dictates the development of a training program to educate existing and potential labor and employment mediators and arbitrators as to the statutes, including substantive, procedural and remedial issues to be confronted, and to train experts in the statutes as to employer procedures governing the employment relationship as well as due process and fairness in the conduct and control or arbitration hearings and mediation sessions.

3. *Panel Selection*

Upon request of the parties, the designating agency should utilize a list procedure such as that of the AAA or select a panel composed of an odd number of mediators and arbitrators from its roster or pool. The panel cards for such individuals should be submitted to the parties for their perusal prior to alternate striking of the names on the list, resulting in the designation of the remaining mediator and/or arbitrator.

The selection process could empower the designating agency to appoint a mediator and/or arbitrator if the striking procedure is unacceptable or unsuccessful. As noted above, subject to the consent of the parties, the designating agency should provide the names of the parties and their representatives in recent cases decided by the listed arbitrators.

4. *Conflicts of Interest*

The mediator and arbitrator for a case has a duty to disclose any relationship which might reasonably constitute or be perceived as a conflict of interest.

5. *Authority of the Arbitrator*

The arbitrator should be bound by applicable agreements, statutes, regulations and rules of procedure of the designating agency, including the authority to determined the time and place of the hearing, permit reasonable discovery, issue subpoenas, decide arbitrability issues, preserve order and privacy in the hearings, rule on evidentiary matters, determine the close of the hearing and procedures for post-hearing submissions, and issue an award resolving the submitted dispute.

The arbitrator should be empowered to award whatever relief would be available in court under the law. The arbitrator should issue an opinion and award setting forth a summary of the issues, including the type(s) of disputes(s), the damages and/or other relief requested and awarded, a statement of any other issues resolved, and a statement regarding the disposition of any statutory claim(s).

6. *Compensation of the Mediator and Arbitrator*

Impartiality is best assured by the parties sharing the fees and expenses of the mediator and arbitrator. In cases where the economic condition of a party does not permit equal sharing, the parties should make mutually acceptable arrangements to achieve that goal if at all possible. In the absence of such agreement, the arbitrator should determine allocation of fees. The designating agency, by negotiating the parties' share of costs and collecting such fees, might be able to reduce the bias potential of disparate contributions by forwarding payment to the mediator and/or arbitrator without disclosing the parties' share therein.

APPENDIX N

THE CODE OF ETHICS FOR ARBITRATORS IN COMMERCIAL DISPUTES

Effective March 1, 2004

The Code of Ethics for Arbitrators in Commercial Disputes was originally prepared in 1977 by a joint committee consisting of a special committee of the American Arbitration Association and a special committee of the American Bar Association. The Code was revised in 2003 by an ABA Task Force and special committee of the AAA.

Preamble

The use of arbitration to resolve a wide variety of disputes has grown extensively and forms a significant part of the system of justice on which our society relies for a fair determination of legal rights. Persons who act as arbitrators therefore undertake serious responsibilities to the public, as well as to the parties. Those responsibilities include important ethical obligations.

Few cases of unethical behavior by commercial arbitrators have arisen. Nevertheless, this Code sets forth generally accepted standards of ethical conduct for the guidance of arbitrators and parties in commercial disputes, in the hope of contributing to the maintenance of high standards and continued confidence in the process of arbitration.

This Code provides ethical guidelines for many types of arbitration but does not apply to labor arbitration, which is generally conducted under the Code of Professional Responsibility for Arbitrators of Labor–Management Disputes.

There are many different types of commercial arbitration. Some proceedings are conducted under arbitration rules established by various organizations and trade associations, while others are conducted without such rules. Although most proceedings are arbitrated pursuant to voluntary agreement of the parties, certain types of disputes are submitted to arbitration by reason of particular laws. This Code is intended to apply to all such proceedings in which disputes or claims are submitted for decision to one or more arbitrators appointed in a manner provided by an agreement of the parties, by applicable arbitration rules, or by law. In all such cases, the persons who have the power to decide should observe fundamental standards of ethical conduct. In this Code, all such persons are called "arbitrators," although in some types of proceeding they might be called "umpires," "referees," "neutrals," or have some other title.

Arbitrators, like judges, have the power to decide cases. However, unlike full-time judges, arbitrators are usually engaged in other occupations before, during, and after the time that they serve as arbitrators. Often, arbitrators are purposely chosen from the same trade or industry as the parties in order to bring special knowledge to the task of deciding. This Code recognizes these fundamental differences between arbitrators and judges.

In those instances where this Code has been approved and recommended by organizations that provide, coordinate, or administer services of arbitrators, it provides ethical standards for the members of their respective panels of arbitrators. However, this Code does not form a part of the arbitration rules of any such organization unless its rules so provide.

Note on Neutrality

In some types of commercial arbitration, the parties or the administering institution provide for three or more arbitrators. In some such proceedings, it is the practice for each party, acting alone, to appoint one arbitrator (a "party-appointed arbitrator") and for one additional arbitrator to be designated by the party-appointed arbitrators, or by the parties, or by an independent institution or individual. The sponsors of this Code believe that it is preferable for all arbitrators including any party-appointed arbitrators to be neutral, that is, independent and impartial, and to comply with the same ethical standards. This expectation generally is essential in arbitrations where the parties, the nature of the dispute, or the enforcement of any resulting award may have international aspects. However, parties in certain domestic arbitrations in the United States may prefer that party-appointed arbitrators be non-neutral and governed by special ethical considerations. These special ethical considerations appear in Canon X of this Code.

This Code establishes a presumption of neutrality for all arbitrators, including party-appointed arbitrators, which applies unless the parties' agreement, the arbitration rules agreed to by the parties or applicable laws provide otherwise. This Code requires all party-appointed arbitrators, whether neutral or not, to make pre-appointment disclosures of any facts which might affect their neutrality, independence, or impartiality. This Code also requires all party-appointed arbitrators to ascertain and disclose as soon as practicable whether the parties intended for them to serve as neutral or not. If any doubt or uncertainty exists, the party-appointed arbitrators should serve as neutrals unless and until such doubt or uncertainty is resolved in accordance with Canon IX. This Code expects all arbitrators, including those serving under Canon X, to preserve the integrity and fairness of the process.

Note on Construction

Various aspects of the conduct of arbitrators, including some matters covered by this Code, may also be governed by agreements of the parties, arbitration rules to which the parties have agreed, applicable law, or other applicable ethics rules, all of which should be consulted by the arbitrators. This Code does not take the place of or supersede such laws, agreements, or arbitration rules to which the parties have agreed and should be read in conjunction with other rules of ethics. It does not establish new or additional grounds for judicial review of arbitration awards.

All provisions of this Code should therefore be read as subject to contrary provisions of applicable law and arbitration rules. They should also be read as subject to contrary agreements of the parties. Nevertheless, this Code imposes no obligation on any arbitrator to act in a manner inconsistent with the arbitrator's fundamental duty to preserve the integrity and fairness of the arbitral process.

Canons I through VIII of this Code apply to all arbitrators. Canon IX applies to all party-appointed arbitrators, except that certain party-appointed arbitrators are exempted by Canon X from compliance with certain provisions of Canons I–IX related to impartiality and independence, as specified in Canon X.

Canon I: An Arbitrator Should Uphold the Integrity and Fairness of the Arbitration Process

A. An arbitrator has a responsibility not only to the parties but also to the process of arbitration itself, and must observe high standards of conduct so that the integrity and fairness of the process will be preserved. Accordingly, an arbitrator should recognize a responsibility to the public, to the parties whose rights will be decided, and to all other participants in the proceeding. This responsibility may include pro bono service as an arbitrator where appropriate.

B. One should accept appointment as an arbitrator only if fully satisfied:

(1) that he or she can serve impartially;

(2) that he or she can serve independently from the parties, potential witnesses, and the other arbitrators;

(3) that he or she is competent to serve; and

(4) that he or she can be available to commence the arbitration in accordance with the requirements of the proceeding and thereafter to devote the time and attention to its completion that the parties are reasonably entitled to expect.

C. After accepting appointment and while serving as an arbitrator, a person should avoid entering into any business, professional, or personal relationship, or acquiring any financial or personal interest, which is likely to affect impartiality or which might reasonably create the appearance of partiality. For a reasonable period of time after the decision of a case, persons who have served as arbitrators should avoid entering into any such relationship, or acquiring any such interest, in circumstances which might reasonably create the appearance that they had been influenced in the arbitration by the anticipation or expectation of the relationship or interest. Existence of any of the matters or circumstances described in this paragraph C does not render it unethical for one to serve as an arbitrator where the parties have consented to the arbitrator's appointment or continued services following full disclosure of the relevant facts in accordance with Canon II.

D. Arbitrators should conduct themselves in a way that is fair to all parties and should not be swayed by outside pressure, public clamor, and fear of criticism or self-interest. They should avoid conduct and statements that give the appearance of partiality toward or against any party.

E. When an arbitrator's authority is derived from the agreement of the parties, an arbitrator should neither exceed that authority nor do less than is required to exercise that authority completely. Where the agreement of the parties sets forth procedures to be followed in conducting the arbitration or refers to rules to be followed, it is the obligation of the arbitrator to comply with such procedures or rules. An arbitrator has no ethical obligation to comply with any agreement, procedures or rules that are unlawful or that, in the arbitrator's judgment, would be inconsistent with this Code.

F. An arbitrator should conduct the arbitration process so as to advance the fair and efficient resolution of the matters submitted for decision. An arbitrator should make all reasonable efforts to prevent delaying tactics, harassment of parties or other participants, or other abuse or disruption of the arbitration process.

G. The ethical obligations of an arbitrator begin upon acceptance of the appointment and continue throughout all stages of the proceeding. In addition, as set forth in this Code, certain ethical obligations begin as soon as a person is requested to serve as an arbitrator and certain ethical obligations continue after the decision in the proceeding has been given to the parties.

H. Once an arbitrator has accepted an appointment, the arbitrator should not withdraw or abandon the appointment unless compelled to do so by unanticipated circumstances that would render it impossible or impracticable to continue. When an arbitrator is to be compensated for his or her services, the arbitrator may withdraw if the parties fail or refuse to provide for payment of the compensation as agreed.

I. An arbitrator who withdraws prior to the completion of the arbitration, whether upon the arbitrator's initiative or upon the request of one or more of the parties, should take reasonable steps to protect the interests of the parties in the arbitration, including return of evidentiary materials and protection of confidentiality.

Comment to Canon I

A prospective arbitrator is not necessarily partial or prejudiced by having acquired knowledge of the parties, the applicable law or the customs and practices of the business involved. Arbitrators may also have special experience or expertise in the areas of business, commerce, or technology which are involved in the arbitration. Arbitrators do not contravene this Canon if, by virtue of such experience or expertise, they have views on certain general issues likely to arise in the arbitration, but an arbitrator may not have prejudged any of the specific factual or legal determinations to be addressed during the arbitration.

During an arbitration, the arbitrator may engage in discourse with the parties or their counsel, draw out arguments or contentions, comment on the law or evidence, make interim rulings, and otherwise control or direct the arbitration. These activities are integral parts of an arbitration. Paragraph D of Canon I is not intended to preclude or limit either full discussion of the issues during the course of the arbitration or the arbitrator's management of the proceeding.

Canon II: An Arbitrator Should Disclose Any Interest or Relationship Likely to Affect Impartiality or Which Might Create an Appearance of Partiality

A. Persons who are requested to serve as arbitrators should, before accepting, disclose:

(1) any known direct or indirect financial or personal interest in the outcome of the arbitration;

(2) any known existing or past financial, business, professional or personal relationships which might reasonably affect impartiality or lack of

independence in the eyes of any of the parties. For example, prospective arbitrators should disclose any such relationships which they personally have with any party or its lawyer, with any co-arbitrator, or with any individual whom they have been told will be a witness. They should also disclose any such relationships involving their families or household members or their current employers, partners, or professional or business associates that can be ascertained by reasonable efforts;

(3) the nature and extent of any prior knowledge they may have of the dispute; and

(4) any other matters, relationships, or interests which they are obligated to disclose by the agreement of the parties, the rules or practices of an institution, or applicable law regulating arbitrator disclosure.

B. Persons who are requested to accept appointment as arbitrators should make a reasonable effort to inform themselves of any interests or relationships described in paragraph A.

C. The obligation to disclose interests or relationships described in paragraph A is a continuing duty which requires a person who accepts appointment as an arbitrator to disclose, as soon as practicable, at any stage of the arbitration, any such interests or relationships which may arise, or which are recalled or discovered.

D. Any doubt as to whether or not disclosure is to be made should be resolved in favor of disclosure.

E. Disclosure should be made to all parties unless other procedures for disclosure are provided in the agreement of the parties, applicable rules or practices of an institution, or by law. Where more than one arbitrator has been appointed, each should inform the others of all matters disclosed.

F. When parties, with knowledge of a person's interests and relationships, nevertheless desire that person to serve as an arbitrator, that person may properly serve.

G. If an arbitrator is requested by all parties to withdraw, the arbitrator must do so. If an arbitrator is requested to withdraw by less than all of the parties because of alleged partiality, the arbitrator should withdraw unless either of the following circumstances exists:

(1) An agreement of the parties, or arbitration rules agreed to by the parties, or applicable law establishes procedures for determining challenges to arbitrators, in which case those procedures should be followed; or

(2) In the absence of applicable procedures, if the arbitrator, after carefully considering the matter, determines that the reason for the challenge is not substantial, and that he or she can nevertheless act and decide the case impartially and fairly.

H. If compliance by a prospective arbitrator with any provision of this Code would require disclosure of confidential or privileged information, the prospective arbitrator should either:

(1) Secure the consent to the disclosure from the person who furnished the information or the holder of the privilege; or

(2) Withdraw.

Canon III: An Arbitrator Should Avoid Impropriety or the Appearance of Impropriety in Communicating With Parties

A.   If an agreement of the parties or applicable arbitration rules establishes the manner or content of communications between the arbitrator and the parties, the arbitrator should follow those procedures notwithstanding any contrary provision of paragraphs B and C.

B.   An arbitrator or prospective arbitrator should not discuss a proceeding with any party in the absence of any other party, except in any of the following circumstances:

(1) When the appointment of a prospective arbitrator is being considered, the prospective arbitrator:

(a) may ask about the identities of the parties, counsel, or witnesses and the general nature of the case; and

(b) may respond to inquiries from a party or its counsel designed to determine his or her suitability and availability for the appointment. In any such dialogue, the prospective arbitrator may receive information from a party or its counsel disclosing the general nature of the dispute but should not permit them to discuss the merits of the case.

(2) In an arbitration in which the two party-appointed arbitrators are expected to appoint the third arbitrator, each party-appointed arbitrator may consult with the party who appointed the arbitrator concerning the choice of the third arbitrator;

(3) In an arbitration involving party-appointed arbitrators, each party-appointed arbitrator may consult with the party who appointed the arbitrator concerning arrangements for any compensation to be paid to the party-appointed arbitrator. Submission of routine written requests for payment of compensation and expenses in accordance with such arrangements and written communications pertaining solely to such requests need not be sent to the other party;

(4) In an arbitration involving party-appointed arbitrators, each party-appointed arbitrator may consult with the party who appointed the arbitrator concerning the status of the arbitrator (i.e., neutral or non-neutral), as contemplated by paragraph C of Canon IX;

(5) Discussions may be had with a party concerning such logistical matters as setting the time and place of hearings or making other arrangements for the conduct of the proceedings. However, the arbitrator should promptly inform each other party of the discussion and should not make any final determination concerning the matter

discussed before giving each absent party an opportunity to express the party's views; or

(6) If a party fails to be present at a hearing after having been given due notice, or if all parties expressly consent, the arbitrator may discuss the case with any party who is present.

C.   Unless otherwise provided in this Canon, in applicable arbitration rules or in an agreement of the parties, whenever an arbitrator communicates in writing with one party, the arbitrator should at the same time send a copy of the communication to every other party, and whenever the arbitrator receives any written communication concerning the case from one party which has not already been sent to every other party, the arbitrator should send or cause it to be sent to the other parties.

Canon IV: An Arbitrator Should Conduct the Proceedings Fairly and Diligently

A.   An arbitrator should conduct the proceedings in an even-handed manner. The arbitrator should be patient and courteous to the parties, their representatives, and the witnesses and should encourage similar conduct by all participants.

B.   The arbitrator should afford to all parties the right to be heard and due notice of the time and place of any hearing. The arbitrator should allow each party a fair opportunity to present its evidence and arguments.

C. The arbitrator should not deny any party the opportunity to be represented by counsel or by any other person chosen by the party.

D. If a party fails to appear after due notice, the arbitrator should proceed with the arbitration when authorized to do so, but only after receiving assurance that appropriate notice has been given to the absent party.

E. When the arbitrator determines that more information than has been presented by the parties is required to decide the case, it is not improper for the arbitrator to ask questions, call witnesses, and request documents or other evidence, including expert testimony.

F. Although it is not improper for an arbitrator to suggest to the parties that they discuss the possibility of settlement or the use of mediation, or other dispute resolution processes, an arbitrator should not exert pressure on any party to settle or to utilize other dispute resolution processes. An arbitrator should not be present or otherwise participate in settlement discussions or act as a mediator unless requested to do so by all parties.

G. Co-arbitrators should afford each other full opportunity to participate in all aspects of the proceedings.

Comment to paragraph G

Paragraph G of Canon IV is not intended to preclude one arbitrator from acting in limited circumstances (e.g., ruling on discovery issues) where authorized by the agreement of the parties, applicable rules or law, nor does it preclude a majority of the arbitrators from proceeding with any aspect of the arbitration if an arbitrator is unable or unwilling to participate and such action is authorized by the agreement of the parties or applicable rules or law. It also does not preclude ex parte requests for interim relief.

Canon V: An Arbitrator Should Make Decisions in a Just, Independent and Deliberate Manner

A.   The arbitrator should, after careful deliberation, decide all issues submitted for determination. An arbitrator should decide no other issues.

B.   An arbitrator should decide all matters justly, exercising independent judgment, and should not permit outside pressure to affect the decision.

C.   An arbitrator should not delegate the duty to decide to any other person.

D.   In the event that all parties agree upon a settlement of issues in dispute and request the arbitrator to embody that agreement in an award, the arbitrator may do so, but is not required to do so unless satisfied with the propriety of the terms of settlement. Whenever an arbitrator embodies a settlement by the parties in an award, the arbitrator should state in the award that it is based on an agreement of the parties.

Canon VI: An Arbitrator Should Be Faithful to the Relationship of Trust and Confidentiality Inherent in That Office

A.   An arbitrator is in a relationship of trust to the parties and should not, at any time, use confidential information acquired during the arbitration proceeding to gain personal advantage or advantage for others, or to affect adversely the interest of another.

B.   The arbitrator should keep confidential all matters relating to the arbitration proceedings and decision. An arbitrator may obtain help from an associate, a research assistant or other persons in connection with reaching his or her decision if the arbitrator informs the parties of the use of such assistance and such persons agree to be bound by the provisions of this Canon.

C.   It is not proper at any time for an arbitrator to inform anyone of any decision in advance of the time it is given to all parties. In a proceeding in which there is more than one arbitrator, it is not proper at any time for an arbitrator to inform anyone about the substance of the deliberations of the arbitrators. After an arbitration award has been made, it is not proper for an arbitrator to assist in proceedings to enforce or challenge the award.

D.   Unless the parties so request, an arbitrator should not appoint himself or herself to a separate office related to the subject matter of the dispute, such as receiver or trustee, nor should a panel of arbitrators appoint one of their number to such an office.

Canon VII: An Arbitrator Should Adhere to Standards of Integrity and Fairness When Making Arrangements for Compensation and Reimbursement of Expenses

A.   Arbitrators who are to be compensated for their services or reimbursed for their expenses shall adhere to standards of integrity and fairness in making arrangements for such payments.

B.   Certain practices relating to payments are generally recognized as tending to preserve the integrity and fairness of the arbitration process. These practices include:

(1) Before the arbitrator finally accepts appointment, the basis of payment, including any cancellation fee, compensation in the event of withdrawal and compensation for study and preparation time, and all other charges, should be established. Except for arrangements for the compensation of party-appointed arbitrators, all parties should be informed in writing of the terms established;

(2) In proceedings conducted under the rules or administration of an institution that is available to assist in making arrangements for payments, communication related to compensation should be made through the institution. In proceedings where no institution has been engaged by the

parties to administer the arbitration, any communication with arbitrators (other than party appointed arbitrators) concerning payments should be in the presence of all parties; and

(3) Arbitrators should not, absent extraordinary circumstances, request increases in the basis of their compensation during the course of a proceeding.

Canon VIII: An Arbitrator May Engage in Advertising or Promotion of Arbitral Services Which is Truthful and Accurate

A. Advertising or promotion of an individual's willingness or availability to serve as an arbitrator must be accurate and unlikely to mislead. Any statements about the quality of the arbitrator's work or the success of the arbitrator's practice must be truthful.

B. Advertising and promotion must not imply any willingness to accept an appointment otherwise than in accordance with this Code.

Comment to Canon VIII

This Canon does not preclude an arbitrator from printing, publishing, or disseminating advertisements conforming to these standards in any electronic or print medium, from making personal presentations to prospective users of arbitral services conforming to such standards or from responding to inquiries concerning the arbitrator's availability, qualifications, experience, or fee arrangements.

Canon IX: Arbitrators Appointed by One Party Have a Duty to Determine and Disclose Their Status and to Comply With This Code, Except as Exempted by Canon X

A. In some types of arbitration in which there are three arbitrators, it is customary for each party, acting alone, to appoint one arbitrator. The third arbitrator is then appointed by agreement either of the parties or of the two arbitrators, or failing such agreement, by an independent institution or individual. In tripartite arbitrations to which this Code applies, all three arbitrators are presumed to be neutral and are expected to observe the same standards as the third arbitrator.

B. Notwithstanding this presumption, there are certain types of tripartite arbitration in which it is expected by all parties that the two arbitrators appointed by the parties may be predisposed toward the party appointing them. Those arbitrators, referred to in this Code as "Canon X arbitrators," are not to be held to the standards of neutrality and independence applicable to other arbitrators. Canon X describes the special ethical obligations of party-appointed arbitrators who are not expected to meet the standard of neutrality.

C. A party-appointed arbitrator has an obligation to ascertain, as early as possible but not later than the first meeting of the arbitrators and parties, whether the parties have agreed that the party-appointed arbitrators will serve as neutrals or whether they shall be subject to Canon X, and to provide a timely report of their conclusions to the parties and other arbitrators:

(1) Party-appointed arbitrators should review the agreement of the parties, the applicable rules and any applicable law bearing upon arbitrator neutrality. In reviewing the agreement of the parties, party-appointed arbitrators should consult any relevant express terms of the written or oral arbitration agreement. It may also be appropriate for them to inquire into agreements that have not been expressly set forth, but which may be implied from an established course of dealings of the parties or well-recognized custom and usage in their trade or profession;

(2) Where party-appointed arbitrators conclude that the parties intended for the party-appointed arbitrators not to serve as neutrals, they should so inform the parties and the other arbitrators. The arbitrators may then act as provided in Canon X unless or until a different determination of their status is made by the parties, any administering institution or the arbitral panel; and

(3) Until party-appointed arbitrators conclude that the party-appointed arbitrators were not intended by the parties to serve as neutrals, or if the party-appointed arbitrators are unable to form a reasonable belief of their status from the foregoing sources and no decision in this regard has yet been made by the parties, any administering institution, or the arbitral panel, they should

observe all of the obligations of neutral arbitrators set forth in this Code.

D.   Party-appointed arbitrators not governed by Canon X shall observe all of the obligations of Canons I through VIII unless otherwise required by agreement of the parties, any applicable rules, or applicable law.

Canon X: Exemptions for Arbitrators Appointed by One Party Who are not Subject to Rules of Neutrality

Canon X arbitrators are expected to observe all of the ethical obligations prescribed by this Code except those from which they are specifically excused by Canon X.

A.   *Obligations under Canon I*

Canon X arbitrators should observe all of the obligations of Canon I subject only to the following provisions:

(1) Canon X arbitrators may be predisposed toward the party who appointed them but in all other respects are obligated to act in good faith and with integrity and fairness. For example, Canon X arbitrators should not engage in delaying tactics or harassment of any party or witness and should not knowingly make untrue or misleading statements to the other arbitrators; and

(2) The provisions of subparagraphs B(1), B(2), and paragraphs C and D of Canon I, insofar as they relate to partiality, relationships, and interests are not applicable to Canon X arbitrators.

B. *Obligations under Canon II*

(1) Canon X arbitrators should disclose to all parties, and to the other arbitrators, all interests and relationships which Canon II requires be disclosed. Disclosure as required by Canon II is for the benefit not only of the party who appointed the arbitrator, but also for the benefit of the other parties and arbitrators so that they may know of any partiality which may exist or appear to exist;

and

(2) Canon X arbitrators are not obliged to withdraw under paragraph G of Canon II if requested to do so only by the party who did not appoint them.

C. *Obligations under Canon III*

Canon X arbitrators should observe all of the obligations of Canon III subject only to the following provisions:

(1) Like neutral party-appointed arbitrators, Canon X arbitrators may consult with the party who appointed them to the extent permitted in paragraph B of Canon III;

(2) Canon X arbitrators shall, at the earliest practicable time, disclose to the other arbitrators and to the parties whether or not they intend to communicate with their appointing parties. If they have disclosed the intention to engage in such communications, they may thereafter communicate with their appointing parties concern-

ing any other aspect of the case, except as provided in paragraph (3);

(3) If such communication occurred prior to the time they were appointed as arbitrators, or prior to the first hearing or other meeting of the parties with the arbitrators, the Canon X arbitrator should, at or before the first hearing or meeting of the arbitrators with the parties, disclose the fact that such communication has taken place. In complying with the provisions of this subparagraph, it is sufficient that there be disclosure of the fact that such communication has occurred without disclosing the content of the communication. A single timely disclosure of the Canon X arbitrator's intention to participate in such communications in the future is sufficient;

(4) Canon X arbitrators may not at any time during the arbitration:

(a) disclose any deliberations by the arbitrators on any matter or issue submitted to them for decision;

(b) communicate with the parties that appointed them concerning any matter or issue taken under consideration by the panel after the record is closed or such matter or issue has been submitted for decision; or

(c) disclose any final decision or interim decision in advance of the time that it is disclosed to all parties.

(5) Unless otherwise agreed by the arbitrators and the parties, a Canon X arbitrator may not communicate orally with the neutral arbitrator concerning any matter or issue arising or expected to arise in the arbitration in the absence of the other Canon X arbitrator. If a Canon X arbitrator communicates in writing with the neutral arbitrator, he or she shall simultaneously provide a copy of the written communication to the other Canon X arbitrator;

(6) When Canon X arbitrators communicate orally with the parties that appointed them concerning any matter on which communication is permitted under this Code, they are not obligated to disclose the contents of such oral communications to any other party or arbitrator; and

(7) When Canon X arbitrators communicate in writing with the party who appointed them concerning any matter on which communication is permitted under this Code, they are not required to send copies of any such written communication to any other party or arbitrator.

D.   *Obligations under Canon IV*

Canon X arbitrators should observe all of the obligations of Canon IV.

E.   *Obligations under Canon V*

Canon X arbitrators should observe all of the obligations of Canon V, except that they may be predisposed toward deciding in favor of the party who appointed them.

F. *Obligations under Canon VI*

Canon X arbitrators should observe all of the obligations of Canon VI.

G. *Obligations Under Canon VII*

Canon X arbitrators should observe all of the obligations of Canon VII.

H. *Obligations Under Canon VIII*

Canon X arbitrators should observe all of the obligations of Canon VIII.

I. *Obligations Under Canon IX*

The provisions of paragraph D of Canon IX are inapplicable to Canon X arbitrators, except insofar as the obligations are also set forth in this Canon.

MODEL RULES OF PROFESSIONAL CONDUCT

Client-Lawyer Relationship

Rule 1.12 Former Judge, Arbitrator, Mediator Or Other Third–Party Neutral

(a) Except as stated in paragraph (d), a lawyer shall not represent anyone in connection with a matter in which the lawyer participated personally and substantially as a judge or other adjudicative officer or law clerk to such a person or as an arbitrator, mediator or other third-party neutral, unless all parties to the proceeding give informed consent, confirmed in writing.

(b) A lawyer shall not negotiate for employment with any person who is involved as a party or as lawyer for a party in a matter in which the lawyer is participating personally and substantially as a judge or other adjudicative officer or as an arbitrator, mediator or other third-party neutral. A lawyer serving as a law clerk to a judge or other adjudicative officer may negotiate for employment with a party or lawyer involved in a matter in which the clerk is participating personally and substantially, but only after the lawyer has notified the judge or other adjudicative officer.

(c) If a lawyer is disqualified by paragraph (a), no lawyer in a firm with which that lawyer is associated may knowingly undertake or continue representation in the matter unless:

(1) the disqualified lawyer is timely screened from any participation in the matter and is apportioned no part of the fee therefrom; and

(2) written notice is promptly given to the parties and any appropriate tribunal to enable them to ascertain compliance with the provisions of this rule.

(d) An arbitrator selected as a partisan of a party in a multimember arbitration panel is not prohibited from subsequently representing that party.

MODEL RULES OF PROFESSIONAL CONDUCT

Advocate

Rule 3.3   Candor Toward The Tribunal

(a) A lawyer shall not knowingly:

(1) make a false statement of fact or law to a tribunal or fail to correct a false statement of material fact or law previously made to the tribunal by the lawyer;

(2) fail to disclose to the tribunal legal authority in the controlling jurisdiction known to the lawyer to be directly adverse to the position of the client and not disclosed by opposing counsel; or

(3) offer evidence that the lawyer knows to be false. If a lawyer, the lawyer's client, or a witness called by the lawyer, has offered material evidence and the lawyer comes to know of its falsity, the lawyer shall take reasonable remedial measures, including, if necessary, disclosure to the tribunal. A lawyer may refuse to offer evidence, other than the testimony of a defendant in a criminal matter, that the lawyer reasonably believes is false.

(b) A lawyer who represents a client in an adjudicative proceeding and who knows that a person intends to engage, is engaging or has engaged in criminal or fraudulent conduct related to the proceeding shall take reasonable remedial measures, including, if necessary, disclosure to the tribunal.

(c) The duties stated in paragraphs (a) and (b) continue to the conclusion of the proceeding, and apply even if compliance requires disclosure of information otherwise protected by Rule 1.6.

(d) In an ex parte proceeding, a lawyer shall inform the tribunal of all material facts known to the lawyer that will enable the tribunal to make an informed decision, whether or not the facts are adverse.

MODEL RULES OF PROFESSIONAL CONDUCT

Law Firms and Associations

Rule 5.5 Unauthorized Practice Of Law; Multijurisdictional Practice Of Law

(a) A lawyer shall not practice law in a jurisdiction in violation of the regulation of the legal profession in that jurisdiction, or assist another in doing so.

(b) A lawyer who is not admitted to practice in this jurisdiction shall not:

(1) except as authorized by these Rules or other law, establish an office or other systematic and continuous presence in this jurisdiction for the practice of law; or

(2) hold out to the public or otherwise represent that the lawyer is admitted to practice law in this jurisdiction.

(c) A lawyer admitted in another United States jurisdiction, and not disbarred or suspended from practice in any jurisdiction, may provide legal services on a temporary basis in this jurisdiction that:

(1) are undertaken in association with a lawyer who is admitted to practice in this jurisdiction and who actively participates in the matter;

(2) are in or reasonably related to a pending or potential proceeding before a tribunal in this or another jurisdiction, if the lawyer, or a person the lawyer is assisting, is authorized by law or order to appear in such proceeding or reasonably expects to be so authorized;

(3) are in or reasonably related to a pending or potential arbitration, mediation, or other alternative dispute resolution proceeding in this or another jurisdiction, if the services arise out of or are reasonably related to the lawyer's practice in a jurisdiction in which the lawyer is admitted to practice and are not services for which the forum requires pro hac vice admission; or

(4) are not within paragraphs (c)(2) or (c)(3) and arise out of or are reasonably related to the lawyer's practice in a jurisdiction in which the lawyer is admitted to practice.

(d) A lawyer admitted in another United States jurisdiction, and not disbarred or suspended from practice in any jurisdiction, may provide legal services in this jurisdiction that:

(1) are provided to the lawyer's employer or its organizational affiliates and are not services for which the forum requires pro hac vice admission; or

(2) are services that the lawyer is authorized to provide by federal law or other law of this jurisdiction.

ABA Model Rules of Professional Conduct, 2007 Edition, published by the American Bar Association Center for Professional Responsibility. Copyright © 2007 by the American Bar Association. Reprinted with permission. Copies of the ABA Model Rules of Professional Conduct, 2007 Edition are available from Service Center, American Bar Association, 321 North Clark Street, Chicago, IL 60610, 1–800–285–2221.

APPENDIX R

UNIFORM MEDIATION ACT

SECTION 1. TITLE. This [Act] may be cited as the Uniform Mediation Act.

SECTION 2. DEFINITIONS. In this [Act]:

(1) "Mediation" means a process in which a mediator facilitates communication and negotiation between parties to assist them in reaching a voluntary agreement regarding their dispute.

(2) "Mediation communication" means a statement, whether oral or in a record or verbal or nonverbal, that occurs during a mediation or is made for purposes of considering, conducting, participating in, initiating, continuing, or reconvening a mediation or retaining a mediator.

(3) "Mediator" means an individual who conducts a mediation.

(4) "Nonparty participant" means a person, other than a party or mediator, that participates in a mediation.

(5) "Mediation party" means a person that participates in a mediation and whose agreement is necessary to resolve the dispute.

(6) "Person" means an individual, corporation, business trust, estate, trust, partnership, limited

471

liability company, association, joint venture, government; governmental subdivision, agency, or instrumentality; public corporation, or any other legal or commercial entity.

(7) "Proceeding" means:

(A) a judicial, administrative, arbitral, or other adjudicative process,including related pre-hearing and post-hearing motions, conferences, and discovery; or

(B) a legislative hearing or similar process.

(8) "Record" means information that is inscribed on a tangible medium or that is stored in an electronic or other medium and is retrievable in perceivable form.

(9) "Sign" means:

(A) to execute or adopt a tangible symbol with the present intent to authenticate a record; or

(B) to attach or logically associate an electronic symbol, sound, or process to or with a record with the present intent to authenticate a record.

SECTION 3. SCOPE.

(a) Except as otherwise provided in subsection (b) or (c), this [Act] applies to a mediation in which:

(1) the mediation parties are required to mediate by statute or court or administrative agency rule or referred to mediation by a court, administrative agency, or arbitrator;

(2) the mediation parties and the mediator agree to mediate in a record that demonstrates an

expectation that mediation communications will be privileged against disclosure; or

(3) the mediation parties use as a mediator an individual who holds himself or herself out as a mediator or the mediation is provided by a person that holds itself out as providing mediation.

(b) The [Act] does not apply to a mediation:

(1) relating to the establishment, negotiation, administration, or termination of a collective bargaining relationship;

(2) relating to a dispute that is pending under or is part of the processes established by a collective bargaining agreement, except that the [Act] applies to a mediation arising out of a dispute that has been filed with an administrative agency or court;

(3) conducted by a judge who might make a ruling on the case; or

(4) conducted under the auspices of:

(A) a primary or secondary school if all the parties are students or

(B) a correctional institution for youths if all the parties are residents of that institution.

(c) If the parties agree in advance in a signed record, or a record of proceeding reflects agreement by the parties, that all or part of a mediation is not privileged, the privileges under Sections 4 through 6 do not apply to the mediation or part agreed upon. However, Sections 4 through 6 apply to a mediation communication made by a person that has not received actual notice of the agreement before the communication is made.

Legislative Note: To the extent that the Act applies to mediations conducted under the authority of a State's courts, State judiciaries should consider enacting conforming court rules.

SECTION 4. PRIVILEGE AGAINST DISCLOSURE; ADMISSIBILITY; DISCOVERY.

(a) Except as otherwise provided in Section 6, a mediation communication is privileged as provided in subsection (b) and is not subject to discovery or admissible in evidence in a proceeding unless waived or precluded as provided by Section 5.

(b) In a proceeding, the following privileges apply:

(1) A mediation party may refuse to disclose, and may prevent any other person from disclosing, a mediation communication.

(2) A mediator may refuse to disclose a mediation communication, and may prevent any other person from disclosing a mediation communication of the mediator.

(3) A nonparty participant may refuse to disclose, and may prevent any other person from disclosing, a mediation communication of the nonparty participant.

(c) Evidence or information that is otherwise admissible or subject to discovery does not become inadmissible or protected from discovery solely by reason of its disclosure or use in a mediation.

Legislative Note: The Act does not supersede existing state statutes that make mediators incompetent to testify, or that provide for costs and attorney fees to mediators who are wrongfully subpoenaed. See, e.g., Cal. Evid. Code Section 703.5 (West 1994).

SECTION 5. WAIVER AND PRECLUSION OF PRIVILEGE.

(a) A privilege under Section 4 may be waived in a record or orally during a proceeding if it is expressly waived by all parties to the mediation and:

(1) in the case of the privilege of a mediator, it is expressly waived by the mediator; and

(2) in the case of the privilege of a nonparty participant, it is expressly waived by the nonparty participant.

(b) A person that discloses or makes a representation about a mediation communication which prejudices another person in a proceeding is precluded from asserting a privilege under Section 4, but only to the extent necessary for the person prejudiced to respond to the representation or disclosure.

(c) A person that intentionally uses a mediation to plan, attempt to commit or commit a crime, or to conceal an ongoing crime or ongoing criminal activity is precluded from asserting a privilege under Section 4.

SECTION 6. EXCEPTIONS TO PRIVILEGE.

(a) There is no privilege under Section 4 for a mediation communication that is:

(1) in an agreement evidenced by a record signed by all parties to the agreement;

(2) available to the public under [insert statutory reference to open records act] or made during a session of a mediation which is open, or is required by law to be open, to the public;

(3) a threat or statement of a plan to inflict bodily injury or commit a crime of violence;

(4) intentionally used to plan a crime, attempt to commit or commit a crime, or to conceal an ongoing crime or ongoing criminal activity;

(5) sought or offered to prove or disprove a claim or complaint of professional misconduct or malpractice filed against a mediator;

(6) except as otherwise provided in subsection (c), sought or offered to prove or disprove a claim or complaint of professional misconduct or malpractice filed against a mediation party, nonparty participant, or representative of a party based on conduct occurring during a mediation; or,

(7) sought or offered to prove or disprove abuse, neglect, abandonment, or exploitation in a proceeding in which a child or adult protective services agency is a party, unless the

[Alternative A: [State to insert, for example, child or adult protection] case is referred by a court to mediation and a public agency participates.]

[Alternative B: public agency participates in the [State to insert, for example, child or adult protection] mediation].

(b) There is no privilege under Section 4 if a court, administrative agency, or arbitrator finds, after a hearing in camera, that the party seeking discovery or the proponent of the evidence has shown that the evidence is not otherwise available, that there is a need for the evidence that substantially outweighs the interest in protecting confidentiality, and that the mediation communication is sought or offered in:

(1) a court proceeding involving a felony [or misdemeanor]; or

(2) except as otherwise provided in subsection (c), a proceeding to prove a claim to rescind or reform or a defense to avoid liability on a contract arising out of the mediation.

(c) A mediator may not be compelled to provide evidence of a mediation communication referred to in subsection (a)(6) or (b)(2).

(d) If a mediation communication is not privileged under subsection (a) or (b), only the portion of the communication necessary for the application of the exception from nondisclosure may be admitted. Admission of evidence under subsection (a) or (b) does not render the evidence, or any other mediation communication, discoverable or admissible for any other purpose.

Legislative Note: If the enacting state does not have an open records act, the following language in paragraph (2) of subsection (a) needs to be deleted:

"available to the public under [insert statutory reference to open records act] or".

SECTION 7. PROHIBITED MEDIATOR REPORTS.

(a) Except as required in subsection (b), a mediator may not make a report, assessment, evaluation, recommendation, finding, or other communication regarding a mediation to a court, administrative agency, or other authority that may make a ruling on the dispute that is the subject of the mediation.

(b) A mediator may disclose:

(1) whether the mediation occurred or has terminated, whether a settlement was reached, and attendance;

(2) a mediation communication as permitted under Section 6; or

(3) a mediation communication evidencing abuse, neglect, abandonment, or exploitation of an individual to a public agency responsible for protecting individuals against such mistreatment.

(c) A communication made in violation of subsection (a) may not be considered by a court, administrative agency, or arbitrator.

SECTION 8. CONFIDENTIALITY. Unless subject to the [insert statutory references to open meetings act and open records act], mediation communications are confidential to the extent agreed by the parties or provided by other law or rule of this State.

SECTION 9. MEDIATOR'S DISCLOSURE OF CONFLICTS OF INTEREST; BACKGROUND.

(a) Before accepting a mediation, an individual who is requested to serve as a mediator shall:

(1) make an inquiry that is reasonable under the circumstances to determine whether there are any known facts that a reasonable individual would consider likely to affect the impartiality of the mediator, including a financial or personal interest in the outcome of the mediation and an existing or past relationship with a mediation party or foreseeable participant in the mediation; and

(2) disclose any such known fact to the mediation parties as soon as is practical before accepting a mediation.

(b) If a mediator learns any fact described in subsection (a)(1) after accepting a mediation, the mediator shall disclose it as soon as is practicable.

(c) At the request of a mediation party, an individual who is requested to serve as a mediator shall disclose the mediator's qualifications to mediate a dispute.

(d) A person that violates subsection [(a) or (b)][(a), (b), or (g)] is precluded by the violation from asserting a privilege under Section 4.

(e) Subsections (a), (b), [and] (c), [and] [(g)] do not apply to an individual acting as a judge.

(f) This [Act] does not require that a mediator have a special qualification by background or profession.

[(g) A mediator must be impartial, unless after disclosure of the facts required in subsections (a) and (b) to be disclosed, the parties agree otherwise.]

SECTION 10. PARTICIPATION IN MEDIATION. An attorney or other individual designated by a party may accompany the party to and participate in a mediation. A waiver of participation given before the mediation may be rescinded.

SECTION 11. RELATION TO ELECTRONIC SIGNATURES IN GLOBAL AND NATIONAL COMMERCE ACT. This [Act] modifies, limits, or supersedes the federal Electronic Signatures in Global and National Commerce Act, 15 U.S.C. Section 7001 et seq., but this [Act] does not modify, limit, or supersede Section 101(c) of that Act or authorize electronic delivery of any of the notices described in Section 103(b) of that Act.

SECTION 12. UNIFORMITY OF APPLICATION AND CONSTRUCTION. In applying and construing this [Act], consideration should be given to the need to promote uniformity of the law with respect to its subject matter among States that enact it.

SECTION 13. SEVERABILITY CLAUSE. If any provision of this [Act] or its application to any person or circumstance is held invalid, the invalidity does not affect other provisions or applications of this [Act] which can be given effect without the invalid provision or application, and to this end the provisions of this [Act] are severable.

SECTION 14. EFFECTIVE DATE. This [Act] takes effect . . . .

SECTION 15. REPEALS. The following acts and parts of acts are hereby repealed:

(1)

(2)

(3)

SECTION 16. APPLICATION TO EXISTING AGREEMENTS OR REFERRALS.

(a) This [Act] governs mediation pursuant to a referral or an agreement to mediate made on or after [the effective date of this [Act]].

(b) On or after [a delayed date], this [Act] governs an agreement to mediate whenever made.

*

INDEX

References are to Pages

ADMINISTRATIVE DISPUTE RESOLUTION ACT OF 1996, p. 9

ALTERNATIVE DISPUTE RESOLUTION (ADR)
Criminal Law Context, 242, 243
Historical Background, 5–11
Pound Conference, 5

ALTERNATIVE DISPUTE RESOLUTION ACT OF 1998, pp. 9, 129

AMERICAN ARBITRATION ASSOCIATION (AAA), 165, 215, 251–253
Code of Ethics for Arbitrators in Commercial Disputes, 438–463
Commercial Arbitration Rules and Commercial Mediation Procedures, 311–366

AMERICAN BAR ASSOCIATION (ABA)
Formal Opinion 06–439, p. 116
Resolutions
Good Faith Requirements, 101
Mediation and the Unauthorized Practice of Law, 141–143

AMERICAN BAR ASSOCIATION MODEL RULES OF PROFESSIONAL CONDUCT
Rule 1.12, pp. 200, 464, 465
Rule 1.2, pp. 47, 48
Rule 1.2(a), p. 15
Rule 1.4(b), p. 35
Rule 1.6(a), pp. 51, 52
Rule 2.4, pp. 108, 116

AMERICAN BAR ASSOCIATION MODEL RULES OF PROFES-SIONAL CONDUCT—Cont'd
Rule 3.3, pp. 200, 201, 466, 467
Rule 4.1, pp. 50, 51, 116
Rule 5.5, pp. 468–470
Rule 5.5(a), p. 140
Rule 5.5(c), pp. 143, 144

ARB–MED, 256, 257

ARBITRATION
Arbitrability, 166–179
Arbitrator
    Ethics, 199–201
    Immunity, 196, 197
    Law Applied by, 198, 199
Award, 201–214
    Judicial Review, 202
    Manifest Disregard of the Law, 203
    New York Convention, 215, 216
    Public Policy, 204
Collateral Estoppel, 208–214
Compulsory, 160–164
Court Annexed, 162
Definitions, 164–166
    Administered, 165
    Final Offer, 165, 166
    Interest, 164
    Non-administered, 165
    Rights, 164, 165
    Tripartite, 166
Employment, 163, 164
Federal Arbitration Act (FAA), 155
Hearing, 197, 198
Historical Background, 154–159
Initiating the Process, 194, 195
International, *See separate heading*
Legal Issues
    Adhesion, 189–192
    Arbitrability, 166–179
    Due Process Protocol, 191
    Federalism, 179–189
    Kompetenz–Kompetenz, 178, 179
    Procedural Arbitrability, 175–179
    Separability, 176–178
    Substantive Arbitrability, 167–175

ARBITRATION—Cont'd
Legal Issues—Cont'd
 Unconscionability, 189–192
Medical Malpractice, 162, 163
Provisional Relief, 192–194
Public Sector, 161, 162
Punitive Damages, 206–208
Res Judicata, 208–214
Revised Uniform Arbitration Act (RUAA), *See separate heading*
Selection of Arbitrators, 195, 196
Traditional Model, 159, 160
Uniform Arbitration Act (UAA), *See separate heading*
Venue, 206

BARRIERS TO SETTLEMENT, 42, 43

BRAZIL, WAYNE, 46

BOULWARISM, 40

CAUCUS, 83, 136, 137

CIVIL JUSTICE REFORM ACT OF 1990, p. 9

COLLABORATIVE LAW, 7

CONCILIATION, 261

CONFIDENTIALITY
Contract, 123–125
Evidentiary Exclusionary Rules, 119
Mediation, 117–130
Negotiation, 60, 61
Privilege, 120, 121

CONFLICT OF INTEREST
Lawyers Serving as Third Party Neutrals, 105–108
Screening, 109

CONSENSUS BUILDING, 262, 263

COURT–ANNEXED ARBITRATION, 220–222

COURT–ANNEXED MEDIATION, 101, 222, 223
Confidentiality Rules, 129

CULTURE
Avruch, Kevin, 45
Brett, Jeanne, 45

CULTURE—Cont'd
Definition, 45
Mediation, 96
Negotiation, 44, 45

DEMAND FOR ARBITRATION (FORM), 431, 432

DISPUTE REVIEW BOARDS (DRB), 263

DISTRIBUTIVE BARGAINING, 18–19

EARLY NEUTRAL EVALUATION, 232–235

ELECTRONIC DISPUTE RESOLUTION (EDR), 261

EMOTIONS, 43, 44
Core Concerns, 44
Fisher and Shapiro, 44
Negotiation, 43
Stone, Patton and Heen, 43

EMPLOYMENT DUE PROCESS PROTOCOL, 433–437

ETHICS
Advertising, 109, 110
Good Faith Requirements, 100, 101
Mediation, 99–111
Model Standards of Conduct for Mediators, 102
Negotiation, 45–55

FEDERAL ARBITRATION ACT (FAA), 155, 193, 390–405

FEDERAL RULES OF CIVIL PROCEDURE
Rule 26(b), p. 61
Rule 16, pp. 61, 62, 270–275
Rule 68, pp. 63, 64, 276, 277

FEDERAL RULES OF EVIDENCE
Rule 408, pp. 60, 268, 269

FIRST OFFER, 38–40

FOLBERG AND TAYLOR, 79, 94

FULLER, LON, 72

GETTING TO YES, 23, 24, 27

GUARANTEED VERDICT AGREEMENT, 58, 59, See Mary Carter
    Agreements

HYBRID PROCESSES, 246–263

INFORMED CONSENT
Mediation, 111, 112

INTEGRATIVE BARGAINING, 19–20

INTERNATIONAL ARBITRATION, 214–216

**INTERNATIONAL CENTER FOR SETTLEMENT OF INVEST-
MENT DISPUTES (ICSID),** 215

INTERNATIONAL CHAMBER OF COMMERCE, 215

JUDICIAL SETTLEMENT CONFERENCE, 61

KOVACH, KIMBERLEE, 78

LABOR MANAGEMENT RELATIONS ACT (LMRA), 192, 193

LAW
Informed Consent, 111, 112
Role of Law in Mediation, 110, 111

LAWYER–MEDIATOR
Ethical Concerns, 104–110

LAX AND SEBENIUS, 24, 26, 28
3–D Negotiation, 34
Value Claiming, 24
Value Creating, 28

LISTENING SKILLS, 38, 90–93

LOG ROLLING, 41

MAGISTRATES, 236, 237

MANDATORY MEDIATION, 103, 104

MARY CARTER AGREEMENTS, 58, 59

MED–ARB, 255, 256

MEDIATION
Advantages, 72, 73
Caucus, 83
Confidentiality, 117–130
Conflict of Interest, 76
Disadvantages, 73, 74
Definition, 70, 71

MEDIATION—Cont'd
Drafting the Mediation Agreement, 84
Enforceability, 130–134
Ethical Issues, 99–111
Evaluative, 88, 89
Facilitative, 88
Historical Background, 68–70
Immunity, 139, 140
Information Exchange, 82, 83
Interest Based, 71
Lawyers, 112–117
    Acting as Mediators, 116, 117
    Representing Clients, 114–116
Liability of Mediators, 134–139
Listening Skills, 90–93
Mediator's Introduction, 79–81
Narrative, 88
Observation Skills, 95
Pre–Mediation
    Client Counseling, 112–114
    Discussions, 75
Process, 74–85
Questioning Skills, 93, 94
Reframing, 96
Rights–Based, 71
Role of the Mediator, 85, 86
Screening, 77
Stages of the Process, 78, 79
Styles and Approaches, 86–89
Transformative, 88
Understanding–Based, 88
Uniform Mediation Act, *See separate heading*

MENKEL–MEADOW, CARRIE, 27

MENTSCHIKOFF, SOIA, 198, 199

MINI–TRIAL, 246–255

MISREPRESENTATION, 49–53
Puffing, 50

MODEL STANDARDS OF CONDUCT FOR MEDIATORS, 102,
    297–310

**MODEL STANDARDS OF PRACTICE FOR FAMILY AND DI-
    VORCE MEDIATION,** 278–296

MOORE, CHRISTOPHER, 78, 79

NEGOTIATED RULEMAKING, 257–259

NEGOTIATED RULEMAKING ACT OF 1990, pp. 9, 258, 259

NEGOTIATION
Adversarial Approach, 23–25
Barriers to Settlement, 42, 43
Concessions and Compromise, 40, 41
Deal-making, 17, 20
Definition, 16
Dispute, 17, 21
Distributive Bargaining, 18, 22
Ethics, 45–55
Exchanging Information, 37
First Offer, 38–40
Generating Options, 38
Integrative Bargaining, 18, 20–22
Interest Bargaining, 19
Legal Negotiation, 15
Log Rolling, 41
Multiparty, 16
Multilateral, 16
Orientation, 23
Planning and Analysis, 33–37
Problem Solving Approach, 25–29
Stages of the Process, 31–42
Transaction, 20
Zero-sum, 19

NEUTRAL EXPERTS, 241, 242

NEW YORK CONVENTION, 215, 216

OMBUDSPERSON, 259, 260

ONLINE DISPUTE RESOLUTION (ODR), 261, 262

REFERENCE PROCEDURES, 254

RESTATEMENT (SECOND) OF CONTRACTS, 50

RESTORATIVE JUSTICE, 242, 243

REVISED UNIFORM ARBITRATION ACT (RUAA), 153, 193–195, 406–430

SCHNEIDER, ANDREA, 25, 26

SETTLEMENT AGREEMENT, 56–60

SINGLE NEGOTIATING TEXT, 85

SOCIETY OF PROFESSIONALS IN DISPUTE RESOLUTION (SPIDR), 97, 98
Mandated Participation and Settlement Coercion: Dispute Resolution as it Relates to the Courts, 367–370
Ethical Standards of Professional Responsibility for the Society of Professionals in Dispute Resolution, 371–377

SPECIAL MASTERS, 237–241

SUMMARY JURY TRIAL, 223–232

SUSSKIND, LAWRENCE, 262

THREATS, 54

TRUTHFULNESS, 48
Puffing, 50

UNAUTHORIZED PRACTICE OF LAW (UPL), 84, 140–144
Multijurisdictional Practice, 143, 144

UNCITRAL
Model Law on International Commercial Arbitration, 216
Model Law on International Conciliation, 261

UNIFORM ARBITRATION ACT (UAA), 155, 378–389

UNIFORM MEDIATION ACT (UMA), 76, 118, 121, 471–481

VANISHING TRIAL, 8

WHITE, JAMES, 48

WILLIAMS, GERALD, 24, 25, 26

ZERO–SUM, 19

†